THE COMPASSIONATE REVOLUTION

DAVID EDWARDS was born in 1962 in Maidstone, Kent. After taking a degree in Politics at the University of Leicester, he worked in sales and marketing management for several large corporations. In 1991 he left the business world to concentrate on writing about human rights and environmental issues. He now works for the International Society for Ecology and Culture. His first book, *Free to be Human: Intellectual Self-Defence in an Age of Illusions*, was published in 1995 (the American edition was entitled *Burning All Illusions*). He is married and lives in Bournemouth.

THE COMPASSIONATE REVOLUTION

Radical Politics and Buddhism

David Edwards

Green Books

First published in 1998 by
Green Books Ltd
Foxhole, Dartington
Totnes, Devon TQ9 6EB

Cover design by Rick Lawrence

Typeset in Bembo at Green Books

Printed by Biddles Ltd, Guildford, Surrey

A catalogue record for this book
is available from the British Library

ISBN 1 870098 70 6

CONTENTS

CONTENTS *(continued)*

ACKNOWLEDGEMENTS

I would like to thank my wife, Silvia, for her long-suffering support, kindness and love; also M, H, Sis, Olly and particularly Lewis, Elly Welly and Rosie for their invaluable advice. Thanks to Mat for being a truly good pal. I'd also like to thank John Elford for his kind and expert help in editing both this book and *Free to be Human*. Where just about every 'left wing' editor would surely have found them 'much too spiritual', and every 'Green/New Age' editor would have found them 'much too political', John leapt at the chance to plunge off the beaten track. Having taken the plunge, he then set about skilfully removing many of the worst howlers marring the original texts. In the process, John has provided me valuable opportunities for practising patience and self-restraint! (See Chapters Six and Seven for more on this.) John has also taught me everything I know about the use of the semi-colon. I can't thank him enough for his help.

We will have to dispense with all sentimentality and day-dreaming; and our attention will have to be concentrated everywhere on our immediate national objectives. We need not deceive ourselves that we can afford today the luxury of altruism and world benefaction... We should cease to talk about vague... and unreal objectives such as human rights, the raising of living standards, and democratisation.

George Kennan, Head of US State Department Planning Staff, 1948

Generate compassion for all living beings; abstain from killing, from stealing, and so on, and give pleasure to all.

Consider, Your Majesty, if, through such mercy, people treated each other as they would treat themselves or their families, whose heart would ever harbour wicked thoughts?

The cause of all disturbance is lack of compassion. It corrupts the body, speech, and mind; it harms the family no less than strangers. If those who strive for Virtue will only remember compassion, only good can result.

The Buddha

PREFACE

This is a book about radical politics and Buddhism, and the relationship between them. For many readers these may seem to make an odd couple; for others, I can imagine that neither will seem of any great relevance to their everyday lives. At an earlier stage in my own life, politics seemed to have nothing to do with me at all, something that important people in suits argued about (incomprehensibly) on the television. Likewise, Buddhism seemed to be concerned with my gaining the realization that I was indivisible from the rest of the universe. This was far more interesting than politics, but again it seemed to have nothing much to do with me. I was concerned with 'real' issues: finding happiness, love, freedom, and a job that would not bore me to death. Also, I was aware of the extremes of suffering, injustice and hypocrisy around me; I suspected that it was probably my responsibility to engage with the world and try to do something about them.

I can therefore sympathise with seekers after progressive social change—civil, human rights and environmental activists—who might feel decidedly uneasy at the prospect of even involving themselves in a discussion of Buddhism. Dissidents are keen to depict themselves as rigorous, hard-headed rationalists. They are wary of laying themselves open to charges of sentimentality, emotionality and idealism. Unfortunately, the attempt to rigidly 'stick to the facts' represents, itself, a kind of emotionality—that of coldness—and it seems to me that there is a danger that this version of 'hard-headedness' can easily degrade into hard-heartedness. As Howard Zinn has pointed out, it would be a mistake to equate this kind of coldness with increased rationality:

> True, emotion can distort. But it can also enhance. If one of the functions of the scholar is accurate description, then it is impossible to describe a war both unemotionally and accurately at the same time... Thus, exactly from the standpoint of what intellect is

supposed to do for us—to extend the boundaries of our understanding—the 'cool, rational, unemotional' approach fails.[1]

Moreover, dissidents can never get away from the fact that, however
much they might seek to emulate the detached rationality of the
'hard' sciences, their efforts are unavoidably attached to the 'softest'
of human sentiments: compassion.

Libertarian dissent, the desire for radical change, is universally
rooted in compassion, in the desire to relieve suffering. The whole
point about writers like Howard Zinn, Ed Herman, Noam
Chomsky, John Pilger, Sharon Beder and Mark Curtis is that they,
unlike many of their mainstream peers, refuse to place their own
personal concerns for wealth, status, respectability, and even physical security, above the needs of the wretched of the earth.
Compassion, the desire to take away misery, to try to help, is the
very basis of what they do. And yet it is like the air they breathe;
they seem rarely to discuss it, or question it, or marvel at what, to
them, is so natural and yet to others is so unusual, so difficult.

Given the way of the world, it seems reasonable that activists
should at least glance at themselves a little quizzically in the mirror
and ask "What am I up to? What is this business of trying to defend
human and animal rights? What do I get out of it? Why is it such a
satisfying thing to do?" And if they decide that they really are motivated by the desire to help others (rather than, say, the desire to be
admired for their good works), then surely the question must be:
Why me? Why not everyone? How can more people be encouraged to be more concerned? What might happen then?

And what does all this have to do with Buddhism?

Buddhism has exactly the same motivation: it asks exactly these
questions, it is the great compassionate movement of human culture. For example, to read Aryasura's work *The Marvellous
Companion* is to read thirty-four sublime tales comprising 350
pages, all carefully designed to convince us that compassion is
always, in every conceivable situation, in the best interests of everyone! For a Westerner to even read such a book with such an aim is
an awesome experience. That such a work can even have been produced by human culture is a cause for great wonderment and hope.

Yet, unlike Western dissidents, Buddhists do not take this compassionate impulse for granted. Indeed, the whole thrust of
Buddhism is to examine this strange phenomenon, to understand

it, and seeing that it is a great boon for all living beings, to cultivate it to its maximum extent.

Buddhists begin by marvelling at the very existence of compassion. In his poem *The Way of the Bodhisattva*, Shantideva opens with an impassioned declaration of astonishment. How can it be that, in this self-obsessed universe plagued by suffering, egotism and the struggle to survive, a determination to relieve the suffering of other beings can arise? How when "Alas, our sorrows fall in endless streams!" can people deliberately put their own problems aside to seek to satisfy the needs of others?

> This state of mind so precious and so rare
> Arises truly wondrous, never seen before.
> The pain-dispelling draft,
> This cause of joy for those who wander through the world-
> This precious attitude, this jewel of mind,
> How shall it be gauged or quantified? [2]

Anyone who has read Shantideva's poem, or Howard Zinn's essays, or Edward Herman and Noam Chomsky's books, will know that this remarkable concern for the well-being of others truly is a "jewel of mind".

In my view it is compassion that marks the difference between mainstream and dissent, between the clichés of conformity and liberating insight, between a murderous status quo and change, between despair and hope.

Recognizing this great value of compassionate understanding, Buddhism then takes us in all our laughable self-importance, greediness and irascibility, and declares that even *we* can work on ourselves to increase our compassion and reduce our selfishness and so begin to act for the benefit of other beings. In the process, we are told, we will experience freedom (from greed, fear, hatred and delusions) and contentment of a kind that were previously unknown to us.

Anyone who thinks this process has anything to do with the kind of 'free love' hedonism and 'drop out' idealism characteristic of the sixties and some modern New Age movements, should think again. Rather, it involves the same discipline, effort and stubborn perseverance in the face of hardship that dissident writers and activists know all about:

The process of self-mastery is the process of learning to subdue self-centred concerns and give to other beings no matter how great the sacrifice. The teachings point to this one aim; when we accomplish it, the destructive emotions lose their hold, and true happiness can arise. [3]

The power of radical dissent to dispel illusions and so combat the horrors of this world lies, I believe, in the compassionate motivation behind it. Buddhism is a two thousand-year-old master class in understanding the nature and true power of compassion even in the face of the worst viciousness and self-serving ignorance. Combined, the two—new and old, Western and Eastern—can constitute an irresistible force for good in the modern world.

David Edwards
Bournemouth
June 1998

INTRODUCTION

Learning to Look After Number One

Golden Silences

Sometimes the truth, which is normally kept at a safe distance from public view, is revealed with dramatic clarity. As this Introduction was being written, it became clear that attempts to agree adequate targets for the reduction of greenhouse gases at the Kyoto convention in Japan had failed, much as similar attempts failed in 1992 at the Rio Earth Summit. Some eight weeks prior to this predictable disappointment, Nobel Laureate Henry Kendall, chairman of the Union of Concerned Scientists, said: "Let there be no doubt about the conclusions of the scientific community that the threat of global warming is very real and action is needed immediately. It is a grave error to believe that we can continue to procrastinate." [1]

The warning could not have been clearer, and the immensity of the threat is not in doubt. How, then, is it possible that no action was taken in response to this dire situation? What prevented it, and why? The unpleasant answer, for once, could not be hidden. John Grasser, Vice-President of the US National Mining Association and member of the Global Climate Coalition, an organization set up by over one hundred major corporations for the express purpose of combating efforts to limit greenhouse gas emissions, had this to say:

> We think we have raised enough questions among the American public to prevent any numbers, targets or timetables to achieve reductions in gas emissions being agreed here...What we are doing, and we think successfully, is buying time for our industries by holding up these talks. [2]

Truly, the whole world can be seen in this grain of sand.

Do we imagine that other environmental and human rights issues are not subject to the same pressures and priorities? After all, the world is brimming with environmental and human rights catastrophes which are real, and in response to which "action is needed immediately". The world is also full of people "buying time for our industries".

Consider the tragedy of Algeria, ruled by a one-party military dictatorship since 1962, and where 80,000 people have been slaughtered since 1991. The massacre of innocents has become a commonplace, with armed attackers descending on unarmed villages at night to cut the throats of women and children. The violence has been characterized by psychotic frenzy, including the dismemberment of tiny infants. But why? By whom? What is the world doing about it? John Sweeney of the *Observer* reports:

> The weight of evidence indicts the state of Algeria. Around 80,000 people have been killed since the generals cheated the people by scrapping the elections in 1991. The government—*le pouvoir*—is corrupt, hated and stays in power by a reign of terror.[3]

Can this be unknown to Western governments and their intelligence services? A Western analyst observes sardonically:

> Western governments know what goes on in Algeria but have remained silent. You might think it is because of Algeria's oil billions.[4]

Perish the thought. Sweeney is quick to resurrect it:

> Let us not underestimate the power of the state of Algeria. It squats on huge oil and gas deposits worth billions. It supplies the gas that warms Madrid and Rome. It has a £1.8 billion contract with British Petroleum. No Western government wants to make trouble with the state of Algeria. Its wealth buys silence, buys complicity. Since the military junta overthrew the country's democracy, 80,000 have been killed: Europe's gas bill.[5]

Britain's Foreign Secretary Robin Cook, famous for declaring that 'New' Labour would "put human rights at the heart of our foreign policy"[6] quickly revealed the truth of what is merely an Orwellian deception. Of the massacres in Algeria, Cook has recently said:

> We have seen no evidence to support allegations of involvement by the Algerian security authorities.[7]

A failure which presumably means that the European Union will continue to supply the Algerian generals with £80 million in aid for restructuring and 'democratisation'.

As with global warming, then, we find those responsible for

"buying time for our industries" close at hand. As ever, the price is paid in blood. It is the same price being paid in Guatemala, El Salvador, Brazil, Nicaragua, Nigeria, Russia, Indonesia, East Timor, Iraq, Vietnam, and elsewhere throughout the Third World. Many Third World dictators would flee into exile, many torture chambers would be emptied, but for the insatiable need of Western industries for "time". We might think that this systemic barbarism built into the very nature of our political and economic systems would be headline news, the subject of outrage and vigorous debate. Instead it is invisible, unknown, unmentioned. Silence, it turns out, is not only golden—it is blood-red too.

Death by Superficiality

The defining political and economic truths about the world we live in are really not complicated or difficult to understand. We do not need to delve very deep before they become obvious, but we do need to go beneath the superficial appearance of things. In what lies ahead I will argue that it is the role of our corporate mass media and political systems to prevent us from doing just that, to ensure that we thrash around in the shallows, leaving the deep delusional supports of state and corporate power well alone. As a result, we are drowning in superficiality.

Though the Third World and our own environment are being demolished before our very eyes, the media remain content to artificially isolate disasters and hang them on an ideational framework of Third World 'developing nations', 'progress', 'sustainable growth' and Western 'leadership of the free world', steadfastly refusing to interpret events as symptomatic of the logic and overwhelming power of the corporate capitalist system. While the notion that we have a free press seems superficially plausible, it only takes a moment of honest reflection to realize that when a world is being ravaged by corporations, a corporate media system is the last place to look for truth. Anyone who believes we live in a free and open society might like to try finding any reference to this argument in the mainstream media.

Systemic realities mean that the role of a profit-seeking corporate media must be to "buy time for our industries" by playing down calls for profit-sapping change and the human rights and environmental 'Scare Stories' (BBC2) behind them; to represent environmentalists, not corporate executives, as being 'Against Nature'

(Channel 4); to represent the West as being engaged in 'The Search for Peace' (BBC2), rather than being in search of suitably venal dictators to protect Western access to Third World natural resources— from the Third World people to whom they belong. We should not be misled by the fact that reporters like John Sweeney are occasionally allowed to report ugly truths, for the strength of the system lies in its willingness to tolerate tiny instances of dissent in a context of overwhelming conformity. The critical factor is the *extent*, not the existence, of occasional media attention to business-unfriendly facts.

On a deeper level, the job of the media is to ridicule the notion that people are capable of organizing a better, more compassionate way of life.

It need not concern us overly that journalists themselves are sometimes (though not always) oblivious to the role they are playing: human beings are capable of near-miracles of self-deception, particularly when the irresistible force of greed meets the immovable object of accountability for suffering. Later, we will read of Andrew Marr, former editor of the *Independent* newspaper, inquiring of Noam Chomsky: "How, how? This is what I don't understand", as the venerable professor patiently attempts to communicate to Marr something of the reality of Marr's own profession.

It appears that Marr really doesn't understand how thought control might be able to exist in the absence of any kind of conspiracy. The truly fascinating subject of how someone in Marr's position can fail to comprehend this argument will be the subject of several chapters here. Indeed, in a sense this whole book is concerned with this tragi-comic human capacity for self-deception, as well as possible antidotes for it.

No level of cognitive dissonance is too much for our propaganda system, which is rooted in this capacity for self-deception. Today, amazingly, we find that the military 'threat' of global communism has been supplanted by the economic 'threat' of none other than global *capitalism*. We wage slaves are now ordered into the economic arena to do battle with tiger economies run by Third World dictators (installed by us), where once taxpayers boldly confronted the 'communist menace' (invented by us). Little did we Cold Warriors know that we were fighting for the right to compete with slave states like Burma, China, Indonesia and the rest; that is, for the right to lose our rights in the name of 'competitiveness'.

Fortunately for our arms manufacturers, Saddam Hussein

remains in the wings "with enough chemical weapons to kill every man, woman and child on the face of the Earth",[8] as the Pentagon tells us, presumably with a straight face. Truly, if the devil did not exist it would be necessary to invent him.

One intended consequence of the creation of globalized competition is that politics has become the PR arm of business, to an extent that is almost beyond the capacity of even the 'free press' to deny. Democracy has been reduced to a choice between two right wings of the same Business Party. Is it possible that, beyond the media, there are still those who believe that prime ministers and presidents champion the interests of the public, when the giant and "immortal [corporate] persons", so feared by Thomas Jefferson, now bestride the world, alert to any and all 'anti-business' political gestures? Imagine that different branches of a Soviet-style Communist Party ran all sectors of an economy; that all major political parties followed the Communist Party line; that Party executives moved freely between party and industry; that all TV, radio, newspapers, magazines, cinema and publishers, were Communist Party productions. What chance would we give an anti-Communist party of achieving any media coverage, let alone power? The level of freedom in our democracy can be gauged by replacing 'Communist Party' with 'business'. Robert Dahl made the point with chilling accuracy:

> Much in the way of political theory... depends on the assumptions one makes about the sources of political attitudes... If one assumes that political preferences are simply plugged into the system by leaders (business or other) in order to extract what they want from the system, then the model of plebiscitory democracy is substantially equivalent to the model of totalitarian rule.[9]

From Systemic Greed to Unconditional Compassion

If we are able to achieve the first requirement of liberation from an oppressive situation—awareness of the existence and true nature of the problem (in our case, an awareness of the institutionalized subordination of people and planet to corporate profit)—we then need to move to the second goal of liberation: identifying a realistic answer to that problem.

Perhaps the beginnings of an answer can be gained from biologists, who tell us that there would be little danger of alien races infecting us with deadly diseases, the biology of an infective agent needing to be sufficiently similar to that of the host for a destructive link to be made. Alien diseases might well be just too foreign to have any kind of relationship with our bodies.

By contrast, it is surely the ethical commonality between you and I and the corporate system standing over us that enables us to be trapped by it. In the last analysis, it is our own wilful ignorance, empowered by our own greed and hatred, that fuel this systemic greed and hatred. There is no possibility of weakening the bonds of delusion without combating our own greed and hatred, on which this system depends. The antidote to ignorance rooted in greed is awareness rooted in compassion.

Strange though it might initially sound, then, I will argue that despite—or rather because of—the ruthless and violent nature of the system facing us, the only realistic individual, social and political antidote to rampant corporate capitalism is radical awareness rooted in unconditional kindness and compassion.

Although we Westerners may find this woefully naïve, presumably not many of us can claim to do so on the basis of personal experience. Can we say that unconditional kindness and compassion have *ever* been at the heart of the Western 'left' response to corporate capitalism? Dissident radicals are famously angry with an economic system that reduces human beings and animals to the status of industrial fodder. While compassion for Third World victims, the domestic poor and factory-farmed animals is rightly a commonplace, corporate executives, bankers and media moguls are seen as 'the enemy' to be loathed as the self-seeking architects of cruelty and exploitation.

The idea that they too should be recipients of compassion on the part of dissidents may well be received with derision, if not utter incomprehension: What on earth could be meant by such a suggestion?

The argument that will be set out in this book is that dissidents should take a long, hard look at what initially appears so ridiculous, so soft-headed; for in reality, I believe, it is dissident anger and bitterness that are naïve, that are in fact the greatest obstacle to what dissidents themselves are trying to achieve.

I hope it will become clear that I am not proposing this compassionate response out of any misguided notion that corporate executives are in reality kindly people, or tragically misunderstood. I am very well aware of, indeed constantly amazed by, the casual indifference of those willing to sacrifice so much truth, so many people—even the stability of the global climate—for what, in the end, amount to the most trivial, transient baubles of personal wealth, status, comfort and power. Yet in my view it is one of the most lethal of Western prejudices (and one fully supported by the propaganda system) to imagine that the natural, or most powerful, response to an awareness of great 'evil' is great hatred. There is, surely, a middle way between naïvety and anger.

Among several systems of thought which understand both these ideas and the angry dissident alternative, I will here be primarily referring to the Mahayana and Theravada traditions of Buddhism. To my knowledge, few left-wing intellectuals have had anything at all to say about these remarkable systems of libertarian thought, or the dramatic rise of Western interest in them over recent years.

The reason for this silence is not difficult to divine: radical dissent in the West has grown out of atheistic socialism and anarchism, out of the understanding that religion is the opiate of the people. Because these same dissidents imagine Buddhism to be a religious 'faith'—with the Buddha as some kind of Eastern God—they have kept a dismissive distance from all possibility of sedative contamination. Misguided though I think these views are, they are certainly understandable. Tolstoy was after all right when, with characteristic honesty and courage, he wrote:

> The religious superstition is stimulated by processions, festivals, monuments and churches, built with the money collected from the people, by music, architecture, images and incense, which drug men, and especially by the maintenance of a so-called clergy, whose occupation consists in bewildering the minds of men, and keeping them in a continual state of stupefaction, by their stage-play, by the pathos of their services and sermons, by their interference in men's private lives, in birth, marriage and death. [10]

As Tolstoy notes elsewhere, because we see nothing comprehensible in all this, we tend to assign supernatural significance to what we imagine is figuratively, indeed literally, 'above' and 'beyond' us.

Whilst, as Buddhist writer Stephen Batchelor has pointed out, elements of these irrational and authoritarian tendencies are certainly to be found in Buddhism (as they are in every system of thought), the foundations of Buddhism are profoundly rational and offer a wealth of insight into the nature of the greed, hatred and delusion on which all forms of authoritarian power are based.

Like all good libertarians, Buddhists are sometimes not happy even with their own 'ism': the Western term 'Buddhism'. Thus Satya Narayan Goenka says: "I teach Dharma, that is, what the Buddha taught. He never taught any 'ism' or sectarian doctrine. He taught something from which people of every background can benefit: an art of living." [11]

Like Goenka, my concern here is not at all to convert anyone to any sectarian doctrine but to suggest that there is a truly vast libertarian potential in the Buddhist contention that working for the happiness of others is the basis and cause of all happiness.

In my view, this notion, or the intellectual and practical investigation of it, when combined with a radical dissident analysis of society, can provide the basis for a genuine and revolutionary antidote to the oppressive forces facing us.

Our problem, however, is that Western cultures that have evolved over the last 500 years have been masters of the art of exploitation; and just as it is said that a pickpocket can see only the pockets of a saint, many Western commentators have failed to see the revolutionary conception of compassion at the heart of Buddhist thought. Consequently, many of us are not even aware that it exists. Psychologist Daniel Goleman notes that the possibility of unbounded compassion on the level of a Buddha is entirely unknown to Western psychological theories. Perhaps the cowherd's explanation to the five pillaging demons who had also not heard of the Buddha's compassion also serves us well:

> Ah, this is rather a wonder, is it not? Yet how strange! The power of our king is famous, yet you have not heard of him! Or is it that you have heard but could not believe? I suspect that your countrymen are not greatly concerned with the quest for virtue. [12]

But then we would not expect demons with "pointed gnashing teeth, fierce red eyes, flaming and squinting", whose taste is for "raw human flesh, freshly cut, and human blood still warm" [13] to believe in, or understand, the possibility of great compassion. Why should we initially expect more from Westerners, from ourselves, steeped as we are in a culture bent on similar plunder?

Fierce-eyed Western academic reviewers have often missed the point entirely. Thus Winston King, in his acclaimed work *In The Hope of Nibbana: Theravada Buddhist Ethics*, was able to write of Buddhism:

Whatever [English] term we adopt [for *upekkha* or equanimity], something of its quality is evident: controlled balance of mind, emotional non-attachment or neutrality, and 'beyondness' with regard to ordinary ethical uncertainties and struggles. It is seemingly a calm detachment of eternity mindedness that has little interest longer in the ordinary affairs of men.[14]

Had he been referring to Western journalists and academics, King of course might have had a point. This indifference to the ordinary affairs of men, however, has nothing to do with Buddhism.

Consider, after all, a key foundation of Buddhist thought, one which has extraordinary resonance in our age of globalizing, self-interested greed and a collapsing global environment:

Whatever joy there is in this world
All comes from desiring others to be happy
And whatever suffering there is in this world
All comes from desiring myself to be happy.[15]

Buddhists believe that all happiness is ultimately rooted in kindness and compassionate understanding, and that all unhappiness and chaos in the world are rooted in selfishness, ignorance and hatred.

What kind of orientation to life does this understanding imply? Does it imply a calm indifference in the face of suffering? The real aspirations of Buddhism are not in any doubt at all:

May all beings have happiness and the cause of happiness.
May all beings remain free from suffering and the cause of suffering.
May all beings remain unseparated from the sacred joy and happiness that is totally free from sorrow.
May all beings rest in the boundless and all-inclusive equanimity that is beyond attachment and aversion.[16]

Notice that *all* beings—the poor and the rich, exploiters and exploited, torturer and tortured—are included, as all are considered victims of the deluded misfortunes of greed, hatred and ignorance.

There is a tenderness of heart and an all-inclusiveness here that are naturally alien to a Western society that is economically and morally rooted, as we have said, in great violence. A society for which this is true:

Since 1945, rather than occasionally deviating from the promotion of peace, democracy, human rights and economic development in

the Third World, British (and US) foreign policy has been systematically opposed to them, whether the Conservatives or Labour (or
Republicans or Democrats) have been in power. This has had
grave consequences for those on the receiving end of Western
policies abroad.[17]

is unlikely to be one for which this will ring true:

> May all beings be at ease, secure;
> May they all be happy in heart.
> Whoever is a breathing being,
> Stable or unstable without exception,
> Long, or those who are large,
> Medium, short, subtle, gross.
> Visible or invisible,
> Distant or near,
> Beings or those yet to be born,
> May they all be happy in heart.[18]

Buddhists recite these phrases over and over again, not as prayers to
a cosmic creator, but to turn idea into habitual thought and habitual thought into fixed character and determined action for the benefit of all.

And what, then, should be our role in fulfilling these aspirations
for all beings?

> The goal is to work absolutely for the well-being of the entire
> community of sentient beings... This is the key work of the bod-
> dhisattvas.[19]

When judged against this yardstick, are Western dissidents all that
different from their corporate counterparts? After all, as we will see,
anarchists and socialists have regularly favoured war and bloodshed
as necessary means, just as mainstream politicians regularly favour a
short, victorious war on the grounds of the 'Falklands factor'.

Normal Mailer made a telling point, I think, when he noted
recently:

> I think the reason that socialism failed consistently was that as long
> as socialism is managed by atheists, you just get the play of egos.[20]

By atheists, Mailer meant the socialist (not the Buddhist) kind of
atheism: the failure to root our values, as he puts it, in a "larger sense

of things",[21] and, I would add, in a *kinder* sense of things.

We need to face the fact that the Western dissident movement has evolved out of a culture that is in many respects deeply uncompassionate. From an aggressive and hard-hearted culture, an aggressive and hard-hearted—and therefore largely impotent—resistance movement has evolved. Cohesive radical movements will never be built on the actions of individuals who view anger and hatred as acceptable, and even empowering. For if rational dissident thought undermines the deceptions of power, it is anger that undermines rational dissident thought. In my view, this psychological poverty of Western radical dissent is one of the great unrecognized achievements of the mainstream propaganda system.

When we look back over the course of human history, it seems clear that 'the problem' is not hatred as against love, but rather conditional kindness as against unconditional kindness. Amnesty International tells us that young men who love and desire the approval of their fathers and peers make highly efficient torturers. We know that the Nazis loved their Fuehrer and the 'Aryan race', that Soviet killers loved their 'revolution'. Conditional love is not a half-blessing, a half-way house to utopia; it lies behind every act of revenge and many of the worst horrors of human life.

We may love our chosen beau, belle, family, class or nation with unbounded passion, but a threat to any or all of these may elicit hatred of equal intensity. Surely the world is in such a terrible crisis precisely because it is *not* enough to love ourselves but not others, to love the poor but grind our teeth at the élite, to love women but not men, to grieve for the tortured but hate the torturer, to adore animals but despise people.

Indeed, in what lies ahead I will argue that it is only by striving to understand the true extent and cause of the suffering of *all*, and by generating compassion for all on the basis of that understanding, that any can be saved. I will not be suggesting that this comes naturally or easily for any of us, only that the benefits, even from partial success, must be enormous.

In truth, could it ever be more obvious than it is today that to love only 'this one' or 'that one' in isolation from the world of beings around us is to abandon all of us, including our loved ones, to the forces of greed, hatred and ignorance? We are living in a time when 'looking after number one' and desiring that "all beings be happy in heart" are revealed to be synonymous.

Chapter One

DEMOLISHING DEMOCRACY
The West and the Third World

It never happened. Nothing ever happened. Even *while* it was happening it wasn't happening. It didn't matter. It was of no interest. The crimes of the US throughout the world have been systematic, clinical, remorseless and fully documented but *nobody talks about them*. Nobody ever has.—Harold Pinter in the *Guardian*, 4th December 1996.

Anyone Seen the Bad Guy?
In our society it is commonly assumed that Britain, the United States and other Western nations are great and passionate defenders of liberty and democracy. The world around us may be in a mess, but not as a result of *our* lack of trying. Powerful though we may be, there is only so much we can do to save people from themselves and their ethnic and religious strife. Burma? Nigeria? East Timor? Colombia? Chechnya? Terrible—but we can only do so much.

Western benevolence is taken for granted to such an extent that it seems almost ridiculous to affirm it. We might also like to mention that breathing is good for our health, that it is nice to have a sun shining on our planet. What could possibly be gained by making such statements, other than the understanding that the individual making them must be disturbed in some way, or making a crude attempt at humour?

After all, in the remarkable display of euphoria that accompanied President Clinton's visit to Ireland in the winter of 1995, the media never tired of describing the US president as "the leader of the free world". The phrase was used reflexively by newspaper, radio and TV commentators; yet the implications are enormous. If the president of the United States is the leader of the "free world", both he and his country must surely be committed to the spread of freedom throughout the world. By inference, then, all these mainstream media entities in Britain, and the West generally, are implicitly assuring us that the United States is indeed dedicated to the spread of justice, peace and human rights.

As President Clinton himself said of US principles: "The violence done to these innocent [Bosnian] civilians does violence to the principles on which America stands." [1]

The statement was received with sober reflection and much head-nodding by the media—no one questioned it. This is not surprising, for Clinton's statement was merely the latest in a long tradition of US claims to the moral high ground. In accepting the presidential nomination in 1988, George Bush observed that:

> This has been called the American Century because in it we were the dominant force for good in the world... Now we are on the verge of a new century, and what country's name will it bear? I say it will be another American Century. [2]

In April 1950, Paul Nitze, head of the State Department Policy Planning Staff, wrote a state paper (NSC 68) contrasting the "inescapably militant" evil of the Soviet "slave state" with the United States "founded upon the dignity and worth of the individual" and characterized by "marvellous diversity", "deep tolerance", "lawfulness", and a commitment "to create and maintain an environment in which every individual has the opportunity to realize his creative powers." On foreign affairs, Nitze wrote:

> The essential tolerance of our world outlook, our generous and constructive impulses, and the absence of covetousness in our international relations are assets of potentially enormous influence. [3]

And Henry Kissinger also left us in no doubt about the profoundly moral basis of US foreign policy:

> In fact, moral purpose has motivated every American war this century... The new approach [in Somalia] claims an extension in the reach of morality... [4]

Not just concerned with basing foreign policy on moral purpose, then, the United States is actually seeking out new moral frontiers to conquer.

Jimmy Carter—leader of what is generally considered the great US human rights administration—assured us that human rights are "the Soul of our foreign policy".

Independent observers outside the US concur with this view.

Financial Times writer Michael Prowse summed up the US position during the Gulf War thus:

> The single most important justification for the US hard line has been to deter future acts of aggression. With the Cold War over, President Bush rightly wants to create a 'new world order' in which weak nations need not fear their stronger neighbours. He is prepared to risk sacrifices today in order to protect future generations.[5]

Bush, then, was willing to sacrifice *Americans*, and not merely for future generations of Americans but for future generations in "weak nations" everywhere, so that they will not need to "fear their stronger neighbours". Truly this is an extension in the reach of the great "Soul" of US foreign policy.

To be sure, the United States is not the only benevolent presence watching over the globe. Moral feeling has long been a motivating force at the heart of the British empire. Churchill once noted "the reputation of the British empire as a valiant and benignant force in the history of mankind." [6]

For Harold Macmillan, the empire was "a strong instrument", "for the preservation of peace and the spread of civilization throughout a great part of the globe".[7]

In similar vein, the chairman and the deputy director of one of Britain's leading academic institutes write:

> The promotion of democratic values through foreign policy is most directly demonstrated by government attitudes to human rights outside Britain. In the nineteenth century the Royal Navy extended the anti-slavery campaign from Britain to the Atlantic and Indian Oceans, enforcing basic standards of civilized behaviour... Human rights issues are no less controversial or difficult today, though British governments have far less capability to intervene in the affairs of other countries.[8]

Australians are no less steadfast in their moral crusade. "All nations should know that the rule of law must prevail over the rule of force in international relations", Prime Minister Bob Hawke once declared.[9]

Little wonder, then, that you and I have grown up with an unshakeable conviction that we are living in countries utterly devoted to the defence of the rights of human beings. It is a view reinforced by the daily outpourings of the entire mass media system.

When President Clinton declares his outrage at the violation of American principles in Bosnia, we see Clinton but we hear the decent and gentle Henry Fonda in *Fail Safe*, the warm and charming Michael Douglas in *The American President*, the passionately moral have-a-go-hero of *Independence Day*. The list could go on forever: John Wayne, tough but tender at the Alamo; Clint Eastwood—unorthodox but right—blasting assorted 'punks' to kingdom come. This is how Americans are, who they are, who *we* are. We know that their culture, and ours, is saturated with moral concern: Hollywood's obsession with sadistic revenge is usually moral at heart. Either these assumptions are somehow being distorted, or they are basically correct: Americans and Britons are fundamentally good, decent, people, incapable of the sort of crimes we see in the world around us. Rousseau's point, however, remains well made.

> I am aware that the English make a boast of their humanity and of the kindly disposition of their race, which they call 'good-natured people'; but in vain do they proclaim this fact; no one else says it of them.[10]   Certainly not the colonialised!

Our deeply entrenched notions of our own benevolence are immediately called into question by imagining what would happen if this benevolence were truly put to the test. What would happen if democratic governments came to power in, say, Saudi Arabia, Kuwait, the United Arab Emirates and elsewhere in the Middle East? Would not truly democratic regimes sequester local oil resources for the benefit of local poor people? Would not local people demand it of their democratic representatives? And would that not threaten the billions of dollars of profit piped away by Western oil companies operating in those countries? Would the West, with overwhelming economic and military power to hand, permit such a situation? As Charles Glass suggests, the answer is clear:

> The United States has one strategic interest in the Middle East: oil. Everything else is gravy, sentiment, rhetoric... American transnational corporations do not care about Israeli settlers and their biblical claims, Palestinians who are losing their land and water, Kurds who are caught stateless between gangsters in Baghdad and Teheran, victims of war or torture in Sudan, Afghanistan, Algeria, South Lebanon...[11]

As Glass also notes, this explains why Arab public opinion is powerless:

Almost every Arab country has become like an Indian princely state, with American bankers, security experts and military advisers running the show for a native potentate. The largest embassy on earth is the American mission in Cairo. America owns the region, for the moment.[12]

Does this not mean, at least in theory, that the West is not merely tolerant but wholeheartedly supportive of authoritarian Middle Eastern regimes which suppress local popular movements—whilst creaming off a percentage and sending the rest back to their Western masters? And if this forcible denial of democracy requires violence, terror and even torture—as it surely must, given the aspirations of discontented people forced to live in poverty—then are Western nations not required to tolerate, and perhaps even actively support, terror and torture?

But then where does this leave the famous Western commitment to human rights, "the Soul of our foreign policy"? And where does it leave the rest of the Third World? Is there any essential difference in the perceived need, motivation and ability to protect the vast profits being hauled away by Western corporations operating out of South America, Africa and Asia? Are not cash crops, minerals, timber and the like merely 'oil' of a different type? In which case, what does this tell us about the logical relationship between the global Western quest for profits and the global absence of democracy? And what does it tell us about the global presence of torture?

To go one step further: if true, where would all this leave our much-vaunted Western 'free press', which never raises such awful questions and possibilities?

Speculative thought aside, there is a further problem with the standard version of Third World-Western relations: the historical facts.

An End to Sentimentality

The reality, even as expressed by state documents, is so different, so utterly contradictory to the mainstream political and media version, that it is breathtaking.

In 1948, George Kennan, head of the State Department Policy Planning Staff, wrote one of the key state papers (PPS 23) in which he secretly explained post-war US foreign policy goals. Chief among them, Kennan explained, was to maintain "the position of disparity" in wealth between the US and other nations.

...We have 50% of the world's wealth, but only 6.3% of its population... In this situation, we cannot fail to be the object of envy and resentment. Our real task in the coming period is to devise a pattern of relationships which will permit us to maintain this position of disparity without positive detriment to our national security. To do so, we will have to dispense with all sentimentality and daydreaming; and our attention will have to be concentrated on our immediate national objectives. We need not deceive ourselves that we can afford today the luxury of altruism and world-benefaction... We should cease to talk about vague and—for the Far East—unreal objectives such as human rights, the raising of living standards, and democratisation.[13]

Note that this is one of the key policy documents of the post-war period. Note, also, of course, that it represents the exact antithesis of the position declared by Clinton, Bush, Kissinger and Carter. Note, further, that although top secret at the time, the document has long been available to the media and yet is almost entirely unknown.

Elsewhere, Defence Secretary Robert McNamara observed in 1963 that in the Latin American cultural environment the US military must be prepared "to remove government leaders from office whenever, in the judgement of the military, the conduct of those leaders is injurious to the welfare of the nation." [14]

McNamara omitted to specify exactly which nation's "welfare" he had in mind, although in the context of the policy goals outlined by Kennan the answer is not in doubt. Already it should be clear that the real goals of US post-war foreign policy have been the maintenance of Kennan's "disparity" by fair means or foul, including the overthrow of other national governments where required. Such a conclusion is no dissident fantasy: we need only take a look at publicly available state documents.

The US stance outlined above was no mere cold war phenomenon. Much earlier, Secretary of State Robert Lansing had commented to President Wilson that the Monroe Doctrine of 1823 was based on "selfishness alone":

The United States considers its own interests. The integrity of other American nations is an incident, not an end.[15]

We are told that President Wilson found Lansing's argument "unanswerable", though he felt it would be "impolitic" to state it openly. [16]

Echoing Kennan, Woodrow Wilson had himself explained exactly what was meant by the United States' "interests":

> Since trade ignores national boundaries and the manufacturer insists on having the world as a market, the flag of his nation must follow him, and the doors of the nations which are closed against him must be battered down... Colonies must be obtained or planted, in order that no useful corner of the world may be overlooked or left unused.[17]

In Britain in the 1890s, similar attitudes held sway, with Cecil Rhodes declaring:

> We must find new lands from which we can easily obtain raw materials and at the same time exploit the cheap slave labour that is available from the natives of the colonies. The colonies would also provide a dumping ground for the surplus produced in our factories.[18]

Churchill said much the same in private:

> We are not a young people with an innocent record and a scanty inheritance. We have engrossed to ourselves... an altogether disproportionate share of the wealth and traffic of the world. We have got all we want in territory, and our claim to be left in the unmolested enjoyment of vast and splendid possessions, mainly acquired by violence, largely maintained by force, often seems less reasonable to others than to us.[19]

What, as individuals, are we to make of all this? It is forever assumed (and regularly declared) in the mainstream media, by those we assume to be the brightest and best of a basically free press operating in a basically free society, that Bill Clinton is indeed the benign leader of a profoundly principled nation which is not prepared to sit by while its principles, including the moral obligation to protect innocent civilians, are violated.

It is a wonderful idea, and it is easy to understand why everyone—journalists and public alike—would want to believe it. Psychologically, human beings have every reason to prefer to believe that great power is in great and kind hands; it makes for a comforting picture of the world. The alternative—that power is in irresponsible and even dangerous hands—makes for a much less comforting picture.

To suggest that the mainstream media view is mistaken is firstly to threaten to take away a highly reassuring picture of the world and to replace it with a highly disturbing one. Secondly, it threatens to undermine the basic assumption that we are living in a free society with a free press, the effect of which may well be to completely undermine our sense of what is real and true. The latter is an awesome prospect, and it is all too easy to understand why few people will even entertain it. The fact that few *are* willing is witnessed by the truly astonishing level of conformity in the mainstream media: there are problems, but at heart the West is a genuinely benign force in the world.

Stranger than Fiction: the South American Paradox

Spectacularly rich in natural resources and blessed with some of the most fertile and abundant land in the world, South America also has the great good fortune of backing onto the most economically and militarily powerful nation the world has ever seen. And, as we have discussed, the United States is no mere common or garden imperial power, but a nation devoted with a passion to the advancement of freedom and democracy.

With only this information to go by, we would surely be forgiven for imagining that South America must be something close to an earthly paradise, a great showcase of democracy and freedom. The reality is very different. As Martha Gellhorn wrote of Brazil:

> All countries are different but Brazil is much too different. It is beautiful and gigantic; two-and-a-half times the size of all Western Europe. The richness of its natural resources matches its richness in land. The population is small, 153 million. Given reasonably honest, intelligent, efficient government, Brazilians should be among the most privileged people on earth. Instead, generation after generation, the great majority (80 per cent, some say) remain poor.[20]

And not merely poor. For much of this century, South America has been a charnel house of horrors; poverty, sickness, starvation, disappearances, torture, mutilation, rape and massacres. The scale of the misery is astonishing.

In Brazil, while perhaps a quarter of the population enjoy a middle-class European standard of living, seventy-five to eighty per cent of the people live in wretched conditions in huge shanty towns around Rio de Janeiro and São Paulo. Peter Evans writes that "the fundamental conflict in Brazil is between the one, or perhaps five, percent of the population that comprises the élite and the eighty percent that has been left out of the 'Brazilian model' of development." [21] It is estimated that eight million Brazilian children under the age of fourteen are homeless and live as beggars, thieves and prostitutes. The Brazilian journal *Veja* reports that over half the population live in families whose incomes are below the minimum wage.

In Guatemala today, some eighty-seven per cent of the population live below the poverty line, according to the Health Ministry; seventy-two per cent cannot afford a minimum diet; six million, from a population of nine million, have no access to health services and 3.6 million lack drinking water.

In oil-rich Venezuela, according to official figures, over forty per cent live in extreme poverty, while the government admits that only fifty-seven per cent of Venezuelans can afford more than one meal a day. In 1991, thirty-three per cent of the population suffered 'critical poverty', defined as the inability to meet half the basic nutritional requirements.

In Nicaragua, a quarter of the children are malnourished. In late 1993, 100,000 people were starving on Nicaragua's Atlantic coast. In Chile, the journal *Apsi* reports that about half the country is becoming a desert. According to the journal *Excelsior*, under General Pinochet the number of poor people rose from one million to seven million, out of a total population of twelve million. In Argentina, forty per cent of the economically active population are unemployed, according to journalists James Petras and Pablo Pozzi. They also report that:

> The speculative economy, reinforced by a neo-liberal economic policy, which impoverishes most of the population while destroying Argentina's internal market and productive capacity, and scarce resources has generated a Hobbesian world, a savage struggle to survive while the rich continue to reap windfall profits. [22]

A University of Mexico census reports that in Mexico sixty per cent of households are unable to meet basic needs. Maude Barlow, chairperson of a Canadian study group on Mexico describes the *maquilladoras* economic regions on the US/Mexican border as "built by Fortune 500 to take advantage of a desperate people". [23]

The tragedy of mass poverty has not lessened since the end of the cold war, so often used to explain the need for harsh economic measures. Leonardo Boff, one of Latin America's best known exponents of liberation theology, has this to say:

> Today the problem is no longer marginalization of the poor but complete exclusion. The question now is how to survive. That's why liberation theology deals with fundamental issues like work, health, food, shelter and how we live.[24]

Though the world is no longer constrained by the need to fend off the evil march of communism, there is still not, it seems, any way to stave off the evil march of poverty and despair—quite the reverse:

> The poor are much worse off today than 30 or 40 years ago... Brazil has 150 million inhabitants. For a third of them the system functions very well. But for the other 100 million it is a disaster.[25]

A disaster indeed, and getting worse. Phil Gunson of the *Guardian* reports that in 1960 the poorest fifty per cent of Brazilians accounted for 17.7 per cent of national income.[26] By 1990, their income had fallen to 10.4 per cent of the total. The picture is not altogether bleak: Brazil's current tally of billionaires is ten, making them ninth in the world league. More generally, Gunson writes that "86 million Latin Americans survive on less than a dollar a day, and if income distribution is to be left to market forces, everything indicates that their numbers can only increase."

What, then, accounts for the strange paradox that is South America? How can we make sense of so much poverty and violence in such a naturally wealthy region? And why has the "world's greatest democracy" not been able to do more to assist its wealthy but tortured neighbour? Why has the "extension" in Kissinger's "reach of morality" not stretched as far as South America?

Realistic answers can be found only if we are prepared to face the ugly realities of power in what we like to imagine are the Western 'democracies'.

Demolishing Democracy: the Western Connection

Beneath the party political circuses designed for public consumption, corporations constitute the real power in the United States, as they do elsewhere in the West. Corporations, of course, are in the business of maximizing profits, and the maximization of profits requires what are known as 'good investment climates'.

In the Third World, a good investment climate is one providing low cost access to natural and human resources, unimpeded by democratic constraints. Low cost access means poverty wages, no welfare safety system (which would give the poor an option other than working for poverty wages), no trade unions (which might seek to improve the condition of the poor), no community organizations (which might threaten to raise costs by enabling peasants to organize and struggle against exploitation). Workers should have minimal rights: no restrictions on hours worked, no safety standards, no restrictions on the use of dangerous pesticides and banned Western products generally, all of which would increase costs. Exploitation of the environment should similarly be allowed to proceed unhindered: conservation, the protection of endangered species and the prohibition of use of dangerous chemicals all impede profitability and are to be avoided as far as possible. As required, peasants have to be forcibly cleared from their homes and land to make way for cash crops and cattle-rearing for export to the West.

Many victims of 'good investment climates' are not merely poor. They may be desperate: required to watch their children die of starvation and easily preventable diseases; to witness their children entering into prostitution, being murdered as 'street children'; to see them sniffing glue to stave off hunger pangs, and so on. A Salvadoran peasant made the point well to Charles Clements:

> You gringos are always worried about the violence done with machine guns and machetes. But there is another kind of violence that you must be aware of too. To watch your children die of sickness and hunger while you can do nothing is a violence of the spirit.[27]

This "violence of the spirit" in the cause of profit is an ugly business—there is no uglier—and the question that automatically arises is: what kind of people would be willing to inflict this kind of suffering on infants, boys and girls, old people, mothers and fathers, husbands and wives, brothers and sisters, cousins, families? The answer is the military and business élites that have long plagued Latin America and the Third World generally.

We could spend a long time listing the dictators supported by the West; the trend is more or less invariable, and never mentioned in the press. Our journalists somehow fail to notice the entire historical record (including state documentation), and find nothing strange in the fact that the West has long supported the likes of

Suharto, Pinochet, the Shah, Papa and Baby Doc, Somoza, Galtieri, Trujillo, Diem and others, whilst simultaneously raging against Castro for his supposed human rights atrocities.

It is no accident that these tyrants prosper under the nose of the greatest democracy in the world; or that they, and the suppression that inevitably follows in their wake, arise in a world where the Western powers have the ability to isolate and cripple, both economically and militarily, Third World countries such as Cuba, Iraq, North Korea and Vietnam. Tyrants of this kind are not only not an unforeseen accident but an essential component of the Western programme of profit maximization, as becomes clear when we consider the result of the subordination of local people for foreign profit.

Slaughtered and starved by Western-imposed dictators, it is not uncommon for desperate Third World people to perceive that they have nothing left to lose, and so they resort to violent resistance. This type of resistance is qualitatively different from civil resistance in the West—these resisters really do have nothing left to lose, and so are much more difficult to suppress.

One consequence is that resistance of this sort can be stopped only by measures even more extreme than the desperation that lies behind it. As Penny Lernoux has noted, the impoverished masses of Latin America "will not stay quietly on the farms or in the slums unless they are terribly afraid".[28]

For the greatest degree of fear to be instilled, it must be done systematically: people must understand that to talk to the wrong person, or simply to be in the wrong place at the wrong time, will lead to their being dragged away, never to be seen alive again.

There have been desperate pleas for help from (and for) South America, but they have rarely been heard in the West where, in order to hide the truth, it is necessary for South America to barely exist in people's consciousness.

For a long time Western values were imposed under the cover of the cold war, with people-versus-profit wars being fought out again and again in places like El Salvador (50,000 dead during the 1980s), Guatemala (200,000 dead since the CIA-backed coup of 1954), Argentina (many thousands dead during the "dirty war" of the seventies and early eighties), Nicaragua, Colombia, Chile, Mexico, Haiti and elsewhere.

The problem, we were told at the time (and most of us believed it), was the 'ruthless and monolithic conspiracy' of communism:

Just as the Indian was branded a savage beast to justify his exploitation, so those who sought social reform were branded communists to justify their persecution.[29]

In reality, communism was simply a convenient catch-all term which applied to any group of individuals threatening Western interests. Even mild reformists seeking to alleviate some of the worst excesses were removed from the political scene by Western powers, not because they threatened global communist revolution, but because they threatened to lift the people from total misery, perhaps instilling hopes of democracy and so threatening to undermine the 'good investment climate' system.

Reformists should note that the reason torture is so widespread in the Third World is that the terrible suffering required for Western profit-maximizing is like a giant pressure cooker: violence constitutes the lid—lift it even slightly, and the people might explode into democratic life. For this reason, even small examples of independent progress which might restore some hope to the desperate are feared by those who have genuine cause to worry: Western state and corporate élites. Some examples from the real world are instructive in this regard.

Taking the "Hard Track"

Elected in 1950, in Guatemala's first ever democratic elections, Jacobo Arbenz's aim was to transform Guatemala "from a backward country with a predominantly feudal economy to a modern capitalist state".[30] As part of this process, Arbenz felt he had a strong mandate to instigate land reforms. According to Paul Farmer, these reforms affected about a thousand plantations, but only sixteen per cent of the country's total idle cultivatable lands in private hands. Around 100,000 peasants received land through the reform; 234,000 acres of unused land owned by the US-owned United Fruit Company (UFCO) were expropriated with the offer of compensation that UFCO found "unacceptable". Displeased by Arbenz's reforms, UFCO began to apply pressure on the US government and the CIA to take action. As Stephen Schlesinger wrote:

> Under the new regime, the Guatemalan Congress approved a mild labour code which forced the United Fruit, among other employers, to improve the wretched working conditions of its peasants. While the code was being debated, the State Department began to

despatch warnings to the Guatemalan President at the behest of United Fruit.[31]

An UFCO lobbyist warned of the threat Arbenz posed to "stability", declaring him to be a communist preparing a "beachhead" for Soviet expansion. In reality, Arbenz was a left-of-centre Socialist; only four of the fifty-six seats in the Guatemalan Congress were held by Communists. In response, however, the US State Department, working closely with the CIA, evolved a covert plan to overthrow Arbenz, with the name PBSUCCESS. One of the brains behind the latter, Secretary of State John Foster Dulles, was an executive partner of Sullivan and Cromwell, the law firm representing UFCO. Dulles's brother Allen, who later became director of the CIA, had also carried out legal work for the same company. A vast propaganda campaign, orchestrated by UFCO through the public relations guru Edward Bernays, was launched to undermine political stability in Guatemala. Richard Immerman writes that:

> He [Bernays] was extremely successful and, in reality, accomplished for the State Department the propaganda component of its own Guatemalan strategy. [32]

As a result, anti-Arbenz propaganda began to appear in major newspapers throughout the US and the world beyond. Meanwhile the CIA selected Colonel Carlos Enrique Castillo Armas to lead an invasion from Honduras. Immerman explains how the US government created the right atmosphere for invasion, working through the US Information Agency (USIA). From May to June 1954 alone:

> The USIA boasted that... it prepared two hundred articles and backgrounders, designed some twenty-seven thousand anti-communist cartoons and posters, and developed both films and scripts for media outlets. By means of wireless file, cable, and fast pouch, this propaganda blitz reached all parts of the globe... Action against Arbenz required a conducive international climate, and the State Department succeeded in establishing it.[33]

Stephen Schlesinger reports that "the [1954] Putsch was conceived of and run at the highest levels of the American Government in closest cahoots with the United Fruit Company and under the overall direction of Secretary of State John Foster Dulles, backed by President Eisenhower." [34]

On June 18, Castillo Armas and his forces crossed the Honduran border; on June 27 Arbenz resigned, and Armas was installed as president. Armas immediately returned land back to United Fruit and abolished tax on interests and dividends to foreign investors. Arbenz was later found drowned in his bath, whereas Armas received a ticker-tape parade in New York City and honorary degrees from Columbia and Fordham universities.

Following the invasion, the military élite took control of the economy and the country more generally, with government troops patrolling both city and countryside in full battle gear. More than 200 union leaders were immediately killed. Within two months of the invasion, some 8,000 peasants had been murdered in a terror campaign that targeted UFCO union organisers and Indian village leaders. The US Embassy lent its assistance, providing lists of "communists" to be eliminated or imprisoned and tortured.

Exiled journalist Julio Godoy, who had worked on the Guatemalan newspaper *La Epoca*, whose offices were blown up by government terrorists, compared conditions in Guatemala with those in Eastern Europe:

> While the Moscow-imposed government in Prague would degrade and humiliate reformers, the Washington-made government in Guatemala would kill them. It still does, in a virtual genocide that has taken more than 150,000 victims [in what Amnesty International calls] 'a government programme of political murder'. [35]

Over the next four decades, as many as 200,000 civilians were murdered by government forces, with disappearance, torture and mutilation the norm. According to Amnesty International, victims were found "with signs of torture or mutilation along roadsides or in ravines, floating in plastic bags in lakes or rivers, or buried in mass graves in the countryside", many of them being from the peasantry and urban poor. [36] Over 440 villages were totally destroyed, with vast areas of the highlands wrecked.

The British Foreign Office—the control room of Churchill's "valiant and benignant force"—recorded some discomfort at the crudity of the operation:

> If the Americans had quietly worked for the overthrow of the Arbenz government, but nevertheless preserved the decencies of international justice, I think a different impression would have been

left behind about the whole affair...We are glad to see Arbenz gone, but, like Henry II with Beckett, we do not like the circumstances attending his removal.[37]

The act of quietly working for the overthrow of a democratically elected government being, according to the Foreign Office, in complete accordance with the decencies of international justice. The FO's abiding concern was with the "impression" that resulted from being too obviously associated with mass murder, rather than with justice.

Despite reservations about style, the British position was never in doubt. A month after the coup, British Foreign Secretary Anthony Eden wrote with due graciousness to the newly-installed presidential office:

Please convey to His Excellency the President the good wishes of Her Majesty's Government and accept the assurance of my highest consideration.[38]

Shortly after the coup, UFCO's man Dulles addressed the US nation on the major TV networks regarding this "new and glorious chapter" in the already great tradition of the United States. Dulles, in an almost eerily exact reversal of the truth, thanked "the loyal citizens of Guatemala who, in the face of terrorism and violence and against what seemed insuperable odds, had the courage and the will to eliminate the traitorous tools of foreign despots." [39]

The reality was very different, as Edward Herman says:

No shred of evidence ever turned up after the [Guatemalan] coup establishing a secret tie to the Soviets.[40]

It was no accident that there were no Soviet troops, advisers, or arms, Herman reports; the Guatemalan government had been extremely careful to avoid any formal diplomatic relations with Soviet bloc countries out of respect for US sensitivities.

No matter, for throughout the cold war the 'threat' of communism always worked well to trigger deep-seated fears regarding the 'Red menace' that had been implanted over many years by corporate TV, newspaper and cinema propaganda. With few other sources of information about the world, the public were not to know that communism was nowhere in sight in Guatemala; many thousands of innocents were being tortured and killed solely for the sake of profit and to prevent hope being raised amongst other peoples in South America by a "good example".

The deception continues to this day. On the Charlie Rose US talk show of March 31, 1995, journalist Allan Nairn confronted Elliot Abrams, Assistant Secretary of State for Latin American affairs in the Reagan administration. Nairn reminded Abrams of some of the facts:

> Across the board, and in the face of the systematic policy of slaughter by the Guatemalan military, more than 110,000 civilians [were] killed by that military since 1978, [in] what Amnesty International has called a 'government programme of political murder', the US has continued to provide covert assistance to the G-2 [the Guatemalan military intelligence service responsible for coordinating the killings] and they have continued, especially during the time of Mr. Abrams, to provide political aid and comfort...[41]

Abrams dithered, but finally responded: "I am admitting that it was the policy of the United States, under Democrats and Republicans, approved by Congress repeatedly to oppose a Communist guerrilla victory anywhere in Central America including in Guatemala."

Nairn replied: "'A Communist guerrilla victory!' Ninety-five per cent of these victims are civilians—peasant organisers, human rights leaders, priests—assassinated by the US-backed Guatemalan army." Abrams, Nairn continued, "would be a fit subject for a ... Nuremberg-style enquiry..." [42]

Abrams laughed.

Readers should not be surprised if some or all of the above is unfamiliar to them. Schlesinger explains:

> What strikes an observer immediately about the Guatemala affair is how history has over the years practically abandoned it. No book has ever explored it; no Senate committee has ever investigated it.[43]

Salvador Allende's Chilean regime met a similar fate. Elected in 1970, Allende, like Arbenz, was bent on mild reform to alleviate the worst symptoms of poverty. A European-style social democrat, Allende's principal aims were to assert Chilean independence and nationalize industry. As part of his plan to combat poverty and malnutrition, Allende instituted a free milk programme for half a million children. During three years of troubled rule, infant mortality dropped by seventeen per cent, deaths of babies from respiratory diseases fell by thirty per cent and malnutrition among children declined by seventeen per cent.

A few days after Allende's victory, however, President Nixon called a meeting of the '40 Committee' with CIA Director Richard Helms and chaired by Henry "moral purpose" Kissinger. Two responses to the 'problem' in Chile were discussed: a 'soft track' and a 'hard track'.

Responsibility for the 'soft track' was assigned to Ambassador Edward Korry, who defined this option as the attempt to "do all within our power to condemn Chile and the Chileans to utmost deprivation and poverty".[44] Or "to make the economy scream", as Nixon put it.[45]

The even less sympathetic second track entailed the organization of an outright military coup, under the pretext—as was standard for the day—that Allende's attempts to relieve the suffering of the poor represented 'communism'.

Egged on by documents forged by the CIA, indicating that communists intended a bloody coup (involving the beheading of the top echelons of the military), Chilean generals were persuaded to take the second track—the bloody coup of 1973. From that time to 1978, US government figures show that the new Chilean dictators, led by Augusto Pinochet, received fully $226.7 million in US economic aid (including arms sales totalling $146.6 million). Of the coup, the Catholic Institute for International Relations (CIIR) reports:

> The single-minded ferocity of the coup and the subsequent deliberate use of torture, 'disappearances' and murder had at that time no parallel in the history of Chile or Latin America, a continent with a long experience of dictatorship and military brutality.[46]

Later still, the United States supported the cruel dictatorship in El Salvador during the eighties for all the familiar, best reasons. In the words of President Ronald Reagan, US support was necessary

> to halt the infiltration into the Americas, by terrorists and by outside interference, and those who aren't just aiming at El Salvador, but, I think, are aiming at the whole of Central and possibly later South America and, I'm sure, eventually North America.[47]

Reagan "thinks" communists were aiming to take Central and "possibly" South America, aiming "eventually", that is, as the final step, at North America, about which he is suddenly "sure". Reagan, then, was more sure of the final result of this evil strategy than he was about the necessary links in the chain by which it could be achieved! Putting this bizarre reasoning aside, we notice the humble use of "I think". In reality, Reagan's position was neither a tentative subjective view nor a personal position; it was a required view, a systemic view rooted in entrenched economic realities: the corporate and allied state determination to control Third World resources and maximize profits. Reagan's position was a vital component of this profit-seeking by other means.

In similar vein, Secretary of State Alexander Haig asserted in 1982 that he had "overwhelming and irrefutable" evidence that the guerrillas were controlled from outside El Salvador. [48]

A few months before Reagan's dramatic declaration, a *New York Times* reporter asked Jose Napoleon Duarte why there were guerrillas in the hills. The reason, Duarte said, was:

> Fifty years of lies, fifty years of injustice, fifty years of frustration. This is a history of people starving to death, living in misery. For fifty years the same people had all the power, all the money, all the jobs, all the education, all the opportunities. [49]

In short, standard Third World 'democracy'. As elsewhere in the Third world, desperate poverty and crude exploitation, not Soviet designs, were at the heart of the conflict, a view confirmed even by the US Ambassador to El Salvador, Robert White:

> The revolution situation came about in El Salvador because you had what was one of the most selfish oligarchies the world has ever seen, combined with a corrupt security force... [50]

Following a series of fraudulent elections, culminating in the 1977 elections which were finally 'won' by the ruling PCN party (the opposition party was said to have lost, won and then lost again), a mass demonstration became a bloodbath when hundreds of protestors were slaughtered by security forces. A war followed; not a civil war exactly, more a war between the poor on the one hand, and international corporate interests and their local élite representatives on the other.

An idea of what conditions were like in El Salvador during this period, and how the reality was kept from the Western public by the 'free press', can be gained by considering the situation facing voters in the elections of March 1982.

International observers from the United States and Great Britain (delegates from forty other nations, including Canada, Japan, and all Western European nations except Britain had declined the offer to observe the elections) reported that they saw no evidence of government coercion on the day of the election. They also reported a large turnout of people determined to vote, which, they assumed, indicated great public enthusiasm for the elections. The media reinforced this impression, with top US TV commentator Dan Rather exclaiming: "A triumph! A million people to the polls." [51] Clark Kerr, President Emeritus of the University of California at Berkeley, declared "I've never seen people so eager to vote." Republican Bob Livingstone called the elections the "most inspiring thing I've ever seen"; while Senator Nancy Kassebaum called them an "exceptionally fair election". [52]

In the United States, observers and media reported free and fair elections; a triumph for democracy.

As Edward Herman and Frank Brodhead explain in their book *Demonstration Elections*, that election day in El Salvador was actually a grotesque fraud; one that took place in the context of a campaign of violence and intimidation on a scale barely imaginable to us in the West, violence which made the election utterly meaningless, quite regardless of what was seen to happen on the day itself.

To take only a few examples: in the eighteen-month period leading up the elections, twenty-six journalists were murdered in El Salvador. The only two Salvadoran newspapers critical of the government, *La Cronica* and *El Independiente*, were closed in July 1980 and January 1981 respectively. In December 1981 the Salvadoran Communal Union reported that eighty-three of its members had been murdered by government security forces and death squads. The entire six-person top leadership of the main opposition party, the FDR, was seized by government security forces in 1980, tortured, murdered and mutilated. More generally, any left-wing political leader or organizer who gained any kind of prominence in El Salvador in the years 1980-83 was liable to be murdered, and many of them were. More generally still, between October 1979 and March 1982, killings of ordinary citizens occurred at the average rate of over 800 per month, on conservative estimates.

To put the immensity of this violence in such a small country into perspective, Herman and Brodhead converted the figures to a country with the population size of the United States. Doing so:

allows us to imagine an election in the United States preceded by the murder of a thousand-odd officials of the Democratic Party; 5,000 labour leaders; 1,200 journalists; and a million ordinary citizens. Internal and external refugee numbers in El Salvador would correspond to a US equivalent of over 30 million refugees.[53]

Throughout this period, massive supplies of aid from the United States poured in to support the tottering dictatorship, as some 50,000 people were being killed.

Shortly before his assassination in 1980, Archbishop Oscar Romero sent a letter to President Carter imploring him to suspend US 'aid' to the generals of El Salvador. The aid, Romero observed:

> will surely increase injustice here and sharpen the repression that has been unleashed against the people's organizations fighting to defend their *most fundamental human rights*. [my emphasis]

Political power, Romero wrote, is "in the hands of the armed forces" who "know only how to repress the people and defend the interests of the Salvadoran oligarchy... It would be totally wrong and deplorable if the Salvadoran people were to be frustrated, repressed, or in any way impeded from deciding for itself the economic and political future of our country by intervention on the part of a foreign power."[54]

Romero received no reply. As Duarte pointed out, US policy makers had bigger fish to fry than the human rights of a few Salvadorans, the intention of their policy being, after all, to:

> maintain the Iberoamerican countries in a condition of direct dependence upon the international political decisions most beneficial to the United States, both at the hemisphere and world levels. Thus [the North Americans] preach to us of democracy while everywhere they support dictatorships.[55]

Beyond the Americas, the CIA employed 'rent-a-mob' to help overthrow the Iranian nationalist Musaddiq in 1952. Once again, Musaddiq's crime was to seek a measure of national independence from Western domination and control over the country's natural resources. In May 1951, Musaddiq nationalized oil operations in Iran, including the Anglo-Iranian Oil company (later renamed British Petroleum), at which point his fate was sealed. In standard fashion, rumours of communist infiltration were moved rapidly to the fore and once again Iran became a country in need of being saved from itself.

In reality, the UK Ambassador noted that the communists in Iran "have played a largely passive role, content to let matters take their course with only general encouragement from the sidelines... they have not been a major factor in the development of the Musaddiq brand of nationalism." [56]

Indeed, in a rare departure from the script, Secretary of State John Foster Dulles later testified that "there was 'no substantial evidence' to indicate that Iran was cooperating with Russia. On the whole, he added, Muslim opposition to communism is predominant..." [57]

"Our policy," a British official later explained, "was to get rid of Musaddiq as soon as possible." [58] As for his preferred Western replacement, an intelligence memorandum in August 1952 suggested that "we should leave the name-suggesting to the Americans... It should not be difficult to bring the Americans' candidate... to power." [59]

The chosen name, unfortunately for the Iranians, was that of the Shah, who came to power with a little help from his friends, as a US general later testified. "The guns they had in their hands, the trucks they rode in, the armoured cars that they drove through the streets, and the radio communications that permitted their control, were all furnished through the [US] military defence assistance program." [60] US Iran analyst Barry Rubin comments: "All in all, only five Americans with a half-dozen Iranian contacts had organized the entire uprising." [61]

It is interesting to compare the standard media depiction of Britain and the US as staunch defenders of peace, democracy and human rights with the subsequent behaviour of the Shah. In 1975 Amnesty International reported that Iran had the "highest rate of death penalties in the world, no valid system of civilian courts and a history of torture which is beyond belief. No country has a worse record in human rights than Iran." This was in a society where "the entire population was subjected to a constant, all-pervasive terror." [62]

Such repression was a necessary price for the West, whose objective was to prevent Iranian oil reserves falling into the hands of local nationalists. As discussed, it has long been understood that Western interests are best served by dealing with dictators rather than with democrats.

The media's role in all this was simply to fail to state the obvious. In a review of press reporting on Iran under the Shah, William

A. Dorman and Ehsan Omad wrote that "We have been unable to find a single example of a news and feature story in the American mainstream press that uses the label 'dictator'." [63]

Instead, the Shah was presented as a great "liberaliser", with *Time* insisting that "the Shah has a broad base of popular support" [64] among, presumably, the same population being "subjected to a constant, all-pervasive terror". Certainly President Carter's support was never in doubt, as was clear from a speech he made at a banquet in the Shah's presence:

> Iran under the great leadership of the Shah is an island of stability in one of the more troubled areas of the world. This is a great tribute to you, Your Majesty, and to your leadership, and to the respect, admiration and love which your people give to you. [65]

The use of the title "Majesty" was surely intended to lend the proceedings a sense of dignity where only greed and violence were present—a trick used throughout the ages to deceive us into treating exploitative power with respect. Note also the term "stability", as used in connection with Armas, Suharto, Pinochet and the rest. Between the years 1973-78 alone, as the torture and brutality reached its peak, the US government shored up this "stability" with some $15,677 million worth of arms.

For the West, the murder and torture of thousands of Iranians under the Shah constituted merely one of the more difficult lessons to be learned at the 'school of hard knocks':

> Underdeveloped countries with rich resources now have an object lesson in the heavy cost that must be paid by one of their number which goes berserk with fanatical nationalism. [66]

Similarly, the real story of Vietnam was the struggle between a radicalized Vietnamese peasantry and the United States and its wholly dependent (and wholly corrupt) local allies. Considered the defining event of the cold war—a collision between communist expansion in Southeast Asia and the US determination to stop it—in reality the CIA found that evidence of Kremlin-directed conspiracy could be found in virtually all countries *except* Vietnam, which appeared to be an anomaly.

According to Major Patti of the US Office of Strategic Services (the forerunner of the CIA), who was stationed in Hanoi in 1945, the Vietnamese at that time were possessed of "an extraordinary pro-American spirit that was everywhere at the birth of Ho Chi Minh's Vietnam".[67] The Vietnamese, Patti reports, "didn't regard America as an imperial power. They thought we were different from the Europeans and they were desperate not to be associated with international communism, not with the Chinese or with the Russians, but with *us* in America." [68]

Ho Chi Minh's repeated and impassioned appeals (as many as twelve) to President Roosevelt and other senior US officials for US support for Vietnamese independence received no written reply— only the subsequent delivery of some 3.9 million tonnes of bombs, on the South Vietnamese 'ally' alone.

The United States was never in doubt that Ho Chi Minh had massive popular support in Vietnam, just as the CIA was not in doubt that Vietnam had no conspiratorial links with the Soviets or Chinese. In 1948, the State Department called for the establishment of "our conception of a democratic state" in Vietnam, noting "we have not urged the French to negotiate with Ho Chi Minh, even though he probably is now supported by a considerable majority of the Vietnamese people." [69]

"Our conception of a democratic state" included a refusal to negotiate with the leading popular representative of the people; it involved, in fact, the complete destruction of democracy and its replacement by a dictatorship serving Western needs. These truths were all suppressed in the understanding that nationalism could not be allowed to succeed in Vietnam—south-east Asian resources had to be kept under Western control. Britain, the US and France agreed that it was important for the economy of Western Europe that trading and business interests in south-east Asia be maintained, since the countries of south-east Asia were extremely rich in natural resources. Naturally enough, then, independent development was a threat that had to be removed.

From Baths of Blood to 'Pots of Money'

The logic of using terror to maintain good investment climates remains unchanged to this day. The Mexican government was recently left in no doubt about its responsibilities with regard to the uprising of starving Indians in Chiapas. The Chase Manhattan Bank's *Political Update on Mexico* of January 1995 made it clear that: "The [Mexican] government will have to eliminate the Zapatistas to demonstrate their effective control of the national territory and security policy."

Chase Manhattan's stance makes sense from an economic perspective, for while South America has sunk into despair, Western
corporations have made huge profits. In his book *The Real Terror
Network*, Edward Herman reported that US direct investment in
Latin America had grown from $12.2 billion in 1970 to $38.3 billion in 1980, with earnings from these direct investments rising
from $1 billion to $4.6 billion. Between 1982 and 1987, about
150 billion dollars were transferred from Latin America to the
West.

Herman reported that Latin American investments had produced nominal rates of return in recent years that averaged between
fifteen and twenty per cent. With billions of dollars at stake, the
Western corporate system was not about to allow the status quo to
be challenged, and the military support of client dictators ensured
that this did not happen. US military aid programmes between
1950 and 1979 transferred $107.3 billion in equipment and services
to friendly Latin American powers, in addition to $121 billion in
arms sales. Unknown to the public, this 'aid' was not directed
towards peaceful, libertarian regimes.

The leading academic scholar on human rights in Latin
America, Lars Schoultz, found that US aid "has tended to flow dis-
proportionately to Latin American governments which torture
their citizens... to the hemisphere's relatively egregious violators of
fundamental human rights."[70]

Herman confirms this view:

> US training and supply have tended to encourage human torture...
> there are significant positive relationships between US flows of aid
> and *negative* human rights developments (the rise of torture, death
> squads, and the overturn of constitutional governments). This is a
> result, not of any US élite attraction to human torture, but rather
> of the demands of the higher priorities (favourable investment cli-
> mate, worker and peasant atomization) that regrettably necessitate
> the support of torturers.[71]

'Aid', then, is in reality a euphemism designed to cover the real
goal—to aid the rich to take from the poor.

An important element of the 'aid' to the tyrants of Latin
America is supplied through the infamous US Army School of the
Americas (SOA), founded in Panama in 1946 and relocated in
1984 to Fort Benning, Georgia. With both instructors and recruits

at the SOA taken from the upper echelons of the Latin American military establishment, the curriculum includes counterinsurgency, military intelligence, interrogation techniques, sniper fire, infantry and commando tactics, 'irregular' and psychological warfare, and jungle operations. The journalist W.E. Gutman writes that Latin American soldiers at SOA are not trained to repel invaders at their borders:

> They are taught—at US taxpayers' expense—to make war against their own people, to subvert the truth, silence poets, domesticate unruly visionaries, muzzle activist clergy, hinder trade unionism, hush the voices of dissidence and discontent, neutralize the poor, the hungry, the dispossessed, extinguish common dreams, irrigate fields of plenty with the tears of a captive society, and transform paladins and protesters into submissive vassals. Even if it kills them.[72]

This is not merely Gutman's view. Republican Joseph P. Kennedy II argues that "SOA graduates include dictators and soldiers implicated in gross human rights violations in Latin America." [73]

In 1989 a Salvadoran Army patrol went on the rampage, bursting into Central American University and killing six Jesuit priests, their cook and her daughter. Nineteen of the twenty-seven Salvadoran officers who took part in the massacre were graduates of the SOA, according to a United Nations Truth Commission report. In fact, almost three-quarters of the Salvadoran officers implicated in seven other bloodbaths during El Salvador's war against the people (including the assassination of Archbishop Romero) were trained by the SOA. Of the 246 officers cited for various crimes in Colombia by a 1992 human rights tribunal, 105 are SOA graduates. Other distinguished graduates of the SOA include Leopoldo Galtieri, ex-head of Argentina's junta, defeated in the Falklands war; Manuel Noriega, ex-dictator of Panama; Roberto D'Aubuisson, late and infamous Salvadoran death squad leader; and Manuel Antonio Calleyas y Calleyas, chief of Guatemalan intelligence in the late 1970s and early 1980s, when thousands of political opponents were assassinated.

"The SOA is seriously hindering the establishment and strengthening of democracy in Latin America," argues Father Roy Bourgeois, a US priest, "the SOA does not screen soldiers who are assigned to it. Known perpetrators of serious war crimes come and go as they please." [74]

A senior analyst, when guaranteed anonymity, confirmed the obvious, telling Gutman that the SOA "has systematically encouraged the transplantation of military structures into, and facilitated the propagation of military power and objectives against, legitimate civilian governments." [75]

The SOA, then, is simply implementing policy outlined by Defence Secretary Robert McNamara when he talked of the need for the military "to remove government leaders from office" as required.

The Adjutant—Britain's Role

Though the truth is rarely stated explicitly in the press, it can sometimes be found sheltering between the lines. In an article in the *Guardian* Mark Tran reported that UN proposals for the creation of a permanent international criminal court, "a world court on war crimes", had been greeted with minimal enthusiasm by the United States and Britain.[76] While Scandinavia, Canada and Australia were leading the call for a judicial body to "prosecute a 'hard core' of abuses, covering genocide, war crimes, crimes against humanity and possibly aggression", the US was "lukewarm", with Washington "nervous that an international court might turn into a loose cannon", preferring a body that "does not act too independently of the Security Council, where the US and its allies hold sway." In similar vein, Britain—that other great "valiant and benignant force"—had "adopted a studious neutrality, arousing suspicion among human rights groups". Naturally, Tran did not explore the reasons why the US and Britain were so reticent, but they are apparent enough.

It would be a mistake, indeed unfair, to suppose that the United States is alone in its single-minded pursuit of profit over independence and democracy in the Third World; it is only the leader of the pack. Since 1945, British foreign policy has similarly been determined not, as is commonly assumed, by the need to deter communist aggression, but by economic priorities rooted in fully 500 years of Western exploitation of the Third World. As historian Mark Curtis writes, the cold war was very much a cover for a hot war for profits:

Britain bears considerable responsibility for many of the horrors which have afflicted people in the Third World throughout the

postwar era. These policies have been based not on whims—or on
the delusions of malevolent individuals. Rather they are the consequence of the rich states' pursuit of their straightforward 'national
interests'.[77]

We can dispense with the argument that terrible things were done
by Britain during the cold war, but only to prevent even worse
things being done by the communists with their devilish designs on
the 'free world'. As we have seen, such designs were always a fiction
(as was the notion of the 'free world' itself). The danger was not military but ideological—the appeal of socialism to the impoverished
people of Asia, Africa and South America. The threat to profits,
then, was not invasion, but the spread of ideas that might encourage the poor to resist exploitation. It was the same threat presented
by Allende, Arbenz and the Sandinistas.

Wherever we look during the cold war we find that the perception of the Soviet military threat expressed in high-level secret
British documents is very different from that which was claimed in
public and repeated *ad nauseam* by the media. In popular mythology, the Middle East, for example, was at perpetual risk from a
lightning Soviet push to the Persian Gulf.

In July 1950, however, the British Chiefs of staff noted that "the
success of indirect or subversive action by the Soviet government...
in any of the Arab states or in Israel is also improbable in the immediate future."[78] Curtis points out that the threat of *direct* Soviet
action was not even discussed as a possibility.

Similarly, the US State Department noted in 1950 that
Communist parties were "non-existent in Yemen and Saudi Arabia;
outlawed in Iraq, Egypt, Syria and Lebanon and apparently unor-
ganized in Jordan". Indeed "throughout the Arab states, at the present time, extreme rightist or ultra-nationalist elements may
exercise greater influence and form a greater threat to maintenance
of a pro-Western orientation than the communists."[79]

The academic version of events, however, was (and is) carefully
tailored to suit the preferred propaganda line. Highly respected analyst Lord Beloff noted as late as 1986 that "the world-wide struggle
against Communism... remains the inevitable core of American policy";[80] not, as US state documents show, the desire to maintain the
differential between US wealth and that of Third World countries,
and to knock down doors in order to plant colonies around the

world. In similar vein, David Watt, former Director of the Royal
Institute of International Affairs, argued that the Anglo-American
special relationship is "conditioned on Britain's remaining the single
most effective adjutant in the task of containing the Soviet Union
and its allies".[81] This is true, if we decode "containing the Soviet
Union" into containing Third World movements for democracy and
independence.

The mainstream press repeated essentially the same line, stoking
up anti-Soviet hysteria in a long-running 'Red scare'. Mark Curtis
argues that the apparent contradiction between the private understanding that there was no military threat, and the public declaration that the threat was real and imminent, is resolved by the need
to hide the fact that:

> Britain's (and the USA's) 'economic interests' in the Third World in
> the post-war period have been synonymous with the systematic
> exploitation and impoverishment of local populations...

He says that this truth is "effectively unmentionable in respectable
circles. Linked with this is an inability to elucidate what the British
policy of establishing friendly regimes after independence actually
meant." [82]

The high-level understanding of the need to keep the reality of
this ruthless exploitation from public understanding is made very
clear in state documents. The Foreign Office noted in 1950 that "if
Soviet pressure were relaxed as a result of some major tactical devi-
ation, the development of the system might be arrested in proportion as the compelling cause of the Soviet danger diminished... the
consolidation of the West, under Anglo-American leadership, might
well be in jeopardy"—the "system" being that designed to ensure
Western control over Third World resources.[83]

Detente was a real fear; it was scrupulously undermined
throughout the cold war. War, including cold war, is good for
business. The real winners of the cold war were the corporations
exploiting the Third World, and of course the high-tech industries—
the vast rearmament programmes guaranteeing industrial production funded by taxpayers. Both the civil aviation and modern
computer industries began their lives as military projects. After
the taxpayer had funded the early research and development,
private companies moved in to reap the benefits from commercial
applications.

Numerous examples of British (and US) interventions abroad show that anti-communist drives were actually pro-profit drives. One of the most reputable analysts of British foreign policy, Ritchie Ovendale, repeats the standard position with regard to the British intervention in Malaya. Britain, Ovendale said, was "fighting the communist terrorists to enable Malaya to become independent and help itself... to prevent the spread of communism and to resist Russian expansion".[84]

Malaya, in fact, was deemed the "greatest material prize in South-East Asia".[85] According to the Colonial Office four years after the beginning of the emergency, "no operational links have been established as existing" between Malaya and Soviet or Chinese communists; nor was material support offered.[86] As so often, independence, not communism, was the real threat.

The British intervention in British Guiana was similarly presented by the Governor in 1953 as an attempt to "prevent Communist subversion of the government" which was "completely under the control of a communist clique... Their objective was to turn British Guiana into a totalitarian state subordinate to Moscow and a dangerous platform for extending communist influence in the Western hemisphere".[87]

Again, such fairy tales aside, the reality centred around Britain's determination to remove the Guianan PPP government which, according to the Commonwealth Relations Office in September 1953, "was in fact elected to power on a mildly socialist programme, the implementation of which would have been in general of great value to the territory". The PPP's programme, the report continues, was "no more extreme" than that of the British Labour Party. "It contains none of the usual communist aims and it advocates industrial development through the encouragement of foreign capital."[88]

There was clearly an urgent need to present this pro-profit intervention as an anti-communist one. The UK delegation to the United Nations cabled the Colonial Secretary a week before the overthrow of the PPP, arguing that: "If our action can be presented as firm step taken to prevent attempt by communist elements to sabotage new and progressive constitution, it will be welcomed by American public and accepted by most United Nations opinion. If on the other hand it is allowed to appear as just another attempt by Britain to stifle a popular nationalist movement... effect can only be bad... To secure desired result some preparation of public opinion seems to be essential." [89]

Following the successful removal of the PPP regime, the transnational company Bookers was assured of "a remarkable degree of control over the economy, both through its dominant position in the sugar industry and through its interests in fisheries, cattle, timber, insurance, advertising, and retail commerce", according to the Latin American Bureau in 1964.

Something Missing in the Middle: Forbidden Frameworks

This, to be sure, is only the briefest of reviews of the relationship between Western profit-making and Third World suffering at the hands of dictators and torturers that have been trained, installed and maintained by Western powers, with the latter protected by their ability to spin the illusion of being far distant from the resultant suffering, and innocent of any blame for it.

We know much about the goals of corporations and about the suffering of the Third World, and yet we cannot put two and two together; we cannot make connections, complete the picture. This inability is indicative of the dramatic extent to which our view of reality can be distorted to suit the needs of the powerful—all without any need for conspiracies or totalitarian control.

We live in a society which, while it permits us to gain access to some information about the world, rarely allows us to gain access to frameworks of understanding that are contrary to the needs of power; yet it is only through such alternative frameworks that the information we receive can be properly understood. State and corporate interests are willing, albeit with some reluctance, to allow us to gain a few isolated, disembodied facts, statistics, reports and ideas; but do not promote a coherent framework of understanding that makes sense of them.

The status quo is preserved by our playing with pieces of the jigsaw, but never being able to complete the picture. In the words of the song: "You get the straight bits, but there's something missing in the middle." [90] The job of the media is to ensure that something remains 'missing in the middle'. This is achieved by depriving us of crucial pieces, by giving us false and confusing frameworks into which we vainly try to fit our pieces, by ridiculing the idea that there is a wider picture anyway, by omitting to mention any wider framework of understanding at all, and so on.

While this chapter was being written, a short section appeared in the *Guardian's* 'News in Brief'.[91] The report, headlined "US trained Latin Americans in torture", was one column wide and nineteen lines (8.5cm) in length. The report begins: "Training manuals used at the United States army's academy for Latin American military and police officers in the 1980s recommended the torture of guerrillas, threats, bribery and blackmail, according to documents made public by the Pentagon at the weekend." According to a secret report, just declassified, the manuals (written in Spanish) advocated tactics including "motivation by fear, payment of bounties for enemy dead, false imprisonment, executions and the use of truth serum". The manuals were compiled in 1987 from material in use since 1982 at the School of the Americas based at Fort Benning in Georgia, mentioned earlier in this chapter. The school has trained 60,000 officers, "including many dictators and military leaders accused of abusing human rights".

And that, more or less, was that. The fact that such horrific news about the 'leader of the free world' should be relegated to 'News in Brief' is revealing in itself. One might have expected some comment, some attempt at explanation: was this an isolated example, or has the United States promoted torture elsewhere? But there was no further discussion, no editorials, no attempt to place the revelations in a deeper context. Certainly there was no reference to the work of Edward Herman, who wrote about all this and much more as long ago as 1982 (see *The Real Terror Network: Terrorism in Fact and Propaganda*, South End Press).

The point is that even though facts of this sort can be discovered tucked away in the media (in this chapter I have quoted important information sourced from the mainstream on a number of occasions), the arguments which have been detailed above are almost completely absent. The report just reviewed is a perfect example of a harmless jigsaw piece: in isolation, it is merely shocking and soon forgotten. As part of a wider framework of understanding of the role of the West in the Third World it undermines all our preconceptions about the reality of modern democratic societies and our 'free press'.

But, for what should be obvious reasons, this kind of picture of the world could never be consistently presented to the public by the corporate media, for they themselves are an intrinsic part of— and dependent on the support of—the corporate system that has this overwhelmingly exploitative relationship to the Third World.

Given that all media entities are primarily profit-seeking corporations, it would run counter to their whole design and purpose to oppose their own self-interest in this way. Consequently, for a corporate media system to consistently present the type of view of the world outlined above would be close to impossible.

This, as we will discuss further in the next chapter, is the reality of what we so casually call our 'free press'.

Chapter Two

STRUCTURAL CONSTRAINTS
The Myth of Press Freedom

The Big Issue

Words like propaganda, brainwashing and thought control are generally assumed to have nothing at all to do with our society, belonging instead to the world of science fiction and foreign totalitarian states. Indeed it is against just these kinds of manipulation that we imagine ourselves to be in determined opposition. Do we not denounce Saddam Hussein, Qaddafi and the like for their opposition to free speech and democracy? In contrast to their society, we are told, ours is a model of freedom and openness. We define ourselves by what we are not: *they* are totalitarians, monsters; *they* slaughter their own people; *they* are not free. Our society is not totalitarian, we are not monsters, we do not slaughter our own people; ergo, we are free.

Alas, while it is true that our society is not like theirs, and freedom is not denied us in this crude way, it does not necessarily follow that we are free. To be opposed, however passionately, to one variety of unfreedom does not guarantee that we are not ourselves victims of a different kind of unfreedom—there is, we are regularly told, more than one way to cook a goose. While it is useful to agree on what we are not, the question of what we actually *are* remains open. Or at least such would be the case in a truly free society.

Consider the issue of press freedom in the context of the following letter sent to more than a hundred magazines by Chrysler Corporation:

> In an effort to avoid potential conflicts, it is required that Chrysler corporation be alerted in advance of any and all editorial content that encompasses sexual, political, social issues or any editorial content that could be construed as provocative or offensive.[1]

Even a moment's reflection on the above obliges us to question the notion that we are the proud inheritors of an advertising-dependent but 'free' press. Try, however, convincing any mainstream journalist or editor that there is any kind of problem here. Yet Chrysler's stance is the norm for corporate advertisers, who are all equally sensitive to "potential conflicts". Moreover, the media are themselves all corporations, all owned by large, parent corporations, all tied into the stock market, all owned by wealthy people with fingers in any number of other corporate and political pies, and so on.

In this chapter we will examine these structural constraints and how they make a nonsense of the perennial media claim to 'objectivity'. Subsequently, we will consider the intriguing question of how it is that such constraints can remain all but invisible, to the public certainly, but also to the many journalists who operate under them on a daily basis. From this we can arrive at a theory of non-totalitarian, 'democratic' thought control rooted, not in a conspiracy theory, but in the human capacity for self-deception.

Respectable Freedoms: the Cantankerous Press

Despite the critical nature of the issue, the neutrality of the modern mass media has long been presented as a truism to be blandly restated rather than a proposition to be tested against fact and logic.

During the Pentagon Papers case in the 1970s, Judge Gurfein declared that the United States had a "cantankerous press, an obstinate press, a ubiquitous press", and that this "must be suffered by those in authority in order to preserve the even greater values of freedom of expression and the right of the people to know." [2]

There is no question, then, that the press is sufficiently free; quite the reverse—the powers forever being hounded by the press must learn to bite their tongues and suffer such freedoms for the sake of democracy.

As for Britain, David Chaney writes that "the British press is generally agreed to have attained its freedom around the middle of the nineteenth century." [3]

In similar vein, advertising guru Maurice Saatchi informs us that we live "in a democracy of information... now nothing is hidden. Now we know everything." [4]

It is commonly assumed that British press freedom is somehow rooted in a proud tradition of libertarianism that began, who knows, perhaps with the revolutions of the seventeenth century, or perhaps with some kind of post-war liberal consensus. A glance at the historical record dispenses immediately with these notions.

eighteenth.

From the early days of the ~~nineteenth~~ century, business and government were resolutely determined to stamp out the free expression of ideas. The first resort were the seditious libel and blasphemy laws, which essentially outlawed all challenges to the status quo. When these failed to have the desired effect, élites turned to newspaper stamp duty and taxes on paper and advertisements to price radical journals out of the market. Between 1789 and 1815, stamp duty was increased by 266 per cent, helping to ensure, as Lord Castlereagh put it, that "persons exercising the power of the press" would be "men of some respectability and property",[5] the point being that these more "respectable" owners of the press "would conduct them in a more respectable manner than was likely to be the result of pauper management", as Cresset Pelham observed at the time.[6]

also refusal to accept
education for all.

The contempt for freedom, democracy, and the majority it might have aided, is open enough as we approach the time when the British press is "generally agreed to have attained its freedom".

The urgent need to crush freedom of speech, if the threat of genuine democracy was to be averted, was well understood and ruthlessly executed. This state-orchestrated financial war on the radical working class press was reinforced by the collaborative refusal of advertisers to support radicalism. In 1817, for example, Cobbett's popular *Political Register* received a total of three advertisements, although its advertising rates were less than one-hundredth of that of "respectable" rival periodicals.

Liberal hyperbole notwithstanding, the question for those who govern us has always been not how to liberate the press, but how to contain it. The Lord Chancellor put it succinctly in 1834: "The only question to answer, and the only problem to solve, is how they [the people] shall read in the best manner; how they shall be instructed politically, and have political habits formed the most safe for the constitution of the country."[7]

With the industrialization of the press, and the associated rise in the cost of setting up and distributing national newspapers, economic pressures ensured that the radical press was quickly pushed to the margins. All national newspapers launched in Britain between 1855 and 1910, and the great majority of new local daily papers, encouraged positive identification with the social system.

One result of the triumph of the corporate media has been extreme conformity of the press. Thus most national newspapers depicted the 1926 General Strike as a conflict between a minority (the strikers) and a majority (everyone else). Newspapers were overwhelmingly hostile to trade unionism, portraying it as the result of alien intervention, communist infiltration and the like. Every daily national newspaper supported the aborted union "reforms" proposed by the government in 1969, and all national newspapers supported Britain's entry into the EEC during the 1975 referendum. In 1980, every national newspaper opposed the TUC's "day of action". In 1985, all national newspapers applauded Neil Kinnock's attack on the "hard left" of his party.

The Truth Business

The modern mass media system is not, as some people casually (and even conspiratorially) like to remark, controlled by corporations; it *is* corporations. Businesses do not control the car industry; the car industry is big business. Likewise, the media is made up of large corporations, all in the business of maximizing profits, all tied into the stock market. This immediately suggests that, at the very least, media corporations might have a tendency to be sympathetic to the status quo, to other corporations, and to the profit-maximizing motive of the corporate system—given that they are part of that system.

Media corporations are also all owned by wealthy people who are generally on the boards of other major corporations, and who have innumerable personal and business contacts. Most of the British press has long been owned by extremely wealthy individuals like Rupert Murdoch, the Maxwells, Lord Stevens, Viscounts Rothermere and Blakenham, 'Tiny' Rowland, the Barclay brothers, Conrad Black *et al.*

Media ownership clearly places enormous power in the hands of the owner. Anyone who has worked in a corporation knows that the owner has the power to hire and fire more or less at will; as corporate veterans will also know, the power system in a corporation is essentially totalitarian in nature—it is top down, with possibly a few bright ideas flowing up the chain, but certainly no control.

It seems a matter of common sense that press neutrality is already seriously compromised by the simple fact that the mass media corporations are owned by wealthy, profit-seeking capitalists. They themselves are happy to admit their influence.

Thus, on his arrival at the *News of the World*, Rupert Murdoch announced: "I did not come all this way not to interfere." [8]

Andrew Neil has disclosed a few details about how wealthy owners are able to compromise press freedom. Referring to Murdoch, his previous boss, Neil writes:

> Rupert expects his papers to stand broadly for what he believes: a combination of right-wing Republicanism from America mixed with undiluted Thatcherism from Britain. [9]

This mixture is far more right-wing than people generally imagine, Neil notes ominously.

Reviewing Neil's autobiography, Alan Rusbridger, Editor of the *Guardian*, indicates the price paid by editors like Neil who fail to ensure that Murdoch's papers stand for what he believes:

> A more serious error [on Neil's part] was to have revealed the way in which British aid had gone to build the Pergau dam in return for a £1.3 billion contract to buy British arms, together with the associated sweeteners. An error because Murdoch badly did not want to fall out with the Malaysian Prime Minister, Mahathir Mohamed, desperately worried, as he was, about his satellite interests in the region... He [Murdoch] berated Neil over the coverage, ordered him not to talk publicly about the story... and eventually moved him out of editing the *Sunday Times* altogether. Neil was later told by a British minister that Mahathir had boasted how he had demanded Neil's head, and that Murdoch had apologized for his 'rogue editor' and promised to sort the problem out. This, then, is the 'subtle' way in which Murdoch controls his editors. [10]

More recently still, the *Observer* reported (March 23, 1997) that "Rupert Murdoch overrode objections of his senior staff to order his flagship newspaper, the *Sun*, into battle on the side of New Labour with a headline which took up almost the whole of Tuesday's front page: 'The Sun Backs Blair'." Murdoch ordered this despite being opposed by four of his most senior journalists, who had already planned their election coverage.

In his review, Rusbridger drew no conclusions about the deeper significance of such events for the whole notion that we have a free (let alone politically neutral) press, or that we live in a democracy (on the assumption that a free democracy is impossible in the absence of a free supply of information), being himself a similarly vulnerable employee of the same system that dumped Neil so crudely. Clearly, *The Times* was not permitted to publish damaging reports about Malaysia, but then what about other Third World nations, where profits might similarly be jeopardized? After all, the Third World is full of similarly touchy totalitarians. And might not an owner's entrepreneurial adventures be similarly damaged by overly critical reports of US and British government policy?

Wealthy ownership apart, what effect might the corporate nature of the media have on the contents of the average newspaper, TV station or magazine?

Consider the former Soviet Union, where all mainstream newspapers were under the direct control of the Communist Party. What kind of view of the world would we expect to emerge from such an arrangement? Naturally we would expect one supporting the goals and values of the rulers of the Communist Party, ideas such as: the Soviet people live in an association of free republics, governed by the people; the Soviet government is devoted to the welfare of the people; the 'evil empire' of the West is dedicated to undermining the 'Motherland'; Afghanistan is being aided in a struggle against imperialism, and so on.

In the West there is no such overt control, but media corporations must sing to the tune of the wider corporate system. After all, they are not only businesses, they are also the property of even larger parent corporations, which are often active in the Third World, and in the arms trade. It seems reasonable to suggest that this ultimate parental power in the media system might have some influence over what comes to be reported. How likely is it that a newspaper or TV station owned by a large arms manufacturer would devote extensive coverage to the morality of the arms business (let alone to the activities of their own parent companies), detailing how arms are regularly sold to Third World dictators? How willing would they be to discuss the activities of those same dictators in suppressing, torturing and murdering their own people? How willing would any media corporation be to discuss these inherent features of the global, corporate capitalist system? The possibility seems remote in the extreme, given that journalists are employed by senior managers of their media company, who in turn are employed by the senior management of the parent company. In their book *Power without Responsibility*, Curran and Seaton have this to say:

This integration of the press into finance and industry created conflicts of interest. It gave rise to no-go areas where newspapers were *sometimes reluctant* to investigate for fear of stepping on corporate toes.[11] [my emphasis]

A dramatic understatement. In reality, newspapers are not merely "sometimes reluctant" to investigate certain areas; they are elements of the selfsame system with the selfsame goals, staffed by individuals employed to achieve those goals, and who are therefore unlikely to even think in terms of stepping on the toes of their corporate colleagues.

In private at least, editors are willing to admit the problem. In a survey by the American Society of Newspaper Editors, about a third of editors admitted that they "would not feel free to run a news story that was damaging to their parent firm".[12]

Guardian Chihuahuas

An important constraint on honest reporting is the reality of how the media make their money. Most newspapers and magazines do not survive by virtue of their cover price but on the strength of their ability to attract advertising revenue. Edward Herman points out that the mass media are intimately linked to the wider business community by their heavy dependence on advertisers, this sponsorship accounting for well over 50 per cent of their gross revenue. The prestigious *New York Times*, for example, is generally made up of around 60 per cent advertising, and could not exist without it. Of this 60 per cent, a sizeable proportion is contributed by the car industry. It comes as little surprise to learn, then, that "*Times* publisher and CEO Arthur Sulzberger admitted that he leaned on his editors to present the auto industry's position because it 'would affect advertising'." [13]

In similar vein, Herman quotes Frank Stanton, president of CBS television, who explained in 1960 that "since we are advertiser-supported we must take into account the general objectives and desires of advertisers as a whole." [14]

And not merely "the general objectives and desires". Gloria Steinem, Editor of *Ms* magazine, reports that Proctor & Gamble made it clear that "its products were not to be placed in *any* issue that included *any* material on gun control, abortion, the occult, cults, or the disparagement of religion." [15]

These are examples of a decisive trend that is shaping the media:

> You name it: the appearance of ads throughout the pages, the 'jump' or continuation of a story from page to page, the rise of sectionalisation (as with news, cartoons, sports, financial, living, real estate), common page size, halftone images, process engraving, the use of black-and-white photography, then colour, sweepstakes, and finally discounted subscriptions were all forced on publishers by advertisers hoping to find target audiences.[16]

It seems a matter of common sense that sponsors are also able to bring enormous influence to bear on TV programming, as Lee and Solomon point out:

> Prospective shows are often discussed with major advertisers, who review script treatment and suggest changes when necessary. Adjustments are sometimes made to please sponsors... corporate sponsors figure they are entitled to call the shots since they foot the bill—an assumption shared by network executives, who quickly learn to internalize the desires of their well-endowed patrons.[17]

The remarkable end result, according to the host of one of PBS's shows being that: "You cannot get a TV or a radio show on the air in America these days unless it targets an audience that corporations are interested in targeting and unless it carries a message that is acceptable to corporations." [18]

This claim was supported by *The Economist* when it noted that (media) "projects unsuitable for corporate sponsorship tend to die on the vine," adding that "stations have learned to be sympathetic to the most delicate sympathies of corporations."[19] How might we expect advertisers to react to extensive, critical media coverage of their activities? In fact there is no need to speculate, as there are clear examples of what does happen.

Business Week reported in 1976 that the *New York Times* has "slid precipitously to the left and has become stridently anti-business in tone, ignoring the fact that the *Times* itself is a business—and one with very serious problems".[20]

One example of the paper's supposed dramatic swing to the left was an editorial recommending an increase in taxes on business to help overcome the city's financial problems. *Business Week* continues: " 'Something like that,' a Wall Street analyst muses, 'could put the *Times* right out of business.'" How? "Following a *Times* series on medical incompetence," a magazine run by the parent company "lost $500,000 in pharmaceutical advertising." [21]

A similar case involves The Media Foundation, a dissident Canadian organization specializing in the production of "subvertisements"—anti-adverts critical of the dominant consumer culture. The Media Foundation bought advertising space for an anti-car advert in the commercial break half-way through a popular Canadian car programme (the equivalent of Britain's *Top Gear*). Understandably upset by subversion of this sort running alongside their own carefully crafted car commercials, advertisers withdrew from the programme which, as a result, collapsed.

The lesson is clear: media which further business interests are boosted by all-important advertising revenue and so tend to flourish. Programmes which damage corporate interests—even if, as in this case, unintentionally—do not, and tend to disappear or retreat to the margins.

In an interview with Ralph Nader, David Barsamian asked:

> Wouldn't it be irrational for them [the media] to even discuss corporate power, since their underwriting and sponsors come from very large corporations?

Nader's reply was:

> Very irrational... [There are] a few instances almost every year where there's some sort of criticism of auto dealers, and the auto dealers just pull their ads openly from radio and TV stations. [22]

The media are extremely vulnerable to business pressures of this kind. While environmental and human rights groups like Greenpeace and Amnesty International are able to generate significant publicity, they are no match for the enormous advertising, public relations and political lobbying power of transnational corporations, which are often more powerful than nation states. Corporations can put pressure on the media and even national governments to ensure that both remain 'objective'; that is, business friendly. Capital and advertising can soon be redirected to more amenable governments and media.

Corporations often come together to form 'flak machines', designed to promote a business-friendly line in media, education and politics. One such organization is Citizens for the Sensible

Control of Acid Rain, which, financed by major electrical utilities and coal companies, battles against restrictions on air pollution.

David Reidnauer at the National Centre for Public Policy Research, a conservative US flak machine, argues that "Environmental education is engaging children in politics in primary school and, frankly, is indoctrination." [23]

Opponents of green reform are powerfully supported by groups such as the Heritage Foundation, a Washington-based flak machine, which recently issued a report entitled *Little Green Lies*. Its author, Jonathon Adler, listed ten so-called eco-myths, including "Recycling is always good" and "There is too much garbage", [24] and claims that acid rain helps eastern forests by providing nitrogen for nutrition.

As a result of this type of pressure, Edward Helmore of the *Observer* writes that teachers have been warned not to discuss subjects such as wilderness preservation, cattle grazing or the reintroduction of the wolf into national park land, in case they cross the interests of the state's powerful ranchers. "If I spoke about it, my job would be in serious jeopardy," says Jon Rachael, a fish and game biologist and visiting school lecturer. "Wolves, grizzlies and salmon restoration have become such hot issues that I don't do school programmes any more." [25]

In Meridian, Idaho, the school board guidelines state: "Discussion should not reflect negative attitudes against business or industry." [26] Teachers are not to promote activism; planting trees, raising money to save whales, writing letters, protesting against polluting industries or rainforest destruction, are all out.

This green "indoctrination" opposed so vigorously by corporate flak machines should be evaluated in the context of the occasional diffident attempts by business to influence education. In her book *Selling Free Enterprise*, Elizabeth Fones-Wolf reports that in 1950 the National Association of Manufacturers (NAM) distributed almost four and a half million pamphlets to students. By 1954, over 3.5 million students watched sixty thousand showings of NAM films. That year school superintendents estimated the investment in free corporate material at $50 million, about half the amount public schools spent on standard textbooks annually.

A further constraint on news reporting is the fact that the media are heavily dependent on state news sources. Fresh news from around the world is expensive to gather and the state effectively subsidizes the media by providing cheap and readily available current affairs sources from terminals such as No. 10 Downing Street, the Pentagon and State Department. Herman reports that 46.5 per cent of the information sources for stories appearing in the *New York Times* and *Washington Post* (the two national daily US broadsheets) between 1949 and 1969 were US government officials and agencies, with the trend toward reliance on government sources moving upward. The business community was the next most important news source.

By subsidizing the production of news in this way, state and corporate power lock reporters into a system of dependency and thus control. The consequences of a newspaper adopting a radically critical line on state or corporate activity in the Third World are severe. The all-important state news sources, on which investigative journalists rely, dry up, starving both them and their newspapers of up-to-date news, to the obvious advantage of competitors. The inevitable result, as David Nyhan of the *Boston Globe* has pointed out, is that our fearsome newshounds are in fact "a docile, not to say boot-licking, lot subsisting largely on occasional bones of access tossed into the press kennel", happy to respond to lies with "worshipful prose".[27]

Servility Pays

Given the amount of power and wealth circulating around the media and political systems, there is a constant incentive for journalists to rationalize any doubts they might have about their profession. As Chomsky has argued, it is difficult to do a media job well if you don't believe what you're saying. The simple solution, then (given the spoils at stake), is to believe it!

Charles Lewis, a former producer of the US current affairs programme *60 Minutes*, who resigned to fund the Centre For Public Integrity, has said: "The values of the news media are the same as those of the élite, and they badly want to be viewed by the élites as acceptable. Socially, culturally, and economically they belong to the group of people they are covering."[28]

A recent report revealed that top newscaster Barbara Walters of ABC is paid in the region of $9 million a year. CBS evening news host Dan Rather receives $5 million. Britain's Martin Bell and Kate Adie of the BBC are reported to have earned between £80–£100,000 per year.

The material rewards of toeing the business line far outweigh any benefits of dissent. Senior reporters are eagerly sought by those with money and connections. In recent years, high profile US journalists have been paid lecture fees of up to $50,000 for a single speech to a business audience.

As Walter Karp writes: "It is a bitter irony of source journalism... that the most esteemed journalists are precisely the most servile. For it is by making themselves useful to the powerful that they gain access to the 'best' sources." [29]

Alongside these 'carrots', a range of 'sticks' means that even independently minded individuals have very little room for manoeuvre. Anthony Bevins, a former political correspondent of the *Sun* and *Daily Mail*, explains the limits imposed by the system as a whole:

> It is daft to suggest that individuals can buck the system, ignore the pre-set 'taste' of their newspapers, use their own news-sense in reporting the truth of any event, and survive. Dissident reporters who do not deliver the goods suffer professional death. They are ridden by news desks and backbench executives, they have their stories spiked on a systematic basis, they face the worst form of newspaper punishment—by-line deprivation... it's much easier to pander to what the editors want. [30]

It is interesting to consider that all of these pressures are obvious, immensely significant, known to all journalists and yet, as we will see, not part of the occasional discussions on press freedom, with journalists instead insisting that they are completely free and independent in their reporting. There are remarkable insights into the human capacity for self-deception to be gained here—for anyone, that is, willing and able to escape from that same tendency.

The Truth is Not Out There: the Great Non-Issue

The controls inherent in a capitalist system, though subtle, are real enough, as Anthony Sampson has noted:

> Journalists have been constrained from reporting or criticising... by pressures from owners, advertisers and public relations men, who helped set the agenda of the business pages. Entrepreneurial owners naturally dislike the critical and investigative function of reporters... [31]

Sampson says "naturally"; in fact observations of this sort are entirely alien to the mainstream—literally so for CBS media critic and sometime cosmologist Jeff Greenfield, who commented that media criticism of this type "to me looks like it's from Neptune... absolutely wacko",[32] confirming perhaps that the truth really is 'out there', even if hard to find here on earth.

Edward Herman and Noam Chomsky's propaganda model of media control, to which Greenfield was referring, focuses on the idea that the corporate nature of the media system in the context of a capitalist society dramatically distorts media content. Since its publication in 1988 in Herman and Chomsky's book *Manufacturing Consent: The Political Economy of the Mass Media*, the propaganda model has been almost completely ignored by the mainstream US and British press.

In a rare review published in the US journal *Atlantic Monthly*, Nicholas Lemann explained that the discrepancies in media reporting described by Herman and Chomsky can be accounted for by the fact that "the press tends to focus on only a few things at a time", and so cannot cover everything.[33] Milan Rai reviews the review, suggesting that although Lemann's analysis is "patently inadequate", it "may well be the most coherent critique of the Propaganda Model to have come out of the mainstream press." [34] A sobering thought. What seems "natural" to Sampson is to mainstream media writers, such as Tom Wolfe, "the most absolute rubbish I've ever heard... patent nonsense".[35]

There are several reasons why the propaganda model should be included in any debate on media freedom. First, highly influential intellectuals have advocated that the media serve an élite propaganda function. In 1947, in his book *The Engineering of Consent*, Edward Bernays—who was later to apply his engineering skills to the task of demolishing Guatemalan democracy—wrote that "any person or organization depends ultimately on public approval, and is therefore faced with the problem of engineering the public's consent to a programme or goal... The engineering of consent is the very essence of the democratic process..." [36]

Likewise Walter Lippmann, considered one of the most thoughtful and cultured of journalists, wrote that: "The common interests very largely elude public opinion entirely, and can be managed only by a specialized class whose personal interests reach beyond the locality. This class is irresponsible, for it acts upon information that is not common property, in situations that the public at large does not conceive, and it can be held to account only on the accomplished fact." [37]

As for the reality of these "common interests", Edward Filene, a spokesperson for industrialists in the 1920s and '30s spoke of the need for industry to "sell to the masses all that it employs the masses to create...The time has come when all our educational institutions... must concentrate on the great social task of teaching the masses not what to think but *how to think*, and thus to find out how to behave like human beings in the machine age." [38]

The self-deception is glaring, with "how to think" being, of course "what to think": namely, that we should desire all that industry "employs the masses to create". How best to "behave like human beings in the machine age" is further clarified by a corporate slogan: "Buy, buy, buy; it's your patriotic duty." [39]

Given that leading élite intellectuals propose that an élite class should "manufacture consent" (Lippmann's term, not Herman or Chomsky's), and that such views are well-received, indeed accepted as truisms, by other élites, it seems reasonable to assert that the propaganda model should be part of the debate.

The propaganda model should also be included because it simply makes sense: a glance at the structure and goals of the media in the context of a capitalist society suggests that the media must serve the dominant centres of power. As Milan Rai has commented, "Media corporations are still corporations. It would be surprising if they worked to undermine corporate interests." [40]

There is also considerable public support for a propaganda analysis of the media. In 1981, a poll for the *Washington Post* found that public complaints were at considerable variance with media complaints. Forty per cent, the largest group, felt that the media were "not critical enough of the government". [41] A Gallup poll carried out for the *New York Times* in 1986 found that 53 per cent of respondents considered the press too often "influenced by powerful people and organizations," [42] including federal government, big business, trade unions and the military.

Edward Herman has focused on the specific inability of the mass media to report the systematic links between the West and human rights abusers in the Third World. In response to these facts, Herman writes, the US media operates according to "what we might call their 'fundamental laws of motion' as a propaganda system," [43] which he sums up as follows:

> Avert the eyes from the terror of friendly fascists; locate and
> devote full attention to the abuses of the enemy. This is an
> extremely important task, given the size and human costs of the
> real [West-sponsored] terror network. The function of the mass
> media, as servants of the dominant power interests of a country
> whose nominal values are liberal, is therefore to obfuscate real-
> ity—to pretend that the NSSs [the National Security States sup-
> ported by the West] and other dependent tyrannies (like the
> Philippines) are not extremely well arranged to serve Western
> interests; to play down the crucial Western involvement in the
> emergence and spread of this Third World fascist Mafia; and, most
> of all, to avoid and distract public attention from the details about
> what is happening to several million peasants and other victims of
> this joint venture.[44]

Analysis of this type has nothing to do with a left/right ideological perspective; it is simply an accurate description of the facts. The
corporate media element of the global corporate system is not
going to provide significant coverage of the inhuman results of
that same system.

Any reports of atrocities by "friendly fascists" would attract
intense criticism from powerful state and business vested interests
determined to protect their investments. As a consequence, the
sources for stories describing abuses must be extremely authori-
tative. Yet most dissident sources—human rights, peasant and
union groups—are inherently unauthoritative and will be vulnerable to contradiction by official sources. The mass media will
occasionally give muted treatment to abuses by friendly regimes;
this isolated, partial coverage helps lend legitimacy to the idea that
we have a free press. Reporting will, however, always be sporadic
and lacking the sort of historical background and rational framework that might allow us to understand the systemic and institutionalized links between the West and Third World human rights
abuses.

The same is true for business-unfriendly environmental issues.
Environmentalists—no matter how accurate or brilliant their facts
and ideas—will always encounter obstacles to the communication
of messages which threaten state and business interests.

This does not mean that the truth will be completely excluded (a feature of the far less sophisticated totalitarian system of control), for we do hear about environmental crises. But we tend to hear about isolated problems, or about larger problems only in passing, while the true severity of those problems tends not to be emphasized. Also, we find that any number of experts are on permanent stand-by to rise up to defend corporate and state interests against 'hysterical' greens with their tendency to 'exaggerate' and 'spread panic' in order to 'increase membership'.

Sharon Beder writes how, in this context, media 'neutrality' becomes a kind of Orwellian euphemism:

> Balance means ensuring that statements by those challenging the establishment are balanced with statements by those whom they are criticising, though not necessarily the other way round.[45]

In the end, journalists and their editors have little option but to serve the needs of state and corporate power. They are bound by the iron logic of a profit-maximizing media system operating within a capitalist society.

There is a margin for dissent in Britain, Mark Curtis suggests, but it is vanishingly narrow:

> Of the five daily broadsheet newspapers in Britain—the *Daily Telegraph, Times, Financial Times, Independent* and *Guardian*... the first three—which account for around 70 per cent of broadsheet readership—systematically fail to elucidate the specific link between British policy and human rights abuses. The *Independent* also regularly portrays the reality of British foreign policy in an inaccurately benevolent light. These newspapers are firmly entrenched within a propaganda system and their reporting implicitly serves to promote the concept of Britain's basic benevolence... Of the five newspapers, only the *Guardian*—with around 17 per cent of broadsheet readership—tends to report on British foreign policy in a more independent manner.[46]

As Cockburn and Silverstein suggest, the corporate media monopoly has dire implications for democracy and freedom of thought in our society:

> Today, any vestige of critical thought in the press has been all but extinguished, and journalists are as much a part of the ruling élite as the politicians and business people they supposedly cover.[47]

This truth, and the refusal to admit this truth, brings to mind R.D. Laing's observation on the secret and unmentionable true causes of mental illness in our society:

> Only by the most outrageous violation of ourselves have we achieved our capacity to live in relative adjustment to a civilization apparently driven to its own destruction.[48]

It is indeed an outrageous violation of reason and truth to assert that we have a free press. It is a falsehood of such audacity that it can be maintained only by the media banishing all rational discussion of the real issues. To discuss those issues honestly would bring down the whole edifice of illusions, an eventuality that the press has been precisely designed (both consciously and by a process of business-biased unnatural selection) to avoid. Ultimately, the truth is that journalists of the 'free press' must declare themselves free because they are not free to do anything else.

"Cold Facts": the Amazing Myth of Media Neutrality

For good reasons, then, few notions are defended with more vigour than the idea that neutrality and objectivity are proud traditions of the 'free press'. Often this happens obliquely: the veteran BBC reporter Martin Bell, who won a seat at the 1997 General Election on an anti-sleaze ticket, caused quite a ruckus by declaring:

> I do not believe we should stand neutrally between good and evil, right and wrong, aggressor and victim.[49]

The assumption being, of course, that the media currently *do* "stand neutrally between good and evil". Despite this, Bell remains committed, the *Guardian* reports, "to the old-fashioned notions of impartiality, fairness and meticulous concern for the facts".[50] Bell assures readers that he is "not a crusading journalist" but "I will happily call myself a founder member of the something-must-be-done campaign."[51]

The message seems more than a little confused: Bell is committed to impartiality but does not want to be neutral; he is happy to be part of a "something-must-be-done campaign" without becoming a crusader for a cause!

As the propaganda model predicts, Bell's call for an end to neutrality was greeted with due seriousness by his corporate colleagues. Thus Jon Snow, presenter of *Channel 4 News*, said: "Martin

[Bell] is dead right"; and Lucian Hudson, senior editor of *BBC World* observed that Bell "sounds to me like a celibate priest who at a certain stage in his life has decided to bonk". Andrew Marr, former Editor of the *Independent*, responded to Bell by noting that " 'engaged' journalism has a long and honourable history and we certainly encourage it in our commentary and opinion pages. But viewers and readers still want *cold facts* and need the time and space to make considered judgements..." [52] [my emphasis]

The subsequent argument raged between journalists and editors defending "our obligation to be impartial" [53] and the idea that "as well as straight reporting there is room—and sometimes a need—for a more engaged form of writing." [54]

Veteran BBC Foreign Editor John Simpson made his feelings known in no uncertain terms: "Martin Bell is talking nonsense and he knows it. He was one of the most objective journalists." Simpson added, apparently with a straight face, "You don't watch the BBC for polemic." [55]

The question, then, is not whether our corporate media system is objective and neutral—that is taken as read—but whether it should sometimes allow itself to indulge in a little subjectivity.

As so often in the mainstream, the truth is hidden by, and beyond, these two opposing arguments. The flaws in both are immediately revealed when we recognize that it is actually impossible for any journalist, even a corporate one, to be objective and neutral. Historian Howard Zinn made the point well in his essay 'Objections to Objectivity':

> The chief problem in historical [and journalistic] honesty is not outright lying. It is omission or de-emphasis of important data. The definition of 'important', of course, depends on one's values. [56]

As Zinn suggests, 'the facts' are *always* value-dependent: data reported, emphasized, headlined, or neglected, are selected—or not—on the basis of what the historian or journalist deems important. There is no way around this, for a journalist must have values, priorities (conscious or otherwise), must filter facts, must report subjectively. Bias and subjective opinions are inherent to the profession of journalism, indeed to human existence, not an indulgence to be avoided wherever possible.

The notion, then, that a journalist can somehow be an "impartial" dispenser of "straight reporting" is a logical absurdity. The deep denial of reality in relation to the issue of media freedom verges on the surreal, and is easily as bizarre as any primitive religious dogma or belief in a flat earth.

This myth of media objectivity is easily exposed by even the briefest of glances at the dismal historical record. In the leaked minutes of one of the BBC's weekly Review Board meetings during the Falklands war, BBC executives directed that the weight of their news coverage should be concerned "primarily with government statements of policy". An impartial style was felt to be "an unnecessary irritation".[57]

The BBC, after all, was founded by Lord Reith in 1922 and immediately used as a propaganda weapon for the Baldwin government during the General Strike, when it became known by workers as the "British Falsehood Corporation". During the strike, no representative of organized labour was allowed to broadcast on the BBC; the Leader of the Opposition, Ramsay McDonald, was also banned. Reith said it was wrong but that he could do nothing about it. The reality being that "to Reith, impartiality was a principle to be suspended whenever the establishment was threatened." [58]

Likewise, at the start of the Second World War, an official wrote that the Ministry of Information "recognized that for the purpose of war activities the BBC is to be regarded as a Government Department." (He added: "I wouldn't put it quite like this in any public statement.") [59]

During the Falklands conflict, a Peruvian plan for a negotiated settlement came close to success. On 13th May 1982 Edward Heath told ITN that the Argentines had requested three minor amendments to the peace plan. According to Heath these were so minor that they could not possibly be rejected, yet Prime Minister Thatcher rejected them out of hand. The interview with Heath was the only time on British television that mention was made of the peace plan; the story was allowed to die.

Intriguingly, recent reports suggest that the BBC is in fact much closer to Bell's position that it should not "stand neutrally between good and evil" than Bell imagines.

Richard Brooks of the *Observer* reported (1st December '96) that "BBC insiders" believed that the corporation was "letting commercial interests influence its coverage of China. Critics claim several recent stories about the occupation of Tibet and on human rights abuses have not been broadcast, although the BBC expressed initial interest or commissioned them." *Newsnight* expressed initial enthusiasm for secret footage of the Panchen Lama's home. The programme changed its mind after "internal consultations". BBC News originally sought Danish footage showing how Tibetan monks were forced to remove pictures of the Dalai Lama. That too was rejected but later shown in many other European countries.

The BBC, Brooks reported, was "anxious not to provoke Beijing", as part of an effort to ensure access to news sources in China in the run-up up to the Hong Kong handover, and also to safeguard trade links which were "currently at an all-time high", with the BBC "negotiating to get World Television back into China" after being dumped by a Rupert Murdoch satellite in 1994. The BBC's foreign affairs editor, John Simpson, was about to be sent to China to cover the booming economy, the Hong Kong handover and the environment but had not asked to discuss human rights, according to Liu Jianchao, First Press Secretary at the Chinese Embassy in London. No surprise, then, that Sino-BBC relations are reported to have improved in recent times. Asked if this would aid commercial deals, Liu replied that balanced journalism helped relationships. Robbie Barnett of the Tibetan Information Network helped to decode the meaning of "balance" in this Orwellian sense when he said "Market forces rule at the BBC now." [60] No standing neutrally between good and evil here, just as there is no doubt about who are plainly the "bad guys".

"Rule A": Don't!

The suggestion being made here is that Western democratic societies are subject to a level of thought control far exceeding anything achieved by Hitler or Stalin, or imagined by Orwell.

The standard objection to this argument is that thought control on this scale would require a vast conspiracy involving many thousands of reporters, editors and proprietors. The problem with this is that, in the real world, journalists are not only *not* party to any such conspiracy but find the whole notion utterly risible. In addition there is the ample evidence of personal experience: we feel completely free, there are no thought police, we have no sensation of being watched, controlled, or manipulated.

What is being argued here, however, is very different. As we have seen, no conspiracy theory is required, merely an understanding of the standard operation of market forces. In fact the theory of 'democratic' thought control not only does not propose a conspiracy but actually requires the *absence* of any such conspiracy. Thought control of this sophistication could not be achieved, let alone maintained, through any kind of conspiracy, for the simple reason that it would quickly be exposed and so made largely impotent (as was the case, for example, in the Soviet Union).

Thought control of the modern kind is dependent, not on crude conscious planning, but on the human capacity for self-deception. This subject is reviewed in some depth by psychologist Daniel Goleman in his book *Vital Lies, Simple Truths: The Psychology of Self-Deception.*

In essence, Goleman's thesis is that human beings have a powerful ability to make a trade-off between anxiety and awareness: we are able to avoid knowing what we would rather not know. The existence of such an ability implies that we are able to gain partial awareness of what we would rather not know, but then refuse to admit such material into full conscious awareness.

In the 1960s, Lester Luborsky used a special camera to track the eye movements of subjects asked to look at a set of pictures. Subjects were asked to rate which pictures they liked and disliked. Three of the pictures were sexual in content, with one, for example, showing the outline of a woman's breast, beyond which a man could be seen reading a newspaper. The response of some subjects was remarkable. They were able to avoid letting their gaze stray even once to the sexually suggestive parts of the pictures. When later asked to describe the content of the pictures, these subjects remembered little or nothing sexually suggestive about them. Some could not even recall seeing the pictures. Goleman concludes:

> In order to avoid looking, some element of the mind must have known first what the picture contained, so that it knew what to avoid. The mind somehow grasps what is going on and rushes a protective filter into place, thus steering awareness away from what threatens.[61]

Psychologist Donald Spence notes the sophistication of this process:

> We are tempted to conclude that the avoidance is not random but highly efficient—the person knows just where *not* to look.[62]

According to Goleman, we build our version of reality around comfortable frameworks of understanding, or schemas: mental ideational structures which we then protect from conflicting facts, experiences and ideas. The more important these schemas are to our sense of identity and security, the less likely we will be to admit to awareness facts and ideas damaging to them.

If at first sight this strikes the reader as mysterious and abstract, it may seem less so if we consider the kind of situations by which we are all regularly faced. It is easy to imagine, for example, that someone passionately committed to the idea of his or her own essential goodness as a human being would have considerable difficulty in seriously entertaining the suggestion that the corporation for which he or she has worked for many years, indeed the entire corporate system of which he or she is a part, is responsible for terrible crimes against humanity and nature. The problem is that such a person may well have dedicated many years of hard work to building a career within that corporate system. Their prestige and sense of self may be closely tied to their status within it; they will quite possibly feel dependent on their position for the financial and emotional security they need to support loved ones, and so on.

In this situation, serious consideration (by which I do not mean a furtive glance at the facts) of the moral status of his or her work would threaten a profound conflict between our employee's moral convictions and his or her emotional and financial needs. Such a person would quite likely sense that they have everything to lose and nothing to gain from giving such an idea serious and honest thought and would be likely to ignore it completely, or dismiss it out of hand as 'paranoia', 'conspiracy theory', 'that old nonsense', or 'someone else's problem'.

Likewise, we can suppose that journalists might immediately reject from awareness the possibility that media corporations are integral elements of a system of social control subordinating the welfare of people and planet to profit. Despite the fact that they will have been made aware—either subtly or openly—that they are to restrict reporting within certain parameters, they may nevertheless remain utterly convinced that they are noble guardians of truth and social liberties. Awareness of the contradiction would simply be too unpleasant and disruptive to be granted serious thought. Again, by 'serious', I do not mean a quick glance and immediate rejection as 'nonsense', but a thorough, on-going analysis of the arguments for and against.

How is this trick of self-deception achieved? Goleman cites

R.D. Laing, who proposed that dysfunctional families plagued by alcoholism and child abuse are able to keep such truths from surfacing and thus interfering with the agreed delusion that they are a 'happy family', by adherence to an outwardly bizarre set of rules. These rules, Laing suggests, are as follows:

Rule A: Don't.
Rule A.1:   Rule A does not exist.
Rule A.2:   Do not discuss the existence or non-existence of
              Rules A, A.1, or A.2.[63]

For a dysfunctional family, Rule A might mean 'Don't talk about the abuse of a child by a parent', and then denying that such a prohibition exists, and so on.

In journalistic terms, Rule A might mean 'Don't discuss the tight structural constraints on free speech inherent in a corporate media system.'

Rule A.1 would then involve denying that there is any such prohibition against discussing any such structural constraints (which do not exist).

But how to maintain this pretence, when such structural constraints are both obvious, and obviously not allowed to be raised for discussion? This requires Rule A.2, which in journalistic terms means not discussing the existence or non-existence of either the structural constraints, the prohibition on discussing them, or the prohibition against discussing that prohibition.

The use of these rules is reserved, as Goleman explains, "for what cannot be noticed, and not noticed that it cannot be noticed... While they shape and limit experience, we do not readily see that they do so, because they operate outside awareness." [64]

The end result is that the corporate media system is declared free and independent in the complete absence of any historical background, evidence, or rational discussion. Who decided that the media are completely free? No one knows. How is media freedom defined and evaluated? No one knows. When and how was it achieved? No one knows. We know nothing at all, except that we are completely free. And yet, just think of it: corporations are arguably the most powerful, influential and destructive organizations active the world over. The free media system depends on these same corporations reporting honestly the activities of their sister corporations. And we think this arrangement so obviously constitutes a free media system that no discussion is required! As we have said, the 'free press' never subjects itself to any kind of serious critical evaluation. As in the case of Laing's dysfunctional families, the very fact of this silence tells its own story, a point made well by a Soviet dissident resisting a very different kind of social control:

The truth is replaced by silence, and the silence is a lie.[65]

Thus, as we have discussed, Herman and Chomsky's propaganda model, despite its striking clarity and plausibility, has been scrupulously ignored by the mainstream press in both Britain and the United States.

It seems plausible that this failure to discuss what is clearly not allowed to be discussed, in the absence of any awareness amongst many (though not all) journalists of the existence and significance of these prohibitions, is explicable in terms of Laing's rules of self-deception in dysfunctional families. It is worth adding that while individuals might allow the fact of informal censorship of their work to come to awareness, they may nevertheless repress the significance of this censorship—the obvious implications will simply not be drawn. The same, incidentally, is true of readers who may recognize the reality that we do not have a free press, without recognizing the implications of this fact as regards our wider lack of social, political and cultural freedom.

It is, then, in this remarkable, conscious-but-unconscious capacity for 'selective inattention' that modern thought control is rooted, and on which it depends. As a result, journalists can laugh at the notion of democratic thought control, while constantly participating in what is actually an extremely sophisticated system of social manipulation supporting vested interests. Likewise, thousands of corporately-sponsored journalists, PR executives and think-tank academics are willing to earn their money to pay for their cars, homes and holidays by consciously seeking to obstruct the vital work of environmentalists and human rights campaigners.

We can see, then, how the terrible political crises afflicting our world are ultimately rooted in psychological forces:

The defences—our bastions against painful information—operate in a shadow world of consciousness, beyond the fringes of awareness. Most often we are oblivious to their operation and remain the unknowing recipient of the version of reality they admit into our ken. The craft of teasing out and capturing defences *in vivo* is a tricky endeavour.[66]

Given this well-documented tendency in human beings, the casual presumption of 'neutrality' and 'straight reporting' among journalists can already be seen to be naive in the extreme. Clearly, what any journalist (indeed any human being) says, cannot be merely taken on trust. But it is just this that our media system manages to persuade us to do.

'God Bless America!': The Additional Problem of Groupthink

Our tendency to self-deception appears to be greatly increased when we join as part of a group. Coming together as a new group creates a sense of belonging, a 'we-feeling', which can provide us with even greater incentives to reject painful truths. As psychologist Irving Janis reports, the 'we-feeling' lends "a sense of belonging to a powerful, protective group that in some vague way opens up new potentials for each of them." [67]

Members are reluctant to say or do anything that might lessen these feelings of euphoria and empowerment. In this situation, even pointing out the risks surrounding a group decision may seem to represent an unforgivable attack on the group itself. This is 'groupthink'. According to Janis, the effect on our ability to perceive reality can be dramatic and disastrous:

> This groupthink tendency can operate like a low-level noise that prevents warning signals from being heeded. Everyone becomes somewhat biased in the direction of selectively attending to the messages that feed into the members' shared feelings of confidence and optimism, disregarding those that do not.[68]

Together with a new sense of strength and confidence, a group can also come to experience a supportive sense of unanimity and solidarity. This is a problem, in that once the group has made a decision, members are reluctant to threaten the sense of togetherness by challenging that decision.

Related to these feelings of empowerment and unanimity, Goleman suggests, is the tendency of groups to be susceptible to an unstated belief in their rightness and morality:

> This glib assumption allows the members to ignore the moral status and consequences of their decisions. This belief follows from

the group credo that 'we are wise and good,' an aspect of its self-image of invulnerability. And, after all, if we are good, then whatever we do must be good.[69]

Thus a journalist is highly unlikely to challenge the ethical basis of his or her work with colleagues, or to raise for discussion any of the many factors that compromise honest reporting. To do so would involve a major disruption of the sense of unanimity and moral rightness; it would be to implicitly accuse fellow group members of wilful self-deception, selling out for money; of a disregard for the truth and for the effect of its suppression on the many victims of power.

As anyone who has worked in a corporation knows, questions of morality do not sit well in any kind of corporate meeting. It is taken as read (but pushed from awareness) that the goal of profit maximization takes precedence over moral standards. Given that we all like to believe that we are basically good people, discussions of moral issues are not welcome during working hours. This understanding is often reinforced by a world-weary cynicism in regard to the innate selfishness and amorality of human beings (this cynicism is also a staple of much media reporting and commentary). To attempt to raise moral issues in this context is to immediately be labelled naive, idealistic, impractical, sentimental: that is, unprofessional. This, of course, is not the case where the affectation of a moral stance—green consumerism, donations to charity, and so on—is seen as a way of generating positive PR.

It is interesting to note how politicians reflexively seek to promote 'groupthink' in the population. Declarations such as 'God bless America' and 'We're backing Britain' are clearly intended to foster the characteristic 'groupthink' sense of empowered unanimity and moral rightness that make all dissent seem 'un-American', 'unpatriotic'. Indeed, from this perspective, the whole notion of nationalism and patriotism can be considered a giant exercise in the promotion of 'groupthink'. Tolstoy understood the utility of this kind of manipulation very well:

Patriotism in its simplest, clearest, and most indubitable signification is nothing else but a means of obtaining for the rulers their ambitions and covetous desires, and for the ruled the abdication of human dignity, reason, and conscience, and a slavish enthralment to those in power.[70]

Given that discordant radical thoughts threaten to create painful internal and external conflicts, to which there are no obvious solutions (other than resignation), it is easy to imagine why a journalist might simply remove such conflicts from awareness.

As a result of these pressures, discussion will be contained within group-friendly parameters; radical dissident views will simply never be raised. Goleman's conclusion is unsettling:

> My belief is that people in groups by and large come to share a vast number of schemas [shared frameworks of understanding], most of which are communicated without being spoken of directly. Foremost among these shared, yet unspoken, schemas are those that designate what is worthy of attention, how it is to be attended to —and what we choose to ignore or deny... people in groups also learn together how *not* to see—how aspects of shared experience can be veiled by self-deceits held in common.[71]

Unfortunately, awareness of the human capacity for self-deception does not necessarily protect us from it—Goleman's book suggests that he is himself subject to the same tendency to self-deception that he describes. Although he writes that "willingness to rock the boat is the essential quality of all those who would remedy delusion", he often fails to do just that.

Thus in his passing mention of the media, Goleman assures us:

> Although about two hundred firms do 85 percent of the business, there is nothing here like the single-minded vision produced by a state monopoly.[72]

This is all he has to say! Apparently no evidence or analysis is required: it's that tell-tale silence again. The sound, as Goleman puts it, of "hushed whispers of thoughts disappearing into silence".[73]

As Goleman notes, these two hundred firms are *all*, indeed, *firms*; that is, they are *all* single-mindedly profit-oriented. Might that not suggest a certain unity of vision? In a tiny footnote tucked away at the bottom of the page (out of sight of mainstream reviewers, perhaps?), Goleman adds: "Still, some biases in publishing and the press may be less than innocent."[74] This is an extraordinarily simplistic addendum for a book ostensibly dedicated to addressing the difficulty of facing the truth. It is interesting to consider, by comparison, Chomsky's analysis of the same media system:

The basic principle, rarely violated, is that what conflicts with the requirements of power and privilege does not exist.[75]

On the deceptions we are fed as 'history', Goleman has this to say:

American textbooks rarely portray the occupation of Indian lands by 'pioneers' as having even the least tinge of injustice. American invasions of Canada, Russia, and Mexico are glossed over, while in the textbooks of those countries those invasions are major events.[76]

Presumably, then, we are to assume that more recent American interventions in Vietnam, Panama, Nicaragua, El Salvador, Iran, Chile, Greece, Guatemala, Brazil, Iraq, Laos, Indonesia, Angola, and on and on, have not been glossed over.

By citing examples from politically ancient history, as opposed to more sensitive modern examples, Goleman fails his own "rock the boat" test. Indeed, he is careful to avoid applying his under-standing of the capacity for group self-deception and fallacious moral rightness to any politically sensitive topics (apart, it must be said, from a context-free analysis of the Bay of Pigs fiasco).

The human capacity for self-deception is a slippery fish indeed, even for those who understand how it works.

Chapter Three

RUMBLE IN THE MEDIA JUNGLE

The fact is that they are deceitful with no wish to deceive, not like Machiavellians, but with no consciousness of their deceit, and usually with the naïve assurance that they are doing something excellent and elevated, a view in which they are persistently encouraged by the sympathy and approval of all who surround them.—Tolstoy, *On Civil Disobedience and Non-Violence.*

Where Egos Dare: Andrew Marr meets Noam Chomsky

According to the propaganda model, the mainstream press will consign the propaganda model to oblivion. It will be met with ridicule, anger and abuse where necessary; with silence where possible—the priority being that all engagement with the idea itself be avoided.

As the model also suggests, however, the mainstream is not monolithic and is not maintained by a conscious conspiracy. The very efficiency of 'democratic' thought control is such that many individuals are completely unaware of the realities of the system by which they are controlled, and so perceive no danger in exposing that system to radical examination. For this and other reasons, damaging rationality and common sense do occasionally slip through the net.

Such was the case recently, when Noam Chomsky, Institute Professor of Linguistics at the Massachusetts Institute of Technology, was interviewed by Andrew Marr of the *Independent*. This encounter was particularly significant, as Chomsky was facing a mainstream journalist convinced that we have a basically free press. Chomsky was very much preaching to the unconverted, and so we had a chance to see how his radical critique held up against what to most people is simple common sense.

The arena was BBC2's *The Big Idea*, on February 14, 1996, one of a series of thirty-minute interviews. It had all the makings of a classic brawl: Chomsky, the street-fighting linguist, who learned his trade in and around New York's anarchist book stores and news-stands.

Marr, the *Independent*'s much-vaunted Columnist of the Year and Chief Political Correspondent (soon to become Editor).

Marr's preparation for the contest appears to have been relaxed to the point of somnolent. Here, after all, was a respected journalist squaring up to Chomsky, a notoriously tenacious intellectual adversary. One prominent British intellectual warned a colleague against getting into a dispute with Chomsky, describing him as "a terrible and relentless opponent"; and a *New York Times* book reviewer wrote: "Reading Chomsky... one repeatedly has the impression of attending to one of the more powerful thinkers who ever lived." And yet Marr, while knowing enough about Chomsky's arguments to debate them, did not know enough to be aware of Chomsky's countless refutations of the objections he planned to raise. Either he had not read Chomsky's political works, or he had read them half-asleep, and, as one reviewer wrote, "Not to have read [Chomsky]... is to court genuine ignorance."

The result was a mismatch, with Marr offering arguments that were meat and drink to his opponent—the sort of misunderstandings and misinterpretations Chomsky regularly uses to illustrate the intellectual bankruptcy of mainstream journalism. More often than not, Marr managed to prove Chomsky's points for him. Older and wiser journalists would surely have advised Marr that an ill-prepared TV debate with Chomsky is to be avoided at all costs. As one reviewer recently noted with regard to Chomsky: "Academe is crowded with critics who have made twerps of themselves taking him on." [1]

What happened to Marr helps explain why such confrontations happen so rarely. The reality of his predicament appeared to gradually dawn on Marr, whose standard response to Chomsky's counterarguments was to let the issue drop and quickly change the subject, only to be subjected each time to a similarly relentless battering.

The interview centred around Herman and Chomsky's propaganda model. The introduction to the programme was indicative of much that was to come. An ominous clip of Big Brother from a film of Orwell's *1984* set the ball rolling. "The idea that Orwell's warning [about thought control and propaganda] is still relevant may seem bizarre", Marr's voice-over intoned, immediately revealing his lack of understanding of Chomsky's views. Marr asked his audience to consider whether it were possible that the media is "designed to limit how you imagine the world?"

Yet Chomsky's whole point—as is well-known to all who have read his books—is that thought control in democratic societies does *not* happen through totalitarian, Big Brother-style mechanisms but is the result of a filtering process empowered by economic and political power operating in a free market system—there is no design, no conspiracy. Through a complex and subtle process, certain ideas and ways of looking at the world are promoted and come to find their way into our heads. This is a sort of negative thought control—we are controlled as much by what is *not* there, as by what is. It is not that we are prevented from choosing business-unfriendly facts and ideas, we just never encounter them and so assume they do not exist. Children are not forced to choose from a wide range of careers within the one corporate system; they are not deliberately brainwashed into believing that this is freedom. They are convinced that they are making a free choice because society functions in such a way that they are unaware of alternatives. Moreover, they are unaware that they are unaware, so that the options confronting them seem to be "just how life is". As Chomsky has pointed out many times, this is way beyond Orwell, who wrote about crude, Soviet-style propaganda and whose understanding of the possibilities of non-conspiratorial, democratic thought control was limited in the extreme.

Continuing his introduction, Marr proceeded to cite the Indonesian genocide in East Timor as an example of Chomsky's propaganda system in action, claiming that Timor's fate was ignored "because we were selling arms to the aggressors".

Unfortunately for Marr, this interpretation is itself a prime example of the propaganda system in action. In reality, Chomsky (like Herman, Pilger, Curtis and Zinn) argues that the slaughter in Timor has gone unreported for two decades for far more deepseated reasons. Firstly, Indonesian dictator Suharto was a Western client originally installed by the United States, which supplied arms, intelligence and other assistance during the Indonesian massacre of some 600,000 'communists' under Suharto, beginning in 1965. In return, Suharto consistently maintained a 'good investment climate' for foreign companies operating in Indonesia; meaning, as we have discussed, low-wage labour, forcible suppression of unions, extrajudicial killings, torture, death squads, minimal environmental protection and the general militaristic control of the economy to suit the élite at home and abroad. East Timor had gained independence from Portugal in 1975 and was looking to remain independent. This, however, Chomsky argues, was not permissible—and is still not—in the post-war world.

There were other reasons: Indonesia was a major Western ally that it was deemed important to keep sweet, following the partial failure of the war in Vietnam. Other motivations include vast reserves of oil and gas in the Timor Gap (Timorese wealth which is currently being divided up between Indonesia and Australia), and indeed the neat profit made by US companies from supplying ninety per cent of the arms used for the "annihilation of a simple mountain people" in East Timor.

The silence over the genocide in Timor was not just about pressure from the arms lobby; it was part of a much deeper silence surrounding the Western programme to install and support Third World dictators to guarantee cheap access to local resources and so maintain the flow of profits from South to North.

Cat Among the Clichés

Marr began his discussion with Chomsky by suggesting that we live in "an age of relative media diversity, in the age of the Internet". Relative to what?, one might ask. There was once far greater diversity in the media than there is now. A good example is the radical press which grew out of the vibrant working class culture of the thirties and forties, which gave genuine expression to working class interests, but which was quickly marginalized by the corporate press.

Marr moved on to suggest that opposition to the Vietnam War was an example of radical ideas being accorded full coverage in the press. What would we have heard, Marr asked, if there were no propaganda system? Pretty much what we heard about the Soviet assault on Afghanistan, Chomsky replied, namely that the United States was not defending but attacking Vietnam, in support of a corrupt and murderous South Vietnamese client dictatorship, by the massive bombing of civilians and outright invasion. Of these realities, Chomsky suggested, the media uttered barely a word.

"What I don't get," Marr continued, "is that all of this suggests—I'm a journalist—people like me are self-censoring."

Chomsky argued that this is not so: journalists are a product of a state- and corporate-run selection system that is operative throughout politics, culture and education. Children are trained to defer to experts, to repeat what they are told by learned authorities, and to suppress their own doubts and independent conclusions. As children and adults rise up the educational and career ladder they are selected for obedience and subservience (such as the willingness, for example, to put aside reservations and do as they are told for the sake of career advancement). Winners are intelligent and free-thinking, but only within certain parameters.

What Marr "doesn't get" is that the propaganda model does not depend on self-censorship, but on a system of filtering maintained by the ability of power to introduce bias by marginalizing alternatives, providing incentives to conform and costs for failure to conform, and by the innate human tendency to rationalize inconsistencies, as discussed in the previous chapter.

But, Marr insisted, "there are a lot of disputatious, stroppy, difficult people in journalism, and I have to say I think I know some of them." Chomsky replied that he also knows some of "the better" journalists and they know it's all a sham and play the system "like a violin", looking for occasional windows of opportunity to get things through. Chomsky accepted that Marr was sincere in his beliefs but then "If you believed something different you wouldn't be sitting where you're sitting."

"Politics Funnier than Words can Express..."

Marr referred Chomsky to the Gulf War, pointing out that he was "very, very well aware of the anti-gulf war dissidents—the 'no blood for oil' campaign."

"That's not the dissident position," Chomsky interrupted.

" 'No blood for oil' isn't the dissident [position]?!" Marr replied incredulously.

As with East Timor, Marr had again unwittingly demonstrated how the propaganda system operates: by presenting a false version of the *actual* dissident view which is ignored, goes unreported and is thus unknown.

Chomsky pointed out that the real dissident argument was that a peaceful, negotiated settlement to the Gulf crisis was possible even from August 1991, and increasingly so as allied forces threatened to wreck havoc on Iraq. It is not simply that sanctions might eventually have worked: they might already have done their job. The real problem was that, far from seeking a peaceful resolution, the Bush administration was fearful that Iraq might pull out before an attack could be launched. Thus all peace initiatives were powerfully suppressed, and simply did not appear in the mainstream US media. Some high-ranking US officials, like Richard Helms, were unable to get media coverage for possible peace initiatives. Even the US State Department, Chomsky argued, considered the problem negotiable, but the press would not cover it.

This is a sample of the real dissident position, not the "No blood for oil" argument. The media did inform us that many people objected to killing for oil, but they never aired the idea that the war might have been part of a plan to remove an obstacle to Western profits, or that peaceful withdrawal was a genuine possibility, and a genuine fear on the part of our leaders.

Marr chose not to respond, and instead moved on to Watergate, generally assumed to be the classic example of how the free press can humble the powers that be. After all, Marr said, "This brought down a president." Chomsky, however, argues that Watergate is a perfect example of just how servile the press is to power. Watergate is, he has said elsewhere, "small potatoes" compared to what the state secret police—the FBI—had long been doing to socialist, black and women's movements under the COINTELPRO programme. "Sorry, you'll have to explain that," Marr chipped in. Exactly! Chomsky replied. He had to explain the meaning of COINTELPRO, whereas Marr knew all about Watergate.

What Marr did not know about was a huge campaign of political subversion that went all the way from bugging, theft and sabotage, to political assassination organized by the FBI under four administrations. By comparison, the Republican Watergate shenanigans were a side-show. The reason the latter became headline news was, as Chomsky explained, that one half of US political power started to mess with the other half, and that is not allowed—hence the fall of Nixon and widespread press coverage.

Watergate showed, not that the US has a free press, but that powerful interests in the US are capable of defending themselves against attack. By contrast, when minority movements without power are attacked, there is no way through the propaganda system and the facts go unreported. Thus, once again, in a way completely contrary to the common understanding, Chomsky argued that:

> There couldn't be a more dramatic example of the subordination of educated opinion to power in England, as well as in the United States.

"It still seems to me," Marr proposed gamely, "that on a range of pretty important issues for the establishment there is serious dissent." Gingrich, for example, has "been pretty savagely lampooned". Again, Marr missed the point. It is fine to lampoon Gingrich, just as it is fine to lampoon Major and Blair. The point is that this type of dissent is restricted within parameters so narrow that all serious dissent is excluded and so real power is unthreatened. Henry Adams explained how it works in a letter to a friend:

> We are here plunged in politics funnier than words can express. Very great issues are involved... But the amusing thing is that no one talks about real interests. By common consent they agree to let these alone. We are afraid to discuss them. Instead of this the press is engaged in a most amusing dispute whether Mr. Cleveland had an illegitimate child and did or did not live with more than one mistress.[2]

It is the job of politicians to act as a buffer between populace and power, to distract us from real issues, from real obstacles to democracy. If necessary, a politician like Nixon can be sacrificed and the myth promulgated that the one 'bad apple' has been purged from an essentially good 'barrel'. Politicians, like journalists, are representatives—not of the people, to be sure, but of corporate interests. They are functionaries who have to abide by the basic rules or leave.

But what about NAFTA (The North American Free Trade Agreement)?, Marr countered. "We were well aware of the [counter] arguments" presented by unions, environmentalists and so on.

"That's flatly false," Chomsky responded, pointing out that the crucial dissident responses, the widespread and profound objections to NAFTA, were suppressed and replaced by "Mexico bashing" and the concern about losing jobs. The real issues: that the treaty was organized and signed in secret in a way that largely circumvented democratic procedures (whereby unions were supposed to be allowed to comment on the treaty, and so on) were ignored. Instead, a barrage of media publicity railed against union strong-arm tactics in pressuring politicians, whilst the massive pressure exerted by corporate lobbyists went unnoticed. The corporate solidarity in favour of NAFTA was such that genuine discussion of the issues was nowhere to be found in the mainstream.

But what about 'sleaze'? Marr asked. Apparently many of the politicians he is acquainted with are "deeply irritated, ranging on furious" about media intrusions into their private lives; and do we not hear no end of tales about sexual misdemeanours and corruption? Sure, Chomsky said, but that's of marginal importance. Corporate power is in favour of 'law and order' (on its terms) and is certainly opposed to corruption, which acts as a drain on profits and interferes with the control of society. In India, fully one-third of the economy is 'black', a fact that is not at all popular with transnationals. Also, as Henry Adams hinted, sex scandals, corruption and sleaze all serve the important function of diverting us from what really matters. While we are focusing on royal love lives, or what politicians like to wear in bed, we are assuredly not focusing on the real, systemic issues which should be central to everyone concerned with democracy—such as the fact that, regardless of the personalities and behaviour of individual politicians, modern democracies are hopelessly compromised by the immense influence of large corporations, which have the power to manipulate governments and economies simply by threat of capital flight and other measures.

By way of a strangely inappropriate concluding question—one which supports Chomsky's contention that "within the mainstream it is barely even possible to hear the arguments"—Marr asked: "What would a press be like, do you think, without a propaganda model [sic]? What would we be reading in the papers that we don't read now?" Chomsky reminded Marr that he had just given dozens of examples; examples, moreover, that had been chosen by Marr. Chomsky could have chosen different ones which might have made his task easier.

Finally, how much hope is there in the Internet? As Chomsky suggested, the struggle taking place for the independence of the Internet is nothing new. First of all it is essentially an élite operation (most of the people in the world have no access to a phone, let alone a computer). More importantly, a similar battle already took place in the 1920s over radio which, initially, was viewed as a public resource. There were no limits on the number of stations, no reason why the airwaves should belong to anyone in particular. Nevertheless, radio fell under corporate control and, today, with the exception of a few marginal voices, there is little dissent.

"Deceived Deceivers"

Barring a grin from Marr and a wry smile from Chomsky, the interview was over. It was a rare and illuminating event. Chomsky was interviewed by Peter Jay on TV in the '70s, and by Bill Moyers in the

'80s, but never have we seen Chomsky discuss the propaganda model in such detail with a mainstream journalist. The public response to these appearances is interesting. The Bill Moyers interview generated 1,000 letters from readers (more than the programme had received for almost any other interview). When Chomsky appeared on TV Ontario in 1985, the phone-in number registered 31,321 calls—a station record. John Pilger, who regularly applies the propaganda model in his journalism, reports that when his Timor documentary *Death of a Nation* was shown on Channel Four, British Telecom registered 4,000 calls a minute to the number displayed at the end of the programme. The producer of the Marr-Chomsky interview reported that: "The audience reaction was astonishing... I have never worked on a programme which elicited so many letters and calls." His office was "inundated".[3] The public enthusiasm for this type of analysis is clear, but that of the corporate media less so.

With Marr's *The Big Idea*, we had a chance to see ideas that have been casually dismissed by the mainstream pitted against one of the media's finest. The result was fascinating. We saw that journalists like Marr are intelligent, lucid and rational, but only within parameters that preclude a deeper understanding of what is really happening in the world. We saw how the illusion of media diversity is maintained by presenting superficial and trivialized versions of the true dissident position. Above all, perhaps, we saw how journalists are intellectual herd animals who instinctively seek safety among the tried but rarely tested clichés of the mainstream: Watergate proves we have an anti-establishment free press, media-coverage virtually ended the Vietnam war, and so on. Normally this tactic succeeds in eliciting eager nods of agreement, or a humble shrug of 'I suppose you're right'. When confronted by a Chomsky, however, the façade of great expertise and intellectuality that is the stock-in-trade of the journalist, and which is normally so intimidating, quickly crumbles. Interestingly, the reaction of the viewer to the spectacle of this intellectual debagging is not surprise but relief: 'My God, I was right all along, and I thought it was just me!'

To listen to, and believe, mainstream journalists like Marr— who is undoubtedly an honest and sincere individual—is to be stifled and bemused by a necessarily superficial, misleading and confusing version of the world that cannot make sense because it cannot address the real issues. Marr is not a liar and he is not a crude propagandist; he is the unwitting product of a system that selects for the ability to talk intelligently and convincingly about anything and everything, so long as it is not genuinely costly to power. The crucial factor is that individuals are able to do this sincerely and with the firm conviction that what they are saying is the uncompromised, freely-expressed truth. This, in the end, is the real genius of the modern system of thought control—it is very subtle, invisible, and its greatest victims are often not the deceived but the deceivers themselves.

Chomsky Vanishes

It was intriguing to see how Marr would react to the experience of interviewing Chomsky. In the months immediately following the screening of *The Big Idea*, Marr wrote several times on media censorship and the objectivity of the press. In the April 1996 edition of *Prospect* magazine, for example, he wrote a piece entitled 'Words and Things' to mark the 50th anniversary of the publication of Orwell's *Politics and The English Language*; according to Marr "an almost holy text for many thousands of journalists".

Marr reminds us that Orwell wrote of how "lizard-eyed power hides behind pretentious sentences," and that "in our time, political speech is largely a defence of the indefensible." Marr agrees, but assures us that "there is no political evil in the world today as great as Stalinism." Survivors in East Timor, El Salvador, Burma, Guatemala, Iraq, Nicaragua and Chechnya might beg to differ. Beyond specific cases, the subordination of human and environmental well-being to 'good investment climates' right around the world, such that forty per cent of Latin Americans live below the poverty line and the natural support systems of planetary life are collapsing before our very eyes, might well be said to far exceed Stalin's crimes. Marr might, at the very least, have used his article to draw attention to some of these lesser "political evils" and might even have urged fellow journalists to give more attention to them.

As ever in this type of mainstream analysis, Marr is full of praise for his fellow journalists: "I suspect we may be living in a silver, if not a golden age, for this kind of prose." This general approval and praise is accompanied by colourful but superficial criticisms: "Tepid clichés, and bland, tasteless UHT thinking gurgle from the radio and curdle on the page."

Word pictures aside, Marr makes no reference to the corporate monopoly on Truth: that corporations hire and fire editors and journalists on the basis of their performance such that important interests are carefully protected. "Ours is not a time of clashing ideology or thrilling ideas," he insists. Marr is clearly disinclined to consider just why it is that clashing ideologies and thrilling ideas are absent in a time when corporations have a monopoly over systems of communication, and so have little to gain from stirring up such excitement. Presumably he prefers to believe the old chestnut beloved of all conquerors: the natives are reconciled, they have seen the value of their new rulers' ways and now history is at an end.

Marr's analysis never rises above the uncontroversial and unthreatening. Britain, he assures us, "remains a country passionately committed to plain speech and instinctive in its hostility to overblown English", although the ardour of corporations is perhaps cooled somewhat where plain speech interferes with profit.

Unsurprisingly to all who understand Orwell's limits and the serviceability of his ideas for Western 'democrats', Marr writes of his tremendous respect for Orwell: "For democracy, his defence of plain English has been an absolute and important good." Orwell indeed "is not just a great writer; he is one of the great political reformers of the century."

Throughout Marr's article, one name is missing; the name which any honest writer, any genuine opponent of "lizard-eyed power", would feel duty-bound to mention as the obvious successor to Orwell. In Marr's world Noam Chomsky does not exist, even though he himself had recently interviewed him—and had his views effectively demolished by him.

In Marr's world, perhaps, Chomsky cannot exist. Marr is just too far down the road of conformity; he has just too much to lose to consider Chomsky and the implications of his ideas. For, surely Marr cannot have been unable to perceive the truth of what Chomsky had to say to him. Perhaps the explanation for Marr's unwillingness to question the required delusions of the mainstream is to be found in a single short announcement appearing in many British newspapers in April 1996: "Andrew Marr Made Editor of the *Independent*".

As for Marr's reputation in the mainstream, Matthew Parris, writing in the *Sunday Telegraph*, has this to say of Marr's book *Ruling Britannia*: "A work of brilliance... lit by a beautiful honesty. Simply to read him is to realise how weasely, self-regarding and conformist is so much of the rest of British political columnism."[4]

The propaganda system is maintained by apparently reasonable people heaping praise on other apparently reasonable people; the end result is our stupefaction and passivity and, for the Third World, the unimaginable horror that goes with it. Terrible inhumanity does not depend on angry words and fist-shaking tyrants alone; it depends on the gentle diversion of people's attention with half-truths and bland entertainments.

"How the Media Undermine Democracy"

Andrew Marr's performance in *The Big Idea* is representative of the mainstream media in Britain and elsewhere. His inability to perceive the narrow parameters of 'respectable' discourse within which he is required to operate is very much the norm.

In a two-page spread in the *Guardian* on April 1, 1996, headlined 'News You Can't Use', James Fallows, Washington Editor of the *Atlantic Monthly*, focused on "How the media undermine American democracy". Fallows began by pointing out that the press is often referred to as "the Fourth Branch of Government", which means that it "should provide the information we need so as to make sense of public problems". As such, he argued, the press "must give people the sense that life is not just a sequence of random occurrences", or that "the foreign news is mainly a series of unexplained and unconnected disasters".

Admirable sentiments. It is indeed unfortunate that the press fails to present sufficient background and historical detail by which sense can be made of domestic and international affairs.

We might imagine that Fallows was referring to the hypocrisy of, say, *The Times* reporting on January 18, 1991, with regard to the Gulf War, that "the cause is simple on a world scale, the defence of the weak against aggression by the strong". After all, *The Times* omitted to mention that the Iraqi invasion took place some eight months after the United States had invaded Panama with 26,000 troops, at the cost of perhaps 3,000 civilian lives, in December 1989. The invasion was in clear violation of international law and was subsequently condemned at the United Nations by seventy-five votes to twenty. *The Times* also failed to note that the US and its allies have a long history of "defending the weak" if and when it suits their interests, and in supporting the strong against the weak when it does not.

In fact Fallows had something else in mind. The real problem, he argued, is that the media have fallen into the habit of "portraying public life in America as a race to the bottom, in which one group of conniving, insincere politicians ceaselessly tries to out-manoeuvre another." This is a problem because "by choosing to present public life as a contest among scheming political leaders, all of whom the public should view with suspicion, the news media help bring about that very result."

Too much negativity is a problem, Fallows continues, "if an awareness of the parts of life that go right is not built into an enumeration of what is going wrong, the news becomes useless, in that it teaches us all to despair." Similarly, what is really irksome is that media celebrities like to make themselves "the centre of attention" by making "fun of the gaffes and imperfections of anyone in public life".

In short, the press is too *hostile* to power, too willing to grab attention at the expense of imperfect politicians. Instead, a more up-beat press should present American public life with more respect and less cynicism.

Are Fallows and the *Guardian* joking? Suspicions (in my case, genuine suspicions) were raised by the fact that the article appeared on April Fool's Day. That Fallows intended his remarks seriously was confirmed by the fact that Michael Elliott, editor of *Newsweek* international, and ex-Washington editor of *The Economist*, was booked to respond to Fallows a week later in order to ask "if the British media are guilty of the same shortcomings as their American counterparts".

This Elliott failed to do, although he did attempt to critique Fallows' "fierce attack" on the American press. Fallows is surely right, Elliott observes, to suggest that the objectivity of high-profile journalists with their "snouts deep in the lecture circuit trough" sometimes "gets lost in the swill"—an observation that presumably has some meaning for high-profile journalists and editors, although precious little for the rest of us. But if some of the detail is right, Elliott continues, Fallows' big picture "just seems wrong". In an apparent reference to Fallows' criticism that the American press reduces news to empty entertainment, Elliott argues cryptically that "it isn't true that American newspapers don't ask their readers to eat spinach—in fact, sometimes the diet is too wholesome for any but a saint."

Elliott continues: "From Bosnia to Bill Clinton's healthcare plan, the American press covers the minutiae of the world's news with diligence, thoroughness, bravery and skill." Indeed, journalists "go the extra mile, do ten interviews instead of three, and check out the facts with a zeal that is exemplary."

To add to the sense of unreality, Elliott observes that there are indeed problems with the attitude of journalists: "their calling is dignified by the constitution", such that "some American journalists tend to think that the only way they can prove themselves worthy of their honour is by a great earnestness."

Sometimes, then, journalists are too honourable, such that they take "their calling" too seriously. Elliott agrees that reporters do try to combine information with entertainment, but then there is no law that says information should be at the expense of giving readers "stuff they will enjoy". It is not a neat business, Elliott concludes, and "we can always do better. But we aren't doing badly."

Note, then, that the parameters of debate stretch all the way from the assertion that, on the one hand, the press is too critical of power; and on the other that the press is doing a difficult job well.

It might seem surreal that these views should constitute a discussion on 'How the media undermine democracy' and yet this represents the norm for discussions of this kind. It is also worth noting that these comments were made by senior editors of two of the most important and influential journals. Yet their arguments are superficial in the extreme. There is nothing here to make sense of, just a discussion so shallow, so disconnected from any rational analysis of the structure and functioning of the media, that no real insights are gained. Significant issues are ignored as if non-existent or irrelevant: the fact that the media are all corporations with a deep interest in the maintenance of the status quo, with intimate links to other large corporations, government and financial institutions, is not considered a significant issue in a discussion of how the media undermine democracy.

With no substance to grasp hold of, the reader naturally assumes that he or she is insufficiently informed, or too unintelligent, to grasp the issues, or to make sense of what is being said. References to high-profile lecture circuits, numbers of interviews carried out, and inside information on just how thorough journalists are, create an impression of specialist insider knowledge intended to intimidate 'outsiders': surely top editors understand the media better than we: they are professionals, specialists, experts. Who are we to question their judgement?

In reality, with high-paid careers at stake, editors like Fallows and Elliott have every reason to rationalize their positions, every reason to believe that they are performing public service roles in an honourable and dignified Free Press. The price of thinking otherwise would be great personal stress, and perhaps the loss of their job, career, reputation and earnings. In fact it is clear that the independent outside observer is in a far better position to evaluate the media than the insider who is selected, employed, highly rewarded by the corporate system—and under permanent threat of dismissal. The insider, after all, has a job to do.

Chapter Four

POLITICAL ANTHROPOMORPHISM

'Getting with the Programme': Globalizing Inhumanity

Today the world is being subjected to a programme of economic conquest described by the much-loved sound bite 'globalization'. Like 'development' and 'modernization', 'globalization' is, in itself, a meaningless term intended to denote progress while actually camouflaging a multitude of horrors. Indeed, a notable feature of this mysterious process of 'globalization' is an emptying of the terms of social and political discourse. What is actually being globalized, of course, is a particular type of economic system, namely corporate capitalism.

Corporations, the elements of corporate capitalism, are the surviving offspring of a system of profit-seeking evolution whereby investors ensure the survival of the most successfully profit-oriented: corporations which make a high, quick return on profit will tend to flourish, while those that do not will tend to be dismantled or taken over.

Corporate capitalism, then, is a system of artificial evolution selecting for maximum profit at any cost. To be sure, there will be restraints on how far profit can be maximized, but the mechanics of corporate capitalism are such that it ceaselessly seeks to circumvent and extend these limits. Were any rogue corporate units to decide to resist this central systemic drive for profit, the system would simply divert capital to a competing unit. To be ethical, for example, is to fail to 'get with the programme' and become 'unfit' by the standards of profit-maximization (as is well-known to all individuals who have made the mistake of straying in that direction). After some five hundred years of continuous evolution, it comes as no surprise that the pre-eminent corporations of modern capitalism are indeed supremely well-adapted to the business of maximizing profits.

Knowing only this, a passing Martian with no knowledge of conditions on planet Earth would surely predict that such a system must have destructive consequences for every last aspect of human and non-human life. A reasonably astute Martian would surely also predict that awareness of the real logic, goals and impact of a profit-maximizing system of this sort—being an obstacle to profit—would likely be unknown to the vast majority of people. Our Martian would expect to find the majority of people convinced that they were completely free in a benign and humane political and economic system.

Little green dissidents aside, what, in the real world, does the existence of an all-powerful economic system designed to subordinate all secondary concerns to profit actually mean for that flexible friend of corporate commentators, 'democracy'?

Democracy Disarmed
Edward Herman and Thomas Ferguson have argued for an 'investment theory' of politics, suggesting that in modern 'democracies' political parties tend to coalesce around the needs and interests of groups of investors. Thus, in the United States, for example, the Republican and Democratic parties tend to coalesce around the interests of larger and smaller businesses respectively.

Ferguson argues that "to discover who rules, follow the gold."[1] By contrast, mainstream analysts argue (with little documentary evidence) that voters' preferences are the driving force behind party competition; the idea being that parties compete by shaping their policies in order to appeal to the average voter. This theory is seriously compromised by perennially low voter turnout, with those who do vote being relatively well-off. In the United States, turnout is around 50 per cent for presidential elections: in 1980, Reagan won a small majority of the popular vote, with 28 per cent of the electorate supporting him. Why the low vote? Chomsky explains:

> When the interests of the privileged and powerful are the guiding commitments of both political factions, people who do not share these interests tend to stay home.[2]

According to Thomas Edsell of the *Washington Post* "the interests of the bottom three-fifths of society" are not represented in the political system.[3]

The idea that parties represent the people is untenable when, as Chomsky reports, half the population thinks that both political parties should be disbanded, with eighty per cent regarding the economic system as "inherently unfair".

It is also made untenable by the wide discrepancy between the policies of both major political parties and what people actually want; the reality being, as Brad Knickerbocker of the *Christian Science Monitor* has written, that "it's almost as if lawmakers looked at what Americans want... and then marched off in the opposite direction." [4]

Substantial majorities support the idea that government should assist the needy and favour extra spending on health, education, help for the poor and environmental protection—priorities contrary to the policies of both major US political parties.

The same is true in Britain, where, as John Pilger wrote prior to the 1997 general election:

> The voters will have the choice of voting yes or no to another term by the Tory government, whose policies are shared by its principal rival [New Labour]. In the long-distant past there was an element of difference that gave people hope. There is none now... The American model has arrived, with the electorate now called upon every five years to ratify one of two factions representing the same wealth and power. [5]

Jonathan Eyal, Director of Studies at the Royal United Services Institute, has observed that the realities of globalized transnational wealth and power have reduced Western party politics

> to a petty bureaucratic squabble: since economic priorities appear pre-ordained, the dispute is only about who is better suited to apply them. Britain's Conservatives are offering Thatcherism without Thatcher; their Labour counterparts are espousing conservatism without the Conservatives. [6]

Erich Shaw explains the logic of the 'investment theory' of politics as applied to Britain's New Labour:

> At the heart of New Labour is a vacuum. The real lessons of the past are that in government the most formidable pressures come not from the unions, or the social lobbies but from the right—from the City, industry, the international finance markets and the media, all of whom will be quick to pounce on any but the most timorous effort to achieve a fairer and more cohesive society. [7]

The public, we note, are absent from their considerations.

It is in the context of these realities that we need to consider

Guardian environment correspondent Paul Brown's attempts to find "excuses that can be made" for the fact that 100,000 species have been extinguished by human activity in the five years since the Rio Earth Summit; why global emissions of carbon dioxide have continued to rise; why deserts are getting bigger, forests smaller, poor people poorer; why, in sum, "everything has got a lot worse".[8]

Brown explains that:

> Voters who a couple of years previously had been worried about the environment suddenly switched to caring only about keeping their jobs... Politicians were prey to that fear.

(This analysis is, it should be noted, a favourite of the multinational industries attempting to undermine any response to global warming. As James May, Director-General of UK Offshore Operations Association Limited, writes in defence of his oil industry: "Our industry meets demand. It supplies the products that people want, to allow them to live the life they lead." [9])

The problem, according to Brown, is that politicians are victims of the changing demands of fickle, self-seeking voters. This is the standard picture of our political system, painted by the mainstream media without exception. It is natural that Brown should reiterate this view: a great deal of his paper's reporting is premised on the assumption that our political process is basically fair and democratic, that we are therefore free and are living in a society in which the status quo is more or less acceptable. In reality, the idea that the public determines political policy is hardly credible.

Thus the 1996 edition of the *British Social Attitudes Survey* found that, contrary to the policies of both major parties, most British people wanted more spending on health, education and social benefits, even if it meant paying more tax. Over 60 per cent favoured 'tax and spend'. A large proportion of people believed that "government should redistribute income from the better-off to the less well-off": 43 per cent of those in the South of England, 51 per cent in London, 61 per cent in the North. A strong majority believed that "big business benefits owners at the expense of workers": 56 percent in the South, rising to 66 percent in Scotland. Samuel Brittan of the *Financial Times* (May 3, 1997) comments that if New Labour were to make "even a fraction of the changes in attitude that Tony Blair has promised... UK capitalism will be far more unconstrained than the electorate really desires."

Brittan's analysis was confirmed by the BBC exit poll broadcast the day after the election, which showed that 72 per cent of those who voted wanted the government to put a penny on the rate of income tax to pay for better education, and 58 per cent wanted the government to redistribute income from rich to poor. David Dimbleby, hosting the BBC election special, commented that these results showed "huge majorities against the things the Tories were standing for".[10] The more important point is that these figures also show huge majorities against the things *New Labour* stands for: no income tax rises and no redistribution of income or wealth. Milan Rai comments:

> The election result is not yet more confirmation that the British people are opposed to justice and equality and freedom. It is yet more confirmation that the present parliamentary system is not democratic: it does not express the needs and opinions of the people of this country.[11]

While voter intention, according to Brown, is a powerful hindrance to political attempts to combat global warming, in fact the political desires of the majority of said voters are simply ignored by all political parties.

The unified media view aside, according to the investment theory, parliamentary politics should be seen as an arm of business; the job of political parties being to promote the interests of élite groups of investors regardless of, and often against, the needs of the vast majority of ordinary people.

As is well known, there is a constantly revolving door between senior state and corporate managers. The tendency of senior British ministers to leave politics and immediately move into high-level positions within the corporations they were formerly responsible for regulating, and even privatizing, has led to calls for controls. The argument against prohibiting moves of this sort has been that ministers deal with a wide range of companies and would be effectively barred from finding any gainful employment after leaving politics. The same would of course also be true were ministers to seriously displease the many corporations they deal with—an incentive to bow to corporate requirements with rather huge implications for what we like to imagine is democratic government serving the people, given the self-confessed corporate ambitions of senior ministers.

The Teeth Behind the Smile: Political Anthropomorphism

According to the dictionary definition, anthropomorphism involves the "attribution of a human form or personality to a god, animal, or thing". It is interesting to consider this definition in the context of parliamentary and corporate politics.

Politicians and corporate executives are human beings with human personalities. The problem, however, is that political and economic managers are not where they are by accident: as with journalists, they are the result of a selection process designed to satisfy the needs of the corporate system. Success within the political and economic system will tend to encourage, and be conditional on, individual conformity to the goals and requirements of the corporate system.

On the other hand, at the point where this conformity breaks down, we can be sure that the system will replace the 'failed' individual with someone more appropriate to its needs. Even high-profile leaders can quickly be dismissed and made to vanish from public view. A good example of this was the fate of Andrew Neil, former editor of *The Times*, who, as we have discussed, fell foul of the profit-maximizing system.

There are any number of similar instances of this type of filtering. In 1945, Wilfred Burchett of the *Daily Express* was the first Western correspondent to reach what remained of Hiroshima after the atomic bombing. Burchett found confusion in the city's two remaining hospitals; doctors had no idea what they were dealing with: "People come in, the symptoms are of dizziness, internal haemorrhage, diarrhoea, and then later there are spots and before death the hair falls out and there is bleeding from the nose." [12]

Burchett described this as an "Atomic plague"—being in fact, of course, radiation sickness. The authorities occupying Japan denied Burchett's reports. A military spokesman insisted that people had died only as a result of the blast; a version of the truth that was widely accepted at the time. The *New York Times* published a report with the headline "NO RADIOACTIVITY IN HIROSHIMA RUIN".[13] The presence of radioactivity was denied "categorically" by the military authorities. Burchett had his press accreditation withdrawn and was issued with an expulsion order from Japan.

John Pilger also cites the admirable example set by Robert White, Ambassador to El Salvador, who, in a speech before the Senate Foreign Relations Committee said: "The chief killers of

Salvadoreans are the government security forces. They are the ones responsible for the deaths of thousands upon thousands of young people who have been executed merely on the suspicion that they are leftists." [14]

As we have discussed, these same government security forces were in receipt of some $2 billion in US 'aid' from 1980 to 1986. Eighty-five per cent of this paid for arms, planes, helicopters, incendiary bombs, oxygen-reduction bombs, phosphorus bombs, napalm bombs, cluster bombs, anti-personnel weapons and munitions, electrified wire, and other horrors. White's comments were clearly not without significance for the reputation of the United Sates as the great defender of democracy. As for our brave dissident: "For saying that", Pilger reports, "White paid with his career." [15]

Elsewhere, former US Attorney General Ramsey Clark has been consigned to media obscurity for his work in exposing US war crimes during the Gulf War. Similarly, Noam Chomsky, despite being described as "arguably the greatest living intellectual", is *persona non grata* as far as the US media are concerned, with Rupert Murdoch's *Times* describing him as "America's most gaunt and humourless intellectual".[16] A sense of humour is certainly essential for anyone with integrity also attempting to gain access to the corporate media system.

As such examples imply, the very fact that a given individual is appearing before us in the role of a media commentator, or political or corporate leader, indicates that he or she has a proven track record of conforming to the requirements of the corporate system. This is true also of our cultural icons: acceptance by the mainstream bodes ill for the honesty and worth of cultural productions. For example, the rebel leaders of rock and pop are often, in reality, as Andy Partridge of rock band XTC has noted, filtered products of a music industry which functions as "a hammer to keep you pegs in your holes".[17]

Whether or not our leaders are pleasant, kindly individuals is largely irrelevant; so long as they appear before us in the mass media we can rest assured they are adequately performing the job assigned to them. Of course such people are free to 'defect', and they sometimes do; in which case, as with Neil, Burchett, White, Clark *et al*, they quickly disappear from sight.

Political and corporate leaders are peculiarly constrained by their public roles. Clearly, you and I—outside work and education, at least—are relatively free to talk as we please. We are free to rail against our economic and political systems and, if convinced by a powerful argument, to agree with that argument. This is patently not true of our leaders, who are under great pressure to act to the benefit of the system by which they have been selected. Writing about spokespeople for the PR and Human Relations industries, Jacques Ellul pointed out that:

> His words are no longer human words but technically calculated words... The presence is not that of the individual who has come forward but that of the organization behind him. In the very act of pretending to speak as human to human, the propagandist is reaching the summit of mendacity and falsification, even when he is not conscious of it.[18]

No surprise, then, that the propaganda system tries with all its might to convince us of the humanity and normality of our leaders. Whether chatting from the fireside, dancing with their spouses, taking off their jackets at a conference (a major news event), playing the saxophone, or saying a silent prayer at the scene of some disaster, we clutch at any evidence of their humanity with palpable relief. Naturally we do not like to imagine that the morality and humanity of our leaders are compromised by the requirements of economic power. It is surely for this reason that such trivial gestures are of such significance to us. But note, also, how we are almost shocked by the sight of our leaders showing genuine humanity and emotion. It is almost as if we cannot believe our eyes, accustomed as we are to a continuous parade of deception and obfuscation.

To expect our leaders to adhere to basic standards of rationality and morality in their public lives is to indulge in a kind of anthropomorphism: they will not, indeed cannot. (Incidentally, I do not mean to suggest that these individuals are somehow subhuman, rather that in their public lives they are constrained from acting with the kind of compassion and reason we associate with the idea of a fully human being.) Their highest priority *must* be the defence of profits, to which logic and morality must be subordinated as a matter of course. Where basic logic and reason threaten profits, our leaders must resort to audacious extremes of illogic and unreason— often carefully wrapped in deliberate obfuscation—to hide the reality as far as possible. Similarly, where elementary rules of human morality and decency threaten profits, our leaders have no choice but to abandon those rules as if they did not exist; or, as in the case of White, to speak the truth and disappear from public view.

Thus, whilst all but a few pathological individuals would agree that it is wrong to torture little children and steal from them in order to feed those who already have far more than they could possible require, our leaders in effect are required to disagree, and to act accordingly. Profit is never satisfied, is the highest priority and, as we saw in the first chapter, stealing food from starving and dying children to give to the greedy is institutionalized within the capitalist system.

To watch as a president, prime minister or chief executive takes to the podium and expect him or her to respond on the basis of rationality and humanity; to expect him or her to behave as a 'normal human being like me', to reflect our concerns for the world and its people, is anthropomorphism. They are simply unable to do so.

Time and again our hopes will be raised and dashed. Indeed, the aim of much of politics is to raise our hopes and then let them drift off into nothingness, into 'business as usual'. We will very likely feel bewildered that our leaders do not admit to the crimes, inhumanity and indifference of which we know they are guilty.

Systemic Crimes, Systemic Lies: Killing East Timor

If the above strikes the reader as extreme, let us consider a few examples. On October 1, 1997 it was announced in the press that more than 1,500 of the world's most distinguished scientists (including 104 of the 138 surviving recipients of Nobel prizes), had signed a declaration urging world leaders to act immediately to prevent the "potentially devastating consequences of human-induced global warming" [19]. Nobel Laureate Henry Kendall, chairman of the Union of Concerned Scientists said:

> Let there be no doubt about the conclusions of the scientific community that the threat of global warming is very real and action is needed immediately. It is a grave error to believe that we can continue to procrastinate. [20]

Dudley Herschbach, another Nobel prize winner and professor of chemistry at Harvard University, said:

> This is a wake-up call for world leaders. Never before has the senior scientific community spoken so boldly on the urgent need to prevent disruption to our climate. [21]

Three days later, in the same newspaper, James May, Director-General of the UK Offshore Operations Association Limited, spoke up on behalf of the oil industry:

> I should make clear at the outset that concern for the environment is something that motivates us all.

However, May notes, "All would admit the science surrounding climate change is complex. One thing is clear, though. This is a global issue, necessitating a global response." [22]

The real meaning of this statement is clear enough. Recall that our world's top scientists are insisting that we be "in no doubt" that the threat facing us is "very real" with "potentially devastating consequences" such that the idea that we can continue to procrastinate would be "a grave error". By "devastating consequences", the world's scientists do not mean that we might fall into recession, that unemployment might rise; they do not mean that war might break out: they mean that we may be stricken by an uncontrollable global catastrophe on an unimaginable scale.

In the face of this unprecedented threat to humanity, to our entire planet, to everything we hold dear, May nevertheless feels it is acceptable to insist that "the science... is complex", which is industry code for: 'more research needs to be done, we can't be sure of the significance of the threat'; and "one thing is clear, though", which is industry code for: 'one thing is not clear: the seriousness of the threat of global warming'; and that "this is a global issue, necessitating a global response", which is industry code for: 'we in the West/Third World are not going to do anything until 'they' in the Third World/West do something', in order that no one should have to do anything.

Is this a reasonable, moral response to the scientific consensus and the awesome seriousness of the threat highlighted by it?

By way of a further, more detailed, example, it may be enlightening to consider a 'Head to Head' exchange of letters between Angie Zelter and Robert Key MP, printed in the *Guardian* on September 7, 1996. It may seem overly pedantic to focus so intensely on such a minor exchange, but it was a classic example of how political executives, like their corporate colleagues, are required to depart from the most basic norms of rationality and morality. It involved, moreover, a splendid display of the standard devices of the propaganda system that keep us in ignorance and passivity. What is so interesting is the primitive nature of these devices: meaningless (and therefore confusing) arguments; high-sounding gestures; grand claims to the moral high ground; the feigning of expertise and esoteric knowledge, all peppered by the liberal use of insults. Unable to employ rationality and truth, the propaganda system relies on its capacity to bamboozle and intimidate, and on our lack of in-depth understanding of the issues, to carry the day.

Angie Zelter is one of four women, all belonging to the Swords to Ploughshares movement, who 'disabled' a British Aerospace Hawk fighter bomber destined for the government of Indonesia and for possible use in East Timor. With household hammers, Zelter and her companions broke into a British Aerospace (BAe) site in Warton, near Preston, on January 29, 1996 and destroyed the display screen in the cockpit and an air speed probe, and made holes in the fuselage, inflicting an estimated £1.5 million of damage. The women decorated the plane with banners and left a 53-page pamphlet and video on the cockpit seat; the latter containing footage of Hawk bombing raids over East Timor. They then phoned a news agency and waited for the police to arrive. Later, the women wrote:

> Filled with joy, we sang, cried, danced and hugged, celebrating the power of ordinary women taking action to prevent export of weapons to a genocidal regime.[23]

Subsequently, at Liverpool Crown Court, the women pleaded not guilty to charges of damaging the plane, citing in their defence the Nuremberg prosecution of Nazi war criminals, the 1969 Genocide Act, and the provision against aiding and abetting murder in the 1861 Offences Against The Persons Act. Under cross-examination, the BAe site manager at Warton, Christopher Foster, was asked "Did you have any concern for the people who might be killed when it was delivered?" "No," Foster replied, "I had no concern." [24]

The *Guardian* 'Head to Head' consisted of an exchange of correspondence between Zelter and Key. It began as follows:

> Dear Robert, A third of the population of East Timor has been killed by Indonesia in its 20-year illegal occupation. Those still living have been corralled into concentration camps, where many die of starvation. Entire tribes have been exterminated and their land settled by Indonesians from hundreds of miles away.

Even government sources confirm what Zelter says. John Pilger interviewed Philip Liechty, who had this to say:

> I was the CIA desk officer at the time. I saw the intelligence that came from firm sources. There were people herded into school buildings by soldiers and the buildings set on fire; anyone trying to get out was shot. There were people herded into fields and machine-gunned. We knew the place was a free-fire zone. None of that got out.[25]

For good reason: ninety per cent of the bullets and machine-guns were supplied by the United States, with extra supplies being rushed in as the killing intensified. The slaughter was not restricted to the years immediately after 1975. A quarter of the population—some 200,000 people—had been slaughtered by 1979, and the remainder were forced into camps where they suffered from famine and one of the highest rates of infant mortality in the world.

Zelter continues:

> Western support for President Suharto's regime from the late seventies to the present day, by re-stocking Indonesia's arsenals has enabled him to carry out genocide in East Timor. Britain continues to support Suharto for strategic reasons and for gold, timber and oil. The mass killings are covered up and excused because the public would be appalled at the extent of British collusion. British Aerospace and the British government know full well that BAe Hawk aircraft have been used to murder unarmed villagers and to terrorise the population. Other British equipment, including tanks and missiles, are regularly used.

As discussed, it would be a kind of anthropomorphism to expect the British government to admit even the most obvious facts relating to the Hawk aircraft. Regularly to be seen at arms fairs brooding over a clutch of anti-personnel weapons and other lethal ordnance, the government is nevertheless happy to defy reason by insisting that Hawks—much admired by unwitting Red Arrows enthusiasts—are training aircraft. Armed forces minister Archie Hamilton assured parliament in 1993:

> There is no doubt in my mind that a Hawk aircraft can do nothing to suppress the people of East Timor. The aircraft is not suitable for that purpose and we have guarantees from the Indonesians that the aircraft would not be used for internal suppression.[26]

These guarantees were dismissed by Alan Clark, former Defence Procurement Minister under Thatcher: "I never asked for a guarantee... A guarantee is worthless from any government, as far as I'm concerned." [27]

As for being able "to do nothing to suppress" the Timorese, retired US Rear Admiral Euegen J. Carroll assures us that "these British aircraft are ideal counter-insurgency aircraft, designed to be used against guerrillas who come from and move among civilian populations." [28] That is: ideal for attacking the people of East Timor.

Mark Higson, a former Foreign Office official, told John Pilger that British ministers lied about the Hawks being "strictly trainers... just as they lied about arms exports to Iraq. Everyone I worked with [at the Foreign Office] knew exactly what they were for." [29]

With regards to the "gold, timber and oil" mentioned by Zelter, recently leaked Australian state documents reveal that Australia gave its full support to the Indonesian invasion of East Timor in the belief that a better deal could be struck on dividing up Timorese oil in the Timor Gap. Australian Ambassador to Jakarta, Richard Woolcott, sent a telegram in August 1975 secretly advising the Australian government that a share of Timor's oil "could be much more readily negotiated with Indonesia... than with Portugal or an Independent East Timor." [30]

Zelter reminds us:

> Britain is currently Indonesia's main weapons supplier. The present Hawk deal has been likened to handing a gun to a serial killer. A thin line held by international law is all that separates legalized killing by soldiers in defence of their country from terrorism. The Indonesian Armed Forces are not engaged in any legitimate war of self-defence. Indonesia is the aggressor illegally occupying neighbouring countries.

After the massacre of children at Dunblane, David Mellor MP said "We must keep our anger burning bright. When the public has forgotten the horror of Dunblane, the gun lobbyists will be coming out with their garbage." [31]

At the time Mellor was speaking, two Hawk aircraft were being made ready to leave for Indonesia. Jose Gusmao, a Timorese now exiled in Australia, saw a Hawk attack on a village in the Matabean mountains of East Timor. "It used its machine guns," he said, "and dropped incendiary bombs." [32] Jose Amorin, another eye-witness, told of how four of his cousins were killed in a Hawk attack. Mellor is listed in the 1996 Register of MPs' Interests as a consultant of British Aerospace and Royal Ordnance, which recently combined to form one of the world's biggest arms companies. Furthermore, this is the same Mellor who, in 1988, exchanged "mutual greetings of friendship and co-operation" with Saddam Hussein. In those days Saddam was 'our man' and Mellor offered him £175 million in trade credits at about the same time that his host was gassing some 5,000 Kurds in the town of Halabaja, many children among them.

Returning to the discussion at hand, Zelter was all but alone in pointing out in the mainstream media that being a nation state does not mean you cannot commit acts of terrorism. Coincidentally, just as news of the women's acquittal was in the news, reports began to filter through of violent repression of the pro-democracy movement in the Indonesian capital. Recall that this was after the bombing in Atlanta, and at a time when there was much speculation that terrorists had downed TWA Flight 800 off Long Island. The obvious story, as Zelter suggests, was the fact that some of the worst terrorism is committed by nation states like Indonesia aided and abetted by nation states like Britain, and that in all the storm of concern about, and fear of, terrorism, the four Hawk disablers were a shining example of how to combat terrorism. Instead, Roy Greenslade of the *Observer* was virtually alone in pointing out that:

> Strangely, the story [of the Hawk acquittal] slipped by the radar of the most popular tabloids. No big headlines, no editorials, no features either lampooning the women as misguided, bleeding-heart do-gooders nor extolling them as courageous, peace-loving heroines.[33]

The bombing in Atlanta, the need to fight terrorism, the repression in Jakarta, the acquittal of the Hawk women, the link between them: naturally no such connection was made. Why? Because it has been decided that nation states, by definition, cannot be guilty of terrorism (unless they happen to be enemy nation states: Iran, Iraq, Libya, etc). Once again we find a truly remarkable and almost uniform rejection of elementary reasoning and rationality, not to mention morality, throughout the media. And not just there. In *The Real Terror Network*, Ed Herman reports an old dictionary definition of terrorism as:

> *a mode of governing*, or of opposing government, by intimidation.[34]

The problem for Western propagandists, Herman points out, is that the italicized phrase inconsiderately encompasses Pinochet's Chile, Garcia's Guatemala, and indeed Suharto's Indonesia and many other Western friends and allies. Intriguingly, this difficulty appears to have been surmounted in recent years: the 1995, ninth edition of the Concise Oxford English Dictionary does not define terrorism at all, but instead describes a "terrorist" as "a person who uses or favours violent and intimidating methods of coercing a government or community." [35] A "person", notice, and not a state: the idea that a government might carry out terrorism has been conveniently defined out of existence.

Herman summarises his enlightening (and hence ignored) study on terrorism as follows:

> If 'terrorism' means 'intimidation by violence or the threat of violence,' and if we allow the definition to include violence by states and agents of states, then it is these, not isolated individuals or small groups, that are the important terrorists in the world. [36]

This observation is so obvious, so reasonable, so important; and yet completely alien to the frame of reference of the mainstream media. This extraordinary situation really does remind us of science fiction, and yet it is a fundamental characteristic of Western 'democracies', or, more accurately, the functioning of concentrated power.

Typical of this widespread form of social self-deception was an editorial in the *Observer* which, following the Atlanta bombing, raged against terrorists: "Society is now exposed to the whims of murderous individuals whose aims can be wholly irrational. They consider their priorities so overwhelmingly absolute that they will put human life indiscriminately at risk to serve their purpose." [37]

It is hard to imagine a more apt depiction of the activities of corporate arms manufacturers and their client dictators in the Third World.

"What is horrifying," the editorial continues, "is the inability of the terrorists to imagine what the pain of those they make suffer must be like and to believe that their own objectives are so correct that the pain is worth such a price. The bonds of any civilization are held together by a capacity to empathise; after all the terms of social exchange are based on reciprocity—and one of the animating forces of reciprocity is the expectation that you should act reasonably because you want reasonable actions in return." [38]

Again, words which might apply to almost any arms manufacturer, for whom "their objectives" are generally so important that the destruction of the Third World is nevertheless "worth the price".

To return to Zelter's letter:

> What is going on in East Timor and also in West Papua is a tragedy. Suharto is a major war criminal; by providing weapons and aid to him the British government is complicit in his crimes. In simple terms, Britain is complicit in mass murder. The sale to Indonesia of weapons and repressive technology, as well as the training of military and police personnel, must end immediately.

Robert Key began his reply to Zelter's first letter as follows:

> Dear Angie, Thank you for your letter. As an elected politician, who as a child narrowly escaped death from a British landmine which killed five of my friends, I need no lessons in piety nor in moral outrage.

Several features are immediately apparent in his response. First is the fact that Key's words just do not make sense. The fact that someone has been elected as a politician clearly has no bearing on whether they "need lessons in moral outrage". The statement is a *non sequitur* and is merely confusing. Nevertheless, when combined with Key's 'authority' as an MP, such confusion can be an extremely potent tool.

Likewise, the fact that Key survived a childhood tragedy says little about his need for lessons in piety, or in the need to take a stand against crimes against humanity. What connection could we make between surviving a tragedy and the development of the capacity for "moral outrage"? Are we more likely to experience moral outrage after surviving a childhood tragedy? If psychotherapists are to believed (a moot point—see my *Free To Be Human* for further discussion), childhood trauma often leads to adult neurosis and even psychosis in later life.

Finally, what are we to understand by "lessons in moral outrage"? Was the aim of Zelter's letter to teach Key to be righteously outraged by immoral acts? Or was Zelter merely participating in a pre-arranged discussion by stating obvious facts about crimes to which we are party?

Key continues:

Don't get me wrong. I condemn the appalling excesses and atrocities which are reported from Indonesia. Of course, Britain does not recognize its sovereignty over East Timor.

Having condemned the "appalling excesses" of a regime that has broken international law by illegally invading Timor, Key, to be consistent, must surely also condemn governments, including his own, which continue to arm that government. Moving on, Key contradicts the historical record when he states that "of course, Britain does not recognize" Indonesia's sovereignty over Timor.

In July 1975 the British ambassador in Jakarta informed the Foreign Office that "the people of Portuguese Timor are in no condition to exercise the right to self-determination" and "the arguments in favour of its integration into Indonesia are all the stronger." The ambassador continued: "Certainly, as seen from here, it is in Britain's interest that Indonesia should absorb the territory as soon and as unobtrusively as possible, and that if it should come to the crunch and there is a row in the United Nations, we should keep our heads down and avoid taking sides against the Indonesian government." [39]

Any possible "crunch" in the United Nations was averted by the likes of Daniel Moynihan, US representative to the United Nations at the time of the Timor invasion, who explained in his autobiography that:

> The United States wished things to turn out as they did and worked to bring this about. The Department of State desired that the United Nations prove utterly ineffective in whatever measures it undertook. This task was given to me and I carried it forward with no inconsiderable success. [40]

The official position of the United Nations therefore meant little, as did Britain's refusal to officially "recognize" sovereignty—such technicalities simply obscuring the realities of acquisition by force.

Note that Key said "of course" Britain does not recognize Indonesian sovereignty. He means to imply that of course Britain does not support illegal acts, let alone participate in them. But as we have discussed, Britain regularly supports illegal acts while, like Key, giving the impression of being passionately committed to international law and human rights. This is no mere academic matter. It is not just a joke, not just a wily old trick practised by politicians. We are here talking about the contemporary slaughter of innocents, of helpless men, women, children. Imagine, after all, how we would respond to this kind of misrepresentation of Nazi atrocities. Key, and so many like him—educated, civilized and far distant from 'the sharp end' though they seem—bear a heavy responsibility for the horrors that afflict our world.

Key continues:

> The question is, what's to be done? Your answer is simple. Ignore the history which created the problem, come to a perverse judgement about Indonesian state institutions and then isolate that nation in the international community. Mine is different.

As with global warming, *doing something* to stop the carnage is rejected as simplistic. In reality, the question for the British government is not "What's to be done?" It is how to keep our heads down, how to sweep the problem under the carpet, so that arms sales can continue and, more generally, trade relations be maintained.

In 1992, a representative spokesman for the East Timor independence movement termed Britain "the single worst obstructionist of any industrialized country".[41] This, indeed, is why it is the British government which is determined to "ignore the history", and not Zelter—yet another example of truth-reversal so favoured by the propaganda system. In her first letter, Zelter focuses on the bloody history of East Timor; it is Key who never mentions it.

Interestingly, while in the previous paragraph Key condemns "the appalling excesses and atrocities" of the Indonesian government, he now derides Zelter's description of Suharto's army as "the aggressor" and of Suharto himself as "a war criminal", as "perverse". If it is "perverse" to consider individuals responsible for "appalling excesses and atrocities" war criminals, whom then should we consider for that title? Yet again, the statement is confusing in the extreme. Also, Zelter does not suggest that the West should "isolate" Indonesia, merely that "the sale of weapons and repressive technology, as well as the training of military and police personnel, must end immediately."

Note that, so far, Key's response has not dealt with the real issues raised by Zelter. This is crucial: Key is not able to deal with the facts and issues at hand, and so must resort to emotion, irrationality and confusion. This is true for all spokespeople for concentrated power and is therefore a key focal point for state education: namely, that it

should not teach us to master the art of penetrative critical thinking. This is not so much a matter of failing to promote the capacity
to analyse problems; it is more a matter of steering us away from
gaining the basic courage and independent-mindedness to step outside the 'truisms' of society. As we will see, central to this programme
is the suppression of our compassion and the promotion of delu-
sion-friendly selfishness (selfish people have little interest in understanding the causes of other people's suffering). We must be
prevented from gaining the ability not to swoon at the sight of the
smile of our imposing leaders and their surrounding pomp and cir-
cumstance. Critical thinking begins where idolatry and selfish greed
end, but about this our education system has nothing to say.

Key continues:

> We cannot turn our European backs on people who were ruled by
> Holland and Portugal, invaded by Japan and then abandoned to
> 'independence' without political structures or institutions to gov-
> ern what is now the fourth most populous country in the world.

Once again Key is arguing his own point, one that was certainly
not made by Zelter who has nothing to say about turning our
backs on anyone. There was indeed a functioning political structure
capable of governing the country under Suharto's predecessor,
Sukarno. The problem, however, was that Sukarno was intent on
building an independent, non-aligned Indonesia unbeholden to
any superpower. As ever, this was entirely unacceptable to the West,
particularly the United States, which assisted in the slaughter of
some 600,000 people, wiping out the possibility of independence
and democracy.

Note, also, that Key's arguments for what has been termed "constructive engagement" do not apply to Cuba or Iraq, or any other
country unwilling to toe the Western line. Instead these are *de*-
structively engaged.

Recent attempts to increase the economic strangulation of
Cuba through the amusingly titled Helms-Burton Cuban Liberty
and Solidarity Act were reported with a straight face in the British
media, along with Clinton's defence: namely, that: "I will do everything I can to help the tide of democracy that has swept our entire
hemisphere finally reach the shores of Cuba." [42]

No mention was made in the *Guardian* report of the fact that
Clinton's "democracy" has left forty per cent of newly "democratized"

Latin Americans living below the poverty line in terrible conditions; nor that his "tide of democracy" has always been red with the blood of human rights, church, union, environmental, peasant organisers and others. Congressman Dan Burton's remarks: "Get out of here Castro...We want you gone!" were reported with a similar lack of comment; with all thoughts of national sovereignty and international law apparently suspended.

It is interesting to contrast Congressman Burton's forthright views with those of others—the Cuban people, for example. An independent 1994 Gallup Poll reported that 88 per cent of Cubans said they were "proud of being Cuban"; 58 per cent considered that "the revolution's successes outstrip its failures"; 69 per cent identified themselves as "revolutionaries" (but only 21 per cent as "communist" or "socialist"); 76 per cent said they were "satisfied with their personal life", and 3 per cent said that "political problems" were the key problems facing the country. This from a country against whose supposed human rights abuses the West loves to rail.[43]

No questions were raised as to just why it is that the United States is so outraged by the alleged Cuban abuses, while dictatorships in Indonesia, China and Saudi Arabia are given red carpet treatment at any number of arms fairs. Customers invited to the Royal Navy and British Army Equipment Exhibition in September 1997 included Turkey, Saudi Arabia, Indonesia and China.

Meanwhile, health experts writing in a US medical journal in October 1994 reported the results of US attempts "to help" Cuba. The Cuban embargo, they note, "has contributed to an increase in hunger, illness, death and to one of the world's largest neurological epidemics in the past century". One author of the report said "Well, the fact is that we are killing people", by denying them food and medicines, and equipment for manufacturing their own medical products.[44]

The agony is on-going. The *Guardian* reported (March 7, 1997) research which showed that "the United States trade embargo has led to needless deaths, left hospitalized children lying in agony as essential drugs are denied them, and forced doctors to work with medical equipment at less than half efficiency because they have no spare parts for their machinery..." with "health and nutrition standards devastated."

Strangely, for a country in such desperate need of traditional Third World 'democracy', "only the pre-existing excellence of the [health] system and the extraordinary dedication of the Cuban medical community have prevented infinitely greater loss of life and suffering", in the words of a report by a team of American doctors and research scientists after a year-long study of the country. This conclusion contrasts starkly with the conditions faced by the rest of the hemisphere already overtaken by "the tide of democracy", where the problem, as we have seen, is not "marginalization of the poor but complete exclusion", with Cuban-style health care an impossible dream.

As for Iraq, another country the West is all too willing to "isolate" and turn its back on, the horror story is even worse. In a letter to the *Guardian* (September 7, 1996), Jean Lennock, a member of the Centre for Economic and Social Rights team investigating the impact of sanctions on health services in Iraq reported "a human tragedy... Hospitals which were once regional centres lack the most basic equipment, including oxygen, anaesthetic agents and foetal monitors. Operations are being performed literally in the dark, because light bulbs can no longer be imported." Lennock continues: "Reliable estimates from the World Health Organisation suggest that half a million children have died as a direct result of sanctions—one every six minutes."

These children are beyond Key's "constructive engagement". He continues:

> From one of the poorest countries, it [Indonesia] has risen well into the middle-income bracket. The astonishing fact is that this mixture of tribes and religions has held together as a nation. But there is unacceptable corruption, limited press freedom and unrealistic restrictions on democracy—I want to help change all that.

The phrase "unrealistic restrictions on democracy" is interesting but without obvious meaning. Instead, we can turn directly to Jeremy Seabrook's report on Indonesia, entitled: 'Revolt in Earthly Hell'.[45]

"Workers are the passionate core of the revolt against military rule in Indonesia," Seabrook writes. "Indonesia has some of the most exploited workers on earth. Their sweat has fuelled the country's 35-year growth and fed President Suharto's billions." Labour costs, Seabrook notes, are often less than ten per cent of production costs.

Not everyone lives in Key's "middle-income bracket":

In Jakarta, in slums and industrial barracks, the workers in the companies that bring wealth to Indonesia huddle in groups of three or four in rented rooms three metres square and talk of how their lot can be improved.

There are factories, Seabrook continues, "where the only jobs available are for sex with management, others where the drinking water is polluted and metal roofs intensify the tropical heat so they are sometimes working in temperatures of 50°C. There are factories where accidents are commonplace but medical treatment is sketchy or unavailable, where exhaustion and malnutrition are part of the uncounted daily cost...The poor have been shifted to wastelands or to factory zones where the sun is perpetually dimmed by smoke, and rows of wooden privies—square boxes with heads and feet of the occupants visible—leach into the black canals."

Key's "astonishing fact" that the country holds together is made less amazing by Amnesty International, which describes Indonesia as a country "ruled with an iron rod, where any dissent is punished by torture, imprisonment or death".[46] The constant threat of torture and death being not quite the state of affairs evoked by Key's "unacceptable corruption" and "limited press freedom"—the word "limited" here being used to replace the word "zero".

"The Indonesian army," Key continues, "is not synonymous with President Suharto. It is loyal to its current political master; but it could have seized power often in the past 40 years. It has not, because the role of their armed forces is defined in law as *dwifungsi*—a dual function defence and socio-political role. It is respected for its 'middle way' by political parties and by the pro-democracy movement."

Again, this makes little sense. *Dwifungsi* aside, there can surely be no law, in the binding sense in which Key uses the word, in a country in which the army "could have seized power often in the past 40 years"; in a country subjected to what Amnesty International, again, has called "human rights violations on a systematic and staggering scale" perpetrated by a regime that is "casual about mass murder".[47] Was the manner in which the role of the armed forces was defined in Nazi German law or Stalinist Russian law of any significance? Obviously, in totalitarian societies of this sort, the law is whatever the military decide it will be.

The idea that the army is respected by people who are dragged off in the night for daring to oppose its violence is hardly to be taken seriously. In June 1995, Amnesty International reported that "advocates of workers' rights have continued to operate under threat of intimidation, arrest, imprisonment, torture and ill-treatment", while demonstrations have been "broken up violently by the police".[48]

Finally, Key writes: "There should be no excuses for the Suharto regime. It should abide by the rule of law, and so should we. Smashing up other people's property is negative and self-indulgent. Why not divert that energy and enterprise into action to improve the situation in Indonesia?"

This is precisely what Zelter is trying to do. Does Key really believe that depriving the Indonesian regime of high technology weapons is irrelevant for the protection of human rights?

With the usual Orwellian twist, it is Key himself who is insisting that there should be "excuses" for Suharto's regime, with his talk of Indonesia's economic success, political stability and public respect for the army, in a country where "the government administers the nation on the level of Chicago gangsters of the 1930s running a protection racket."[49]

Note Key's use of truth-reversal: it is he, not Zelter, who is interested in "improving the situation" in Indonesia. It is Zelter, not he, who is indifferent to the suffering of the people there. Likewise it is Zelter, not he, who is "negative" and "self-indulgent". While Zelter is indulging her love of smashing up military aircraft, it is he, Key, who is putting self-interest aside for the sake of others. There is almost nothing but confusion and dissembling here, and yet this is a Member of Parliament writing in a national newspaper. There was of course no public outcry.

Zelter continues the 'Head to Head' with her second letter. It is accurate and informative and so is perhaps worth reviewing at length:

> Dear Robert, General Suharto is a military dictator who came to power in a bloody military coup. He consolidated his dictatorship by killing over a million Indonesians. The West actively supported him, and we have yet to come to terms with this shameful part of our post-colonial history.
>
> You condemn the atrocities, asking what can be done. Yet you ignore British weapons and torture equipment sales. How can

democracy flourish at the end of a gun? We should distinguish in our aid and trade between supporting the people of Indonesia, who are very poor, and adding to the coffers of Suharto's family, worth over £10 billion. The weapons sold to Indonesia are used in the forceful exploitation of land, resources and labour against the people's will.

I certainly agree with your last paragraph. Suharto is negative and self-indulgent. We disarmed a Hawk jet to prevent it dropping more missiles and cluster bombs on the people of East Timor and they have thanked us for this.

What they cannot understand is why four ordinary women had to do it and why the British police or Attorney General did not ensure compliance with the arms export guidelines, the 10 UN resolutions and international law. If our democratic and legal institutions worked properly the British government would be prosecuted for supplying weapons to Suharto. How can you justify support for this arms trade?"

Again, Zelter's second letter is reasonable and rational and seeks to address points made in Key's first letter.

Key's second response is as follows:

Dear Angie, Thank you for your reply. In spite of all your wild allegations, no one—including the UN—has found any reliable evidence of British arms or equipment being used for repressive purposes. I am not surprised, because we have such a tight licensing regime for arms exports in line with international guidelines.

Zelter's allegations are anything but wild: they describe the facts based on eye-witness accounts and state documentation. So far, in the space of some seven paragraphs, Key has described Zelter and her actions as "perverse", "negative", "self-indulgent" and "wild".

"The UN resolutions which condemned the occupation of East Timor in 1975," Key continues, "did not impose an arms embargo."

However, the Declaration of Principles of International Law Concerning Friendly Relations and Co-operation among States (1970), and the Resolution on the Definition of Aggression passed unanimously by the UN General Assembly (1974), do have something to say about benefiting from criminality: "No territorial acquisition resulting from the threat or use of force shall be recognized as legal", and "no special advantage resulting from aggression shall be recognized as lawful."

As ever, Key, like so many politicians, is out to impress with talk of the UN and "resolutions", as though this were some august, independent body above mere earthly power politics. Also, as most people have little idea of the history of these resolutions, or of how they were arrived at, or what they might actually mean, Key is able to impress us with facts to which the public is not generally privy. Again, we need only recall Moynihan's comments on his role and success in stifling any UN response. The basic rule about the UN is as simple as 2+2 = 4; or, as Chomsky has pointed out: "UN=US." [50] Edward Herman fills in some details of the equation:

> The rules are: when these [the UN and international law] can be used to meet our ends, we are their dedicated advocates; but when the votes are going the wrong way, or international law interferes with our plans, the UN and international law are treated with disdain or are blithely ignored. And the establishment experts and media fall into line without a peep. [51]

Key continues:

> Given the nature of the country and its welcome role in UN peace-keeping operations, Indonesia has a legitimate interest in having well-trained and properly-equipped armed forces. By training their military and police with our professional forces in the UK, eyes will be opened, best practice learned and seeds sown back in Indonesia.

Violent dictatorships, of course, have no "legitimate interests". As for the last sentence, here Key is trotting out the standard argument used by all determined to do business with human rights abusers.

The Washington director of Human Rights Watch/Asia assures us that Indonesian officers have been trained in the US since the 1950s with no "discernible improvement" in their behaviour. [52] Many of these US-trained officers were responsible for the very worst massacres during the massive bloodbath in Indonesia following the CIA-backed coup of 1965. Recall, also, our discussion in Chapter One regarding atrocities in El Salvador, the infamous US Army's School of the Americas and its long-standing record of opening eyes and setting examples of "best practice" to the region's subsequent assassins, torturers and mass murderers.

Key continues:

How strange you think democracy doesn't flourish under oppression. I believe the desire for democracy always defeats dictatorship and repression. What about South Africa? Megawati Sukarnoputri, the Indonesian opposition leader, said only a month ago that the armed forces must continue to play a central role in politics. She explained: 'They come from the grass roots. They are part of the soul of the country.'

Wise words from someone with what amounts to a gun pointing at her head, in a country with a long track record of murdering opposition leaders. Again, the idea that democracy flourishes under oppression does not add up. Democracy does not flourish under oppression, it flourishes under freedom. Democracy might struggle to survive under oppression, but that is hardly to flourish.

With this, the meaningful part of the exchange was largely at an end. Key's responses, like the media's response to human rights and environmental issues, are essentially determined by the requirements of power. In the next chapter we will see how the same requirements have long suppressed our capacity for compassion, our understanding of what a double-edged blessing kindness is in human affairs.

Chapter Five

DEMOLISHING COMPASSION

It need not surprise you that politicians speak so scornfully of the people, and philosophers profess to think mankind so wicked.—Rousseau, *Emile*

The Virtues of Plagiarism

Writing in a small dissident journal, an American reviewer of my first book *Free To Be Human*—actually, to my knowledge, *the* American reviewer of my first book!—noted that there were over 200 footnoted quotations at the back of the book. This made him wonder how many ideas were mine, and how many "merely parroted from those he quotes".[1]

It seems to me that this criticism reflects a general tendency among libertarian activists. The central premise of my first book was that 'the problem' is exploitative, concentrated power, and that such power depends on a series of potent illusions which hide its ugly truths from the general public. The solution, I argued, was to strive to undermine these illusions as far as possible. Sanity, hope and freedom depend, I suggested, on the extent to which we are successful in this. My objective was to inspire as many people as possible to undertake this task. In particular, I offered the ideas in my own book as tools on which, others, I hoped, would be able to improve.

Others may judge the degree of originality, or otherwise, of the book, but the real point, surely, is... So what!

If there is any truth in the premise on which the book is based—of the nature and needs of power and the key role of illusions—then as many people as possible should be copying, digesting, repeating, refining, improving on my ideas, Chomsky's ideas, Fromm's ideas, and so on, as much as they possibly can. The issue is not originality, but effectiveness: whether any given idea, any book, my book, helps as an antidote to the illusions of power.

Of course, if my book had been merely a regurgitation of the familiar ideas of others, presumably it would be unhelpful to those who had read Chomsky, Fromm, Campbell, Buddhism and Tolstoy. But even if that had been the case, it might still have been of help to people (the overwhelming majority) who have encountered Chomsky but not Fromm, or who have never even heard of either or them.

The intriguing question is why, given the obvious premise of the book, would someone even raise the issue? Does it say something about our tendency to idolize—are we looking for a uniquely gifted individual to admire? We are, after all, products of a culture determined to brainwash us into adoring and seeking salvation from some special 'star' or 'leader'.

Does it say something about our egotism? Given the way that we all have to struggle for a living (in the case of libertarian activists, often under quite frustrating and arduous conditions), it sometimes happens that we come to perceive other activists as 'the competition', as a threat, or at least as a benchmark against which we measure ourselves and our own chances of being heard, getting published, finding an audience, being taken seriously. It is an amazing fact that radical groups sometimes see the arrival of new members as a threat, rather than as the whole point of their activities!

And here we arrive at another central premise of my first book: the idea that one of our biggest obstacles is the propaganda system working secretly and unsuspected *within our own heads*. Very often our libertarian activities will actually be founded on ideas and values imported from the propaganda system, which we drag along with us like a counter-activist shadow.

The tendency to see others as competitors and threats is a kind of perverse inheritance from a corporate capitalist system which encourages us to fight for status. Should we not welcome anybody who may wish to use our ideas, our quotations, our material? The important thing is that ideas capable of combating the great illusion factories of the mainstream be distributed as far and wide as possible. The idea that we might be stepping on other people's toes, taking advantage of their work, encroaching on their territory, make perfect sense in the corporate world but are just crazy in the context of activism. It is interesting to consider, here, the central Buddhist principle of a virtuous life:

> Give every gain and victory to others; take upon yourself all their troubles and suffering.[2]

From the mainstream perspective, this advice is naïve and idealistic to the point of incomprehension, for capitalism is based not on helping others, but on exploiting them. It is based not on the idea of happiness resulting from kindness, but from self-aggrandisement. In our society, many wealthy people do not even assist their own parents, children, brothers and sisters, because it goes against the whole thrust of our social conditioning. In our society it is somehow understood that people have to make their own way: 'there are no free lunches', almost as if life were some kind of test to be passed.

And yet the Buddhist principle of unconditional generosity, which seems so outlandish from a conventional perspective, makes perfect sense in the context of dissent. If we truly care about the suffering of others, and believe that the dissolution of the deceptions that maintain exploitative power (for example, by suppressing our capacity for compassion) is a key way to aid that suffering, then seeking to involve and support our fellow activists as far as we are able—encouraging, advising, assisting in any way we can—is the best way to achieve that end. It is here, indeed, that we begin to encounter the astonishing congruence between very old Buddhist strategies and quite modern dissident ones, for revolutionizing society.

I therefore humbly invite all readers to plagiarize Herman, Chomsky, Curtis, Beder, Zinn, Pilger, Fromm, Tolstoy and indeed me, to the fullest possible extent—and then attempt to produce something similar, and hopefully better. Even repetition is a wonderful contribution: consider, after all, the mind-numbing level of repetition facing us in the mainstream!

It seems clear that the central need of our times is that we collectively stop looking out for ourselves and start devoting ourselves to helping each other; so making life better—that is, bearable—for us all. Our all-important motivation for doing so is the issue that will concern us in these last three chapters.

No one should imagine that this re-orientation is being recommended on grounds of stoic self-sacrifice or sentimental ideals of 'niceness'. It is a tough challenge, for it requires much self-awareness, honesty and introspection; but above all the slow erosion of our naïve faith in selfish living as a viable source of personal happiness.

Compassion is the Root of all Dissent
It is one of the wonders of the modern age that so many people have been persuaded to restrict their concerns within a shallow orbit

of personal issues. We know that this has not always been the case, for the simple reason that if it had been, you and I would not possess even the limited freedoms that we do.

In his book *A People's History of the United States*, Howard Zinn reviews some of the massive, vibrant popular political movements that have struggled to bring about a more compassionate society over the last few centuries. It is remarkable to realize that views which are strange and extreme by today's standards were the common sense of even sixty years ago. Consider, for example, the words of Emma Goldman:

> Verily, poor as we are in democracy how can we give it to the world?... a democracy conceived in the military servitude of the masses, in their economic enslavement, and nurtured in their tears and blood, is not democracy at all. It is despotism—the cumulative result of a chain of abuses which, according to that dangerous document, the Declaration of Independence, the people have the right to overthrow...[3]

Or as Helen Keller explained to a suffragette in 1911:

> Our democracy is but a name. We vote? What does that mean? It means that we choose between two bodies of real, though not avowed, autocrats. We choose between Tweedledum and Tweedledee... You ask for votes for women. What good can votes do when ten-elevenths of the land of Great Britain belongs to 200,000 and only one-eleventh to the rest of the 40,000,000? Have your men with their millions of votes freed themselves from this injustice? [4]

To Goldman and Keller, the idea that the only relevant issues for our personal happiness involved personal relationships, levels of consumption, levels of pay, quality and location of housing, and so on, would have seemed a kind of madness. At the time, it was understood that society is a kind of pond and if that pond is poisoned by economic slavery and autocracy, everyone is bound to suffer.

Our modern indifference is one of the great achievements of the propaganda system, one of the primary aims and results of the endless hammering of corporate media and politics. A retailing analyst explains corporate priorities:

> Our enormously productive economy... demands that we make
> consumption our way of life, that we convert the buying and use
> of goods into rituals, that we seek spiritual satisfaction, our ego sat-
> isfaction, in consumption... We need things, consumed, burned up,
> worn out, replaced, and discarded at an ever increasing rate.[5]

We are trained to be passive consumers, not active thinkers, citizens
and moral agents. We all have equal responsibility for the world's welfare, but there is a widespread assumption that the way the world is run
is really someone else's concern. We blush at the idea that we should
'get involved' in anything beyond production and consumption; after
all, we are 'just us'. But then our society never stops persuading us that
we are not supposed to be people in any full sense, as the CEO of
Prism Communications notes of his younger target market:

> They aren't children so much as what I like to call 'evolving
> consumers'.[6]

Consumers, particularly evolving ones, have no business asking
moral questions: a consumer produces to earn, to buy, to consume.
Where do compassion and critical thought fit into this programme?
Nowhere at all, except for the parading of such capacities on charity days and times of great disaster, so that we are able to believe
that we are compassionate, critical thinkers, so that we do not
become aware of how little we really do care. Thus Tony Blair will
talk of the need to create "a compassionate Britain", just as George
Bush talked of the need to "make kinder the face of the nation",
before turning the face of that nation in the direction of the con-
scripts, and the women and children of Iraq.

The goal of personal salvation regardless of the fate of others
remains a delusion; not only for the many, who can only dream of
a higher quality of life, but also for the few, for a life built on such
selfish foundations represents a high standard of living but a low
quality of life, necessarily deprived as it is of the sense of kindness,
sympathetic joy, compassion, solidarity and belonging on which
real happiness depends. When the ecologist and activist Helena
Norberg-Hodge began living amongst the Buddhist villagers of
Ladakh in Northern India, she was bewildered by the strange fact
that everyone was always, well, smiling!

> At first I couldn't believe that the Ladakhis could be as happy as
> they appeared. It took me a long time to accept that the smiles I

saw were real. Then, in my second year there, while at a wedding, I sat back and observed the guests enjoying themselves. Suddenly I heard myself saying, 'Aha, they really are that happy.' [7]

According to Norberg-Hodge, the Ladakhis' extraordinary happiness is rooted in their Buddhist belief system, which is characterized by extraordinary levels of kindness and compassion and the absence of hatred, egotism and grasping possessiveness. According to her, the Ladakhis achieved levels of happiness and well-being almost unimaginable to us in the West.

The difference between the happiness of Ladakhi and Western societies links with another question: what is the essential difference between Emma Goldman and most modern individuals; between, say, a Noam Chomsky and an Andrew Marr? How is it that one intelligent person can be unable to recognize the truth about the logic of power, while to another it is overwhelmingly obvious? How can one be keenly aware of the moral irresponsibility attendant on participating as part of the propaganda system, while the other remains blissfully unaware? What is the difference? It is surely not merely a question of intelligence.

The answer, in my view, can be traced to the extent to which an individual feels the suffering of others to be an issue of fundamental significance in their own lives. If we feel that the suffering of others is something which we, personally, should try to alleviate as best we can, two consequences follow.

The first is that we will feel powerfully motivated to seek out the deepest causes of that suffering. We will find ourselves simply unable to accept the bland, confused, clichéd media account of the world, which always seems to suggest that the status quo is more or less acceptable, that nothing much can, or needs, to be done: the problem is over-population, Third World stupidity, that people just want jobs—any old job will do—and money. Secondly, this critical thinking will be relatively unhampered by the tendency to self-deception rooted in personal greed and ambition.

What seems clear is that our capacity for critical thinking, for seeing through the illusions that hide the world's horrors, is to a large degree determined by the extent of our compassion.

We know from the military history of Nazi Germany, Stalinist Russia, Britain, China and the United States, and of many other countries—that mindless conformity and the absence of compassion fit hand in glove. Selfishness, greed and uncritical thinking are of a piece. By contrast, in an old Buddhist tale we are told that the immoral instructions of a venerated teacher conflicted profoundly with the compassionate impulses of the young Buddha-to-be "whose innate goodness would not allow him to accept his teacher's advice, though it had been accepted as a duty by the other students."[8]

The tale is clear that, while this conflict and disobedience embarrassed and distressed the future Buddha immensely, his deep sense of the life and death importance of compassion outweighed his natural human tendency to indulge in mindless 'groupthink'. It outweighed the miserable ease of fitting in, belonging, being approved of, and achieving 'success'.

If critical thinking with the power to unmask the delusions of power begins anywhere, it begins here, in an understanding that compassion for others overrides all notions of duty, etiquette and justice. Duty has no validity apart from justice, and justice has no validity apart from compassion.

But the question remains: why should we concern ourselves overly with the suffering of others? Is this not a matter only for self-righteous martyrs and goody-goodies? The answer, instead, seems to be that, as in the case of the Ladakhis, truly compassionate individuals are those who somehow sense that their capacity for compassion is also *fundamental to their own well-being and happiness*, to their own integrity and humanity. They sense that "without goodness man is a busy, mischievous, wretched thing; no better than a kind of vermin."[9] They understand that to be merely busy, mischievous and wretched is to abandon all hope of sanity, happiness and fulfilment.

It is this identification between personal well-being and concern for the welfare of others that makes activists so persistent in the face of ostensibly impossible odds, because from this perspective they and everybody else gain from their efforts. It is this understanding of the mutually beneficial nature of compassionate concern that provides the enormous motivating force and strength required to enable dissidents to penetrate the blanketing delusions of mainstream reporting, politics and entertainment and to perceive the truth sheltering in the gaps and silences of the mainstream world-view.

By contrast, where compassion for others is subordinated to a self-centred concern for maximizing one's own happiness, an individual will lack the motivation to seek the truth of human suffering, will therefore not feel prompted to look beneath the surface of mainstream fictions, and so will perceive no gaps, silences or hypocrisies.

Earlier, we reviewed an argument which suggested that the desire to avoid anxiety is the root of human self-deception. But an excess of self-cherishing over compassion is also a great cause of self-deception. It is the hardest thing to suddenly choose to risk a career for the sake of truth. Where great concern for the suffering of others is absent, it is surely all but impossible.

If compassion for others marks the ultimate difference between living in thrall to, and freedom from, the lies of the propaganda system, then what the world is in desperate need of is more compassion, more motivation to look deeper, to notice the uncomfortable truth and to sacrifice comfortable conformity for the sake of the happiness of others.

It is troubling, then, that dissidents are a famously irate bunch, keen to stick to facts and political discussion, but unwilling to look closely at their own motivation. They are also, as we will discuss, notoriously angry and full of hatred for those they deem responsible for our woes. In the chapters that follow, we will discuss the importance of compassion, and why, as the greatest threat to power, it has been largely banished from Western understanding.

A Tale of Two Types of Indian

It is no accident that killers who destroy other people for profit often come to feel contempt for their victims, deeming them responsible and deserving of their fate. It appears to be something of a law of human conduct that before life (both human and animal) can be subordinated to greed, the capacity of the exploiter to feel compassion for the exploited must be 'knocked out'. Mike Jempson comments on a typical device for achieving this goal:

> Mass media coverage of the Vietnam War introduced the world to what might be termed 'the gook syndrome', 'gook' being a derogatory term used by the American soldiers to describe their opponents. By defining the enemy as objects, or at least subhuman, it is easier to order their destruction and to persuade those who must do the killing that their actions are not subject to the moral constraints that rule out murder or torture as acceptable human behaviour.[10]

The same is true of victims who need to be exploited economically. In 1916 Lewis Terman noted that a dismally low level of intelligence:

> is very common among Spanish-Indian and Mexican families of the South-West and also among negroes. Their dullness seems to be racial, or at least inherent in the family stock from which they come... Children of this group should be segregated in special classes... They cannot make abstractions, but they can often be made efficient workers.[11]

This denigration-for-exploitation mechanism was used with striking efficiency by Cristobal Colon (Columbus) and his compatriots in the course of their first and second voyages to the 'new world'. On first meeting the local Taino 'Indians', Colon was greatly impressed by their humanity and hospitality: "They are the best people in the world," he wrote, "and above all the gentlest... All the people show the most singular loving behaviour and they speak pleasantly... They love their neighbours as themselves, and they have the sweetest talk in the world, and are gentle and always laughing." [12]

But then the first expedition to the new world was a voyage of discovery; the goal being to first locate, rather than immediately plunder, Indian wealth.

The goal changed with the second expedition, however, and with it the perceived nature of the Tainos. Formal instructions for the second voyage issued to Colon in May 1493 are significant, Kirkpatrick Sale writes, in that they constitute "the first statement of the colonial strategies and policies of empire that were eventually to carry Europe to every cranny of the earth." [13]

These instructions have been largely ignored by historians— unsurprisingly, given that the strategies outlined therein remain more or less identical to those pursued by Western powers to this day; the fine moral words of politicians, academics and journalists notwithstanding.

The statement, Sale reports—remarkable for its similarity to those made secretly by modern US politicians George Kennan and Robert McNamara reviewed in Chapter One—did not give any thought to the rights, or conditions, of the Indians, being almost entirely concerned with "establishing the means of exploitation and trade, providing no suggestion of any other purpose for settlement or any other function of government".[14]

The overriding concern was then, as now, for gold. Where the first expedition had consisted of just three ships, the second, bent on pillage, comprised fully seventeen ships, with a large band of soldiers armed with crossbows, arquebuses and cannon on board. Guillermo Coma of Aragon records the necessary change in perception of the Indian victims-to-be. Indians who once had been the "best people in the world and above all the gentlest" [15] had undergone a Jekyll and Hyde transformation:

"These islands", wrote Coma, "are inhabited by Canabilli, a wild unconquered race which feeds on human flesh... They wage unceasing wars against gentle and timid Indians to supply flesh; this is their booty and is what they hunt. They ravage, despoil, and terrorize the Indians ruthlessly." [16]

As is so often the case with conquerors, the people to be destroyed are declared to be in need of protection from themselves by the heroic slaughter of the 'bad' element among them. During the Vietnam war, 'good' Vietnamese ostensibly being defended from 'internal aggression' were often indistinguishable from the 'gooks' to be destroyed. B52 bombers were deployed to rain fire and brimstone on some of the most densely-populated regions on earth, such as the Mekong Delta, revealing the distinction to be false and merely a deception (if often a self-deception) of an army with goals and priorities that actually had nothing to do with the protection and well-being of Vietnamese of any kind.

As in the subsequent days of the Wild West, it turns out that the 'bad' Taino Indians were one and the same with the 'good' Taino Indians; the distinction merely being designed to facilitate the massacre of innocents for profit.

The origin of the change in perception is not in doubt:

> Now, on the Second Voyage, Colon seems to have decided *in advance*—although he could have had no possible way to know it...—that the islands he came to were populated by Caribs [cannibals]...The idea of fierce and hostile Caribs, in short, was never more than a bogey, born of Colon's own paranoia or stubborn ferocity...[17]

Or, more to the point, of his need to rationalize the horrors that lay ahead for kindly Indians to be plundered of their gold, and which could hardly have been in doubt. The spinning of the cannibal illusion was vital:

> It permitted the denigration, and thus the conquest and exploitation,

of peoples whose lands were seen as increasingly desirable in European eyes. It is always convenient to regard foreign populations as inferior, more convenient still to regard them as animalistic, or bestial, especially when you have decided to enslave or eliminate them; how positively fortuitous, then, to discover that they are all anthropophagi [cannibals] and provide evidence of their inferiority—indeed, even their unhumanness—three times a day, with every meal.[18]

And so the cannibals, invented by those who had need of them, entered popular mythology as real; a powerful illusion that served well the purposes of exploitation over the next few centuries. Later, as we have seen, the 'cannibals' and 'bad' Indians shape-shifted to become 'communists' and 'terrorists'. As for the immediate task of slaughter for material gain, the delusions certainly worked their spell in silencing the voice of conscience and compassion in the hearts of the invaders. The silence was evident enough to the Indians, for obvious reasons:

> What perplexed the Tainos of Española most about the strange white people from the large ships was not their violence, not even their greed, nor in fact their peculiar attitudes toward property, but rather their coldness, their hardness, their lack of love.[19]

The Limits of Genius

The notion that scientific enquiry has been sufficiently objective to lead the struggle against the necessary illusions required for this type of exploitation and violence need not detain us overly long. The great Swedish naturalist Linnaeus, for example, was sufficiently objective to make the following remarks:

> The American is obstinate, contented, free; the European, mobile, keen, inventive; the Asiatic cruel, splendour-loving, miserly; the African sly, lazy, indifferent. The American is covered with tattooing, and rules by habit; the European is covered with close-fitting garments and rules by law; the Asiatic is enclosed in flowing garments and rules by opinion; the African is anointed with grease and rules by whim.[20]

Surprisingly enough it is Linnaeus's own racial category, the European, which turns out to be keen, inventive and law-abiding. The rest are all conveniently dumped in the usual categories reserved for the exploited: cruel, lazy and obstinate.

Other masters of scientific inquiry similarly failed the test of objectivity and humanity. Sir Francis Galton, the founder of eugenics, once wrote that "there exists a sentiment, for the most part quite unreasonable, *against* the gradual extinction of an inferior race." [21] This has often been echoed by our political leaders: US President Taft said of Latin America that "the day is not far distant" when "the whole hemisphere will be ours in fact as, by virtue of our superiority of race, it already is ours morally." [22]

As the last citation suggests, it is sometimes difficult to decide just what race we are talking about, just who really qualifies as 'white' and 'superior'. In an ironic twist—given that Colon, one of the first great 'civilizers', may well have been Genoan—we find that in 1917 a member of the US State Department described Italians as "like children who must be [led] and assisted more than almost any other nation". [23]

But perhaps after all there is an explanation of the strange matter of Colon's origins. Henry Fairfield Osborne, president of the American Museum of Natural History and, we are assured, one of America's most eminent and prestigious palaeontologists wrote:

> The northern races invaded the countries to the south, not only as conquerors but as contributors of strong moral and intellectual elements to a more or less decadent civilization. Through the Nordic tide which flowed into Italy came the ancestors of Raphael, Leonardo, Galileo, Titiano; also, according to Gunther, of Giotto, Boticelli, Petrarca, and Tasso. Columbus, from his portraits and from busts, *whether authentic or not*, was clearly of Nordic ancestry. [24] [my emphasis]

The possibility that the portraits and busts might in fact not be authentic is not allowed to obstruct the desired conclusion.

Parlez-Vous Français?

In reality, of course, it is not primarily the colour or shape of facial features that determines our supposed worthiness, rather it is a matter of who happens to be the most convenient target for exploitation and hatred. In 1813 E.M. Arndt indicated with admirable clarity the illogic of hating people merely on the basis of colour:

> Hatred of the foreigner, hatred of the French, of their trifling, their

vanity, their folly, their language, their customs; yes, burning hatred of all that comes from them, that must unite everything German firmly and fraternally... Only bloody hatred of the French can unite German power, raise again the German glory, bring out the noblest traits of the people and submerge all the lowest. This hatred must be imparted to your children and your children's children as the palladium of German freedom...[25]

A position neatly summed up by Ludwig Jahn:

It comes to the same thing if one teaches his daughters French or trains them for whores.[26]

Rocker points out that views of this sort were not merely tolerated but eagerly embraced by what was considered to be the 'intellectual élite' of 19th and early 20th Century German society. This resolves the much discussed 'mystery' of how a monstrosity like Nazism could have evolved out of a civilized European nation that had nurtured the likes of Mozart and Goethe, for the true hallmarks of civilization are surely the capacity for independent critical thought and compassion, not the capacity to produce sophisticated music, literature, or technological gadgets.

Rocker points out that the lesson of the German example is lost if we imagine it to be an isolated phenomenon. In reality it is ubiquitous: a prime function of political and intellectual élites is always to justify the actions of power, and to obscure them from the general public. To be sure, there is no shortage of examples.

The *Westminster Gazette* of 1898, for example, reported of an expedition to Sudan:

Now and then I caught in a man's eye the curious gleam which, despite all the veneer of civilization, still holds its own in man's nature, whether he is killing rats with a terrier, rejoicing in a prize fight, playing a salmon or potting Dervishes. It was a fine day and we were out to kill something. Call it what you like, the experience is a big factor in the joy of living.[27]

In his book *Voli sulla ambe*, published in 1937, Mussolini's son Vittorio described war as "the most beautiful and complete of all sports". "It was", he said, "diverting to watch a group of Galli [Ethiopian tribesmen] bursting out like a rose after I landed a bomb in the middle of them." [28]

In 1966, as upwards of 600,000 Indonesians (mostly peasants) were being slaughtered by Suharto's Indonesian army, in what the CIA called a "boiling bloodbath", the then British Ambassador, Sir Andrew Gilchrist, wrote to London: "I have never concealed from you my belief that a little shooting in Indonesia would be an essential preliminary to effective change." [29]

In the event, there was more than a little shooting. On 24 November, British officials reported that "men and women are being killed in very large numbers". Some victims "are given a knife and invited to kill themselves. Most refuse and are told to turn round and are shot in the back." [30]

In similar vein, as some quarter of a million Iraqis lay freshly slaughtered by Western bombs, the *Boston Globe* saluted the "victory for the psyche" and the new "sense of nationhood and projected power" achieved by the leadership of George Bush who was "one tough son of a bitch", having shown that the United States remained "a select people, with a righteous mission on this earth". [31]

Given the nature of power, particularly in our own time, the intellectual élite are very often required to be the priests of intolerance and hatred. The words that communicate their cold cynicism at us from magazines and newspapers are products, not of a dispassionate, hard-headed, objective grasp of reality, but of the terrible needs of power and violence.

Women, too, of course, have not been exempt from the need to denigrate the victim:

> True feminine genius is ever timid, doubtful, and clingingly dependent: a perpetual childhood. [32]

Sometimes, the denigration of women and other 'children of a lesser God' has been neatly combined. In 1869 anthropologist McGrigor Allan noted that "the type of the female skull approaches in many respects that of the infant, and still more that of the lower races." [33] And Charles Darwin commented that "some at least of those mental traits in which women may excel are traits characteristic of the lower races." [34]

Elsewhere, and presumably with a straight face, the French craniologist Pruner noted that "the Negro resembles the female in his love of children, his family and his cabin... the black man is to the white man what woman is to man in general, a loving being and a being of pleasure." [35]

Whether dismissed as children, cannibals, obstinate, miserly, sly, lazy or cruel, the insult itself is unimportant; the point is that real people with real feelings, who suffer every bit as much as any well-dressed Nordic male, be declared somehow inhuman, in order that inhumanity can be committed against them without offending the compassionate instinct within us all.

Steam-Fist Futurist: the Noise of a Little Spring

As we know, the same has also been true for non-human victims of exploitation. In an article with what may well strike us as the humorous title of 'The Moral Standing Of Insects and The Ethics of Extinction', published in the *Florida Etymologist* in 1987, the authors reported that the answer to the question: "Can Insects Feel Pain?" was a resounding 'Yes'. This conclusion was supported by C.H. Eisemann *et al*, in 'Do Insects Feel Pain? A Biological Review', published in *Experientia* in 1984. Elsewhere, a team of researchers at the University of Utrecht in the Netherlands concluded that fish also feel pain and fear comparable to what we would experience were a fish hook to pierce our upper palates.

Further up the sentience scale, we now know that pigs are remarkably intelligent, to the extent that they have out-performed dogs and even chimpanzees in computerized intelligence tests in the USA, involving the manipulation of a joy-stick to obtain rewards.

Despite what many might prefer to think, then, ants do have feelings, fish are certainly tortured on the end of fishing hooks and pigs are sufficiently sensitive and intelligent to suffer intense misery from our treatment of them. As Sharon Salzberg has noted in her book *Lovingkindness*:

> We tend to hold the view that the value of life increases according to the size of the being. So we encounter something like a fly and find it easy to kill.[36]

It might seem a matter of common sense that animals have feelings, and yet for much of Western scientific history not just flies, but all animals everywhere, from dogs to dolphins, have been dismissed as clockwork mechanisms to be abused at will. Descartes, among many others, declared animals "thoughtless brutes", arguing that it was mere sentimentalism to credit them with actual feelings. An unknown contemporary of Descartes described one result of this conviction:

The [Cartesian] scientists administered beatings to dogs with perfect indifference and made fun of those who pitied the creatures as if they felt pain. They said the animals were clocks; that the cries they emitted when struck were only the noise of a little spring that had been touched, but that the whole body was without feeling. They nailed the poor animals up on boards by their four paws to vivisect them to see the circulation of the blood...[37]

Although clearly groundless, the conviction that animals are without feelings has gone largely unchallenged to this day. As Masson and McCarthy suggest in their book *When Elephants Weep: The Emotional Life of Animals*:

So persistent are the forces that militate against admitting the possibility of emotions in the lives of animals that the topic seems disreputable, not a respectable field of study, almost taboo.[38]

To be sure, this is not for lack of evidence: "The scholarly literature on animals contains many observations, accounts, anecdotes and stories that suggest interpretation in terms of the emotions the animals may be experiencing or expressing, or call for further research into this possibility. Little to none is forthcoming." [39]

The issue has simply been ignored. Of the research that might have been carried out, Masson and McCarthy report simply that "there is almost none".[40] Modern society has been happy to passively accept centuries-old dogma as 'common sense fact'. But why? Surely it could not be through a lack of scientific objectivity, through the influence on scientists of vast economic and political forces requiring a particular view? The answer is almost as obvious as the question:

Dominant human groups have long defined themselves as superior by distinguishing themselves from groups they are subordinating. Thus whites define blacks in part by differing melanin content of the skin; men are distinguished from women by primary and secondary sex characteristics. These empirical distinctions are then used to make it appear that it is the distinction themselves, not their social consequences, that are responsible for the social dominance of one group over the other.[41]

Artificial divisions and compassionate cut-off points often go together. In an admirable display of humanitarian concern, the 1954 Protection of Birds Act states:

If any person keeps or confines any bird whatsoever in any cage or their receptacle which is not sufficient in height, length or breadth to permit the bird to stretch its wings freely, he shall be guilty of an offence against the Act and be liable to a special penalty.[42]

This appears to represent a significant move towards the Five Freedoms demanded for animals by animal rights activists: freedom to stand up, lie down, turn around, groom themselves and stretch their limbs. These fine words are followed by a small proviso: "Provided that this subsection shall not apply to poultry." [43]

Why this exception? The answer is provided by the briefest of glances at the poultry factory-farming system.

More than 700 million chickens are currently reared and killed in Britain each year. A standard modern broiler unit consists of four sheds, with the floor of each carpeted by some 30-40,000 birds. For efficiency, today's broilers have been designed to grow at twice the rate of 30 years ago. Their legs and hearts, however, have not. The result is that the chicken rapidly outgrows its skeletal strength such that its legs literally break under the weight; crippling joint pains and other skeletal problems are inevitably legion. Research published in 1992 in the Veterinary Record reported that 90 per cent of birds had detectable abnormalities in walking; in about 26 per cent of cases birds were likely to have suffered chronic pain. The hearts and lungs of broilers are similarly stressed by their rapid body growth: the Agriculture and Food Research Council estimates that about seven million birds simply drop down dead for this reason every year. About two and a half million birds die while being 'harvested' for slaughter, with half dying of heart failure and a third from physical injuries: many birds have their femurs dislocated at the hip as the result of being carried by 'catchers' 'harvesting' them by one leg. This generally causes internal bleeding and, in a third of cases, actually drives the bone up into the abdomen.

In the trucks on the way to slaughter, birds are crammed into plastic drawers, where more deaths and injuries occur as necks are crushed when the drawers are closed. At the end of this journey, the chickens are shackled and have their heads dipped into water with an electric current running through it. This is said to render the majority of victims unconscious, after which their throats are slit.

Similarly, birds bred for egg-laying are kept in sheds housing some 30,000 birds, where they are pumped with antibiotics and food which may contain processed feathers, the remains of other chickens and so on. To prevent maddened birds confined in tiny spaces from pecking and injuring each other, farmers slice off their beaks with red-hot blades. Joseph Mauldin, a poultry scientist from the University of Georgia, says: "There are many cases of burned nostrils and severe mutilations due to incorrect procedures, which unquestionably influence acute and chronic pain..." [44]

Danny Penman notes that a hen's beak is not, as many people imagine, merely a horny growth but is an extremely sensitive organ designed to explore the animal's immediate environment—more like a human finger-tip than a finger-nail. There are of course other horrors too numerous to mention here.

Nevertheless, at the end of the day, we are able to sit down and enjoy a nice boiled egg—albeit with the yellow of the yolk achieved by the use of 'designer' colorants added directly to the chicken feed. Manufacturers provide a colour chart enabling the farmer to choose the precise shade of healthy gold for his otherwise appropriately pale and unhealthy-looking yolks.

The attitude required by the poultry industry in general was summed up by the *Farmer and Stockbreeder* in 1982:

> The modern layer is, after all, only a very efficient converting machine, changing the raw material—feedingstuffs—into the finished product—the egg. [45]

Similarly, while farmers have long suspected that pigs are unusually intelligent, it has been considered wise not to look too closely into the subject. It is, after all, these sensitive and inquisitive creatures that we keep penned in cruelly restrictive farrowing crates and crowded together in vast, darkened sheds in miserable conditions. Transported in packed lorries, it is common for pigs to collapse and die from heat-stroke and stress-induced heart attacks on the way to slaughter. On arrival, they are herded in groups into a stunning room where they watch their fellows being individually electrocuted by electric tongs placed across the head. Subsequently, they are shackled by a hind leg and carried away to have their throats cut. According to a study published in *Meat Manufacturing and Marketing* in 1993, nearly twenty per cent of pigs were improperly stunned or showed signs of recovery before being bled to death.

Likewise the modern dairy cow, forever portrayed as grazing contentedly in verdant fields, is in fact subject to some of the worst horrors of intensive farming. Blood and pus have become significant components of the milk we drink because mastitis (a cripplingly painful inflammation of the udder) is rampaging through the dairy herd: between thirty and thirty-five cases per hundred cows are recorded every year. About thirty per cent of the dairy cows in Britain are lame, partly as a result of laminitis. According to a leading cattle vet, the latter would feel like "crushing all your fingernails in the door then standing on your fingertips".[46]

Both mastitis and laminitis result from the huge stresses placed on the cow by the pursuit of ever higher milk production. As a result of these pressures, most dairy cows have to be culled at five or six years of age. Consequently, as George Monbiot writes, "Agony is the resting state of the modern dairy cow."[47]

Some may find the issue of animal suffering of marginal importance, or even sentimental, and yet this suffering is the result of the same logic at work at the heart of all capitalist operations: South American nations and peoples are "converting machines" changing human and natural resources into profit. The corporate mass media system of newspapers, TV, radio, books, magazines and films is a "converting machine" changing the raw experiences and possibilities of human existence into a web of business-friendly delusions and deceptions. Parliamentary politics is a "converting machine" changing the raw human desire for genuine happiness and freedom into a 'moderate' desire to select from profit-friendly options. Schools are "converting machines" processing human beings into obedient producers and consumers—and so on through every modern political, social and economic institution.

The mainstream has therefore had to continue to perpetrate the myth that animals lack all feelings, for the simple reason that vast fortunes have long been made from causing them great misery and suffering, and the system of institutionalized greed and cruelty does not want to face—or deal with the cost of others facing—that ugly truth.

In short, both animals and people tend to come to be viewed in ways that justify the behaviour of those sacrificing them out of greed, hatred and ignorance. This is the remarkable distorting and deluding effect of greed, discussed in such detail by Buddhists, among others. People doing terrible things in the name of greed do not like to recognize the truth of their actions. The solution? To spin a web of illusions upon which everyone can agree and which can come to be accepted as obviously true, requiring no discussion or examination, such that the process of destruction and brutality can proceed with a clean conscience.

Everybody's Bad but You and Me—and I'm Beginning to Wonder about You!

That the supposed superiority of humans over animals, whites over blacks, men over women is part, not of a hierarchy of excellence, but of a system of necessary illusions supporting power, is indicated by the fact that wealthy white, male humans are also subject to an identical system promoting a sense of inferiority in the service of power. The superior, white, mobile, keen, inventive, law-abiding Nordic 'wheat' sieved from the Third World, animal and female 'chaff' also needs to be denigrated in order that he might be exploited. Machiavelli put it well:

> Whosoever founds a republic (or any other state) and gives it laws must recognize that all men are wicked, and that all without exception will express their innate wickedness as soon as a safe opportunity offers itself.[48]

Or, as Kant put it:

> Man is an animal which, when living among others of its kind, needs a master. For he surely abuses his freedom in the presence of his equals, and although as a reasonable being he desires a law, his beastly selfish nature leads him to exempt himself whenever he can. Hence he needs a master who will break his individual will and compel him to obey a generally accepted rule whereby everyone can be free.[49]

Once again, the intellectual élite plays its role with great gusto. Rudolf Rocker explained the rationale of this all-pervasive idea of original sin with great elegance:

> The doctrine of original sin is fundamental not only in all the great religious systems, but in every theory of the state. The complete degradation of man, the fateful belief in the worthlessness and sinfulness of his own nature, has ever been the firmest foundation of all spiritual and temporal authority.[50]

Power always strives to suppress compassion. Power is the antithesis of compassion; they cannot coexist. If power is to function unhindered, our compassion for ourselves, and for each other, must first be disabled. Chomsky puts it well:

> It is necessary to destroy hope, idealism, solidarity, and concern for the poor and oppressed, to replace these dangerous feelings by self-centred egoism, a pervasive cynicism that holds that all change is for the worse, so that one should simply accept the state capitalist order with its inherent inequities and oppression as the best that can be achieved. In fact, a great international propaganda campaign is underway to convince people—particularly young people—that this not only is what they *should* feel but that it is what they *do* feel, and that if somehow they do not adopt this set of values then they are strange relics of a terrible era that has fortunately passed away.[51]

It is an important and perennial deception that, given our sickly human natures, we are assuredly in the best of all possible worlds; to strive for more, to reach for more freedom and happiness, would be to fly too close to the sun and invite catastrophe. Best, then, to turn away from all such thoughts before they even become fully conscious, and work on what is far more feasible, far safer: dedication to improving our lot within the system as it is. Perhaps, even, if we embrace the system with all our hearts and souls our efforts will be rewarded and we will be granted the same privileges as those who top the commanding heights (where, we assume, some kind of happiness can be found).

Given the realities and goals of power, it is not hard to appreciate that in a society such as ours, compassion for others cannot be seen as a virtue to be nurtured, but is rather perceived (beneath the rhetoric) as an obstacle and a threat to 'moderate', 'pragmatic', 'realistic' considerations.

No surprise, then, that in the age of the information superhighway we find ourselves afflicted by a chronic and debilitating condition known as 'compassion fatigue'. A kind of moral ME, this fatigue is said to account for the weary, short-lived nature of our attempts to reduce suffering in a world overflowing with misery. We have been persuaded that self-seeking cynicism is 'cool' and 'sharp', and kindness sentimental. It is *de rigeur* for the cultural icons of our time to stare in cold contempt at the camera. Catwalk models stride with icy coldness, rock stars snarl and spit their rugged individualism, movie characters chat away about trivia before kicking in a door and 'blowing people away' without a care.

According to a study by the Glasgow Media Group, children can recall large sections of dialogue from *Pulp Fiction*. "Many youngsters regard it as cool to blow people away", according to Greg Philo, author of the report.[52] Youngsters regarded the two hitmen, Vincent (John Travolta) and Jules (Samuel L. Jackson), as the 'coolest' characters. As one put it "Vincent was cool because he's not scared. He can go around shooting people without being worried." [53] Another youngster pointed out "Drugs are drummed into your head like they are bad. But not violence." [54]

Young people are attracted to this violence (*Pulp Fiction* "was the most frequently cited cult film",[55] watched by 42 per cent of 10-16 year olds) not because we are innately psychopathic, but because the conditions of an exploitative society are such that plausible, healthier alternatives are invisible, unknown, or scorned. We should not fool ourselves that this fantasy violence is dissociated from the real thing: it is as much a product of the requirements of exploitative power as the death squads of South America. We have to be persuaded to abandon our youthful compassion and critical thinking and the protests to which these might otherwise lead; they have to be persuaded to abandon their resistance to a life in purgatory.

It is undeniable that the propaganda campaign to which Chomsky referred has been spectacularly successful in our time. This is not surprising, given the volume, reach and sophistication of corporate communications. Today, the ranks of the young are packed with corporate 'rebels'—ostensible free spirits, kitted out with corporate jeans, corporate trainers, caps, cigarettes, logos. The fashionable rebel, of course, is a contradiction in terms, an oxymoron: to consciously follow any kind of fashion is to be a conformist. Most often, today, to deliberately follow the latest fashion, however 'rebellious', is to be a corporate dupe. Indeed it is amazing to see the extent to which the young have literally bought the truly audacious deception that corporate logos somehow signify streetwise rebelliousness and cool!

The problem with compassion fatigue, it is assumed, is that the practice of compassion involves a draining exertion, the flexing of a feeble muscle competing against our brute selfishness and soon exhausted. We may give charitably to Ethiopia, Bosnia, Timor, tip the taxi driver, but then our compassion runs out and we throw up our hands and credit cards: "What's the use!"

And what, indeed, is the use of contributing amounts of income and energy which, while tiny in the grand scheme of global suffering, may constitute significant proportions of our disposable supply? The world will surely be overflowing with misery and suffering long after we have made our contribution, dropping it into a bottomless well from which we may never hear so much as a thank you.

Some might reply that it is all very well talking like that; yes, our money and effort may make little difference, but it is our 'moral responsibility' to do what we can, to sacrifice some of our wealth to aid those in need of help. Unfortunately, because many Westerners are uncertain whether there is a real basis on which moral responsibility rests—Who says who is responsible for what? Who says anyone is responsible for anything? 'Compassion fatigue' is the norm, with our vestigial capacity for giving occasionally jerked into spluttering life by the odd catastrophe.

The message for the young is not inspiring, and is not intended to be: it is 'nice' to be compassionate if you can afford it, if it does not overly tax you, but otherwise there is no overly compelling reason to be so. Peter Singer, one of the great popularisers of ethical and animal rights philosophy in recent years, wrote a book titled *How Are We To Live? Ethics in an Age of Self-Interest*. One of his key conclusions is:

> Do good to those who do good to you, and harm to those who harm you.[56]

His basis for this recommendation?

> To be nice to someone who is not nice to you is to allow yourself to be a sucker. Where there are suckers, cheats prosper. Conversely, if there are no suckers, cheats do badly... To be a sucker is bad, not only for oneself, but for everyone.[57]

In our society, to be more deeply compassionate than this is viewed with great suspicion. We Westerners actually cringe in the face of compassion: we feel far more comfortable on the familiar ground of honest-to-goodness selfish behaviour. It is even a running joke between public and politicians: of course it's all a sham, they're only in it for themselves and the corporations, but at least they're genuine about their phoniness!

No Such Thing as 'Smart' Hate

The consequences of demolishing the capacity for compassion are extraordinarily damaging for society. Regarding parent-child relationships, sociologist D.B. Straus points out that:

> Since physical punishment is used by authority figures who tend to be loved or respected and since it is almost always used for a morally correct end when other methods fail, physical punishment teaches that violence can and should be used under similar circumstances. The intriguing question is whether this legitimization of violence spills over from the parent-child relationship to other relationships in which one has to deal with persons who persist in some wrongdoing, such as a spouse or a friend.[58]

Straus argues that this spill-over does in fact take place. For example, the more physical punishment is authorized in schools, the higher the rate of assault by children in those schools.

In 1988 Baron *et al* reported that in a western US state whose citizens scored highly on three tests measuring exposure to violence—in the media, in state legislation, and participation in violent pursuits such as hunting—women were eight times more likely to be raped than women in an eastern state, whose inhabitants scored low. The authors concluded that legitimate violence "tends to be defused to relations between the sexes".[59] They also suggested that to reduce levels of violence in society, attention must be paid to socially approved violence and not just criminal violence.

This is a problem, Felicity de Zulueta of Amnesty International comments, because, as we know, "economic and racial inequality, physical punishment, mass media violence, capital punishment and other forms of legitimate violence are woven into the fabric of American culture and increasingly into that of other Westernized cultures." [60]

Straus and Baron's findings are corroborated by research from Birmingham University examining whether media violence is linked to real violence. According to the report's author, Dr. Kevin Browne, "Videos cannot create aggressive people, but they will make aggressive people commit violent acts more frequently." [61]

In short, then, there is no such thing as laser-guided 'smart' hate. When our leaders insist that murderers need to be sent to the electric chair as a 'deterrent', or that Saddam Hussein is a "bully" who needs a "punch in the face",[62] or that juvenile criminals need to be administered a 'short, sharp shock', such promotions of hate, revenge and punishment send uncompassionate ripples throughout society: husbands decide that their wives need to be 'taught a lesson', that their children need a corrective 'dose of corporal punishment'.

When the media supports these strategies with endless 'shoot 'em up' films, the incidence of violence is only increased. The moral implications are extraordinary and clear: to even make films like *Pulp Fiction*, to even talk this way, is actually to do violence to the people around us.

While supporters of capital punishment focus on the deterrent effect of state-sanctioned violence on a criminal minority, the huge demonstration effect on society as a whole is ignored.

The findings of Straus, Baron and Browne confirm conclusions arrived at independently by Edward Herman, who, in a typically incisive exposure of hypocrisy, writes:

> Conservative governments focus heavily on 'law and order' and its doublespeak partner, 'crime in the streets'. These code phrases signify the purported threat posed by poor blacks and other minorities to white safety and jobs. Conservative policies *generate* disorder, crime and job scarcity by increasing unemployment, withdrawing the safety net from the weak, unleashing greed, encouraging corporate abandonments, and returning society to the law of the jungle. The conservative 'solution' to increased crime and violence is more police, prisons, and an end to 'coddling'. This is a feedback process, in which basic policies and attitudes encourage alienation, hopelessness, and crime, which the conservatives then attack only at the level of symptoms...[63]

It is interesting to find the same understanding communicated several thousand years ago in a Buddhist tale in which a great king, conscious of his good fortune, thought it advisable to offer a great sacrifice of human and animal life, and thereby ensure the continuance of his prosperity. The king's Buddhist chaplain, being utterly opposed to such cruelty, dissuaded him, pointing out that continued good fortune would be better assured by taking preventative action against the causes of criminality. In modern parlance, the chaplain urged that the king be "tough on crime and tough on the causes of crime". This, though, is a Buddhist kind of toughness, being best achieved by removing the economic causes of discontent:

To farmers the king should issue a subsidy of food and of seed-corn. To merchants and tradesmen he should make available sources of capital which they could invest in their businesses. To those in government service he should give adequate wages and supplies of food. If this were to be done there would be no danger of subversion of the state by malcontents, but on the contrary, the king's revenue will go up; the country will be quiet and at peace; and the populace, pleased with one another and happy, dancing their children in their arms, will dwell with open doors.[64]

The king followed the chaplain's advice, and all happened as he had predicted.

Or consider the sublime advice given to an ancient Tony Blair or Bill Clinton by a Buddhist wise man:

Generate compassion for all living beings; abstain from killing, from stealing, and so on, and give pleasure to all. Consider Your Majesty, if, through such mercy, people treated each other as they would treat themselves or their families, whose heart would ever harbour wicked thoughts?[65]

Our instinctive reaction is surely to appreciate that these measures do indeed represent a genuinely tough response to crime and its causes, as opposed to a tough response to the criminals who are often also victims of the same causes.

Thus with the reversal of truth common to all systems of concentrated power, it is the parties of 'law and order' which are actually the greatest causes of crime and disorder in society. It is they who generate desperation, crime and chaos for the sake of short-term profits for the wealthy, by reducing equality, increasing poverty, stripping down the social security system, increasing unemployment, and above all, perhaps, by keeping from the people an understanding of the importance of critical thinking and kindness.

In 1978 Ainsworth *et al* found that a quarter of the population of the United Kingdom had been "subject to rearing practices which are detrimental to their capacity to 'tune into' others and to form satisfactory relationships. They are also aggressive toward others."[66]

In former West Germany, a thousand children died in 1988 "as a result of being beaten up by their parents".[67] In Britain, at least four children die every week as a result of abuse and neglect, and one child in ten is sexually abused.

In the United States, where around 90 per cent of parents use physical punishment on their children, Gelles estimated that of forty-six million children between the ages of three and seventeen years old living with both parents in 1975, 46.5 per cent had been pushed, grabbed or shoved, 71 per cent had been slapped or spanked and about 7.7 per cent (about 3.5 million) had been kicked, beaten or punched by their parents. About 4.2 per cent (around 1.9 million) had been 'beaten up'. Around 2.8 per cent (1.2 million) of American children have had their parents use a gun or a knife on them.

The result of all this, as Stanley Milgram reported in 1974, is that:

> The kind of character produced in American democratic society cannot be counted on to insulate its citizens from brutality and inhumane treatment at the direction of a malevolent authority. A substantial proportion of people do what they are told to do, irrespective of the content of the act and without limitations of conscience, so long as they perceive that the command comes from a legitimate authority.[68]

In short, a substantial proportion of the population of the US and other Western societies has been successfully inoculated against compassion. No surprise, then, that dissidents too have little interest in the issue of compassion, and have been happy to vent their hatred and anger on specific individuals and organizations deemed to be responsible for the horrors of our world.

It is from an understanding of this wider social context that we need, in my view, to begin to think seriously about compassion. The first conclusion is that you and I should be extremely sceptical about any scepticism we may feel towards the subject. We have been subjected to a ceaseless propaganda barrage since the day we were born, persuading us that anger and revenge are reasonable and rational.

It may appear somewhat bizarre for me to assert, as I do, that compassion—not anger, nor facts, nor action, nor protest—should be at the heart of any effective struggle for freedom and democracy. It is for this reason that you and I are virtual beginners at democracy. In my view, we have barely begun to understand what democracy entails, because we have barely begun to understand that democracy has no meaning at all unless it is based on a deep understanding of compassion; that the extent of our civilization is measured by the extent of our compassion. Our capacity for compassion is hobbled, vestigial, a fact that explains our failure to generate effective resistance to the forces of greed and hatred currently laying waste to our planet.

Chapter Six

REDISCOVERING THE MORAL WHEEL

All the joy the world contains
Has come through wishing happiness for others
All the misery the world contains
Has come through wanting pleasure for oneself.
—Shantideva, *The Way of the Bodhisattva.*

Marriage Made in Hell—"My Fiancée, Revolution"

As we have seen, many of the horrors of our world are institution-alized, the direct or indirect result of politics and economics serving the needs of concentrated power. Western governments and oil companies stand impotently by while the Nigerian dictators murder Ken Saro-Wiwa, declaring themselves unable to intervene in the domestic affairs of another nation.

The idea that the West is committed but helpless is a thin but effective deception: Iraq can be crippled, Nicaragua can be wrecked, Vietnam can be bombed to pieces, Haiti can be stifled—all by the exercise of Western economic and military power; Nigeria, however, stands supreme in its ability to resist Western pressure. Why? Because, of course, there is very little: the West can rely on the Nigerian dictators to keep the oil flowing, and that is what matters. Change of any kind threatens to raise costs, and so is not an option.

We have seen how it is a mistake to expect the mainstream media to report independently and honestly the destruction wreaked by the corporate system. The influence of corporate economic and political power is sufficient to ensure that the public is unable to know enough to care about what is being done in their name in the Third World and at home. It is sufficient, also, to ensure that we do not know that we do not know.

Our political system is subject to the same influences, ensuring that political parties, their leaders and the breadth of political debate are strictly limited by the needs of corporate power. The media, business, political, educational, social institutions of our society are everywhere tailored to support the business programme, built though it is on Third World misery, injustice and on a lethal subordination of environmental integrity to the needs of short-term profit. One result, as we have also seen, is that our capacity for compassion—and our understanding of its central significance in human affairs—has been hobbled to suit the requirements of a society built on necessary illusions.

What kind of resistance can we imagine arising out of such a society?

The first (and for many people the most immediately compelling) response would surely be to hit back in some way, as our society never tires of teaching us to do. It is easy to imagine that we would see the answer in seeking to punish those we deem responsible for the terrible injustice and inhumanity.

Anarchists are primarily infamous for their promotion of just this solution. Bakunin may be considered representative:

> I await my... fiancée, revolution. We will be really happy—that is, we will become ourselves, only when the whole world is engulfed in fire.[1]

The solution to burning injustice, then, is to plunge the world into even more fire. It is interesting to note the close congruence of Bakunin's strategy with those advocated by the executives of concentrated power, against whom Bakunin deemed himself to be in complete opposition. US President Theodore Roosevelt, for example, wrote to a friend in 1897: "In strict confidence... I should welcome almost any war, for I think this country needs one." [2]

Concentrated power thrives on violence and hatred; anarchists like Bakunin duly obliged. This is the same Bakunin who described himself "a fanatical lover of Liberty; considering it as the only medium in which can develop intelligence, dignity, and the happiness of man".[3] Unfortunately, to gain "intelligence, dignity and the happiness of man", Bakunin argued, meant revolution, and:

> Revolution, the overthrow of the state means war, and that implies the destruction of men and things.[4]

Engels had this to say:

> A revolution is certainly the most authoritarian thing there is; it is the act whereby one part of the population imposes its will upon

the other part by means of rifles, bayonets and cannon—authoritarian means, if such there be at all; and if the victorious party does not want to have fought in vain, it must maintain this rule by means of the terror which its arms inspire in the reactionaries.[5]

It is the famous formula for social change with which the twentieth century is so familiar: in the name of the ultimate public good, all extremes of evil are permissible. Arthur Koestler had his fictional Soviet revolutionary of *Darkness At Noon* ask himself exactly where this attempt to destroy oppression by violence had taken the people:

> What happened to these masses, to this people? For forty years it had been driven through the desert, with threats and promises, with imaginary terrors and imaginary rewards. But where was the Promised Land?... wherever his eye looked, he saw nothing but desert and the darkness of night.[6]

Indeed, Engels' assertion that revolutionary terror leads merely to a new terroristic status quo is supported by much that has happened over the course of the present century, making a nonsense of Bakunin's notion that engulfing the world in fire and hatred can somehow purify it to a condition where "intelligence, dignity and the happiness of man" predominate.

In reality, 'revolutionary violence' is an oxymoron. All violence, indeed all anger and hate, is inherently counter-revolutionary, acting to powerfully reinforce the oppressive status quo which will always "welcome almost any war".

Discussing the series of anarchist terrorist acts inspired by the views of Bakunin and others, which reached a peak during the 1880s and 1890s, Peter Marshall has written:

> These acts of terrorism not only sparked off repressive measures against anarchists in general but gave the anarchist cause a reputation for violence which it has never been able to live down. It has consequently done enormous harm to the movement.[7]

A dramatic understatement. It was the anarchist movement itself that was annihilated by the bomb-throwing adventurers of the nineteenth century; to such an extent, indeed, that the name has become a term of abuse and can hardly be used today without eliciting derision.

But the anarchist response is at least understandable to all who have seen something of the truth of the society in which we live. Anarchist violence was often not merely a mindless resort to bloodshed; it was often rooted in compassion for the victims of power, born of a sense of outrage at what was happening and a desire to take strategic action, to do something—anything—to stop it.

What is so important about anarchism (as it is commonly understood—most modern anarchists are not at all bent on terrorism), is that this violent response was as much a product of a society dominated by concentrated power as were the moral outrages provoking it.

Power Source: the Greed-Hate-Ignorance Complex

Systems of exploitative power do not spring out of thin air: they are the product of psychological forces which they, in turn, serve to reinforce. Ultimately, all systems of concentrated power are manifestations of greed, hatred and ignorance. As we saw in the case of the Columbus expeditions, these come as a package: selfish greed for personal gain generates contempt for and hatred of those who threaten to get in the way, wilful ignorance of their humanity, wilful ignorance of the effects of our actions in causing suffering to others—all are mutually dependent, and mutually supportive.

If greed, hatred and ignorance are the ultimate wellsprings of concentrated power, and if concentrated power is the perennial source of oppression, then violence is clearly not only not the solution but very much part of the problem.

As we saw in the last chapter, hatred is not a happy bedfellow of enlightenment and compassion; it is both the result and cause of greed and ignorance. It is not possible to fight for peace, to murder our way to freedom, to torture in the name of kindness.

In response, some might point to the example set by peasant resistance in Vietnam which, at the cost of some 2-3 million Vietnamese and around 60,000 American lives, is said to have at least won freedom and independence from US oppression and colonialism more generally. The reality is very different. Today, Vietnam is once again being colonized by the forces of exploitation; this time, not through napalm and high explosive bombs, but through the globalization of trade. Michel Chossudovsky explains:

> The achievements of past struggles and the aspirations of an entire
> nation are [being] undone and erased...The seemingly neutral and

scientific tools of macro-economic policy constitute a non-violent instrument of recolonisation and impoverishment.[8]

When seventy per cent of the Vietnamese population live in absolute poverty with half its children severely malnourished, when Western corporations can now be assured that "Vietnam's open door invites you to take advantage of its low standard of living and low wages",[9] then we must surely agree with Gabriel Kolko that the Vietnam War has finally ended in "the defeat of all who fought in it—and one of the greatest tragedies of modern history." [10]

Also, as state documents make clear, the bloody nose received by Western power in Vietnam led only to a vast increase in the paranoia, brutality and blindness of that power, and to a redoubling of efforts to crush all opposition, to 'stop the rot'.

The ruthlessness of the slaughter of 600,000 people from 1965 onwards in Indonesia was in large part motivated by a desire to avoid another Vietnamese-style 'loss' of natural resources to independent nationalism. The massacres in East Timor from December 1975, following hard on the heels of the final defeat in Vietnam, came at a time when no quarter was being shown to independent nationalists. Referring to US support for the Indonesian invasion of East Timor, US columnist Jack Anderson reported:

> The United States had suffered a devastating setback in Vietnam, leaving Indonesia as the most important American ally in the area. The US national interest, [President] Ford concluded, 'had to be on the side of Indonesia'.[11]

It seems equally clear that the fanaticism of the subsequent Western-backed assault on libertarian movements in Nicaragua, Guatemala, Chile, El Salvador, Argentina and elsewhere, was at least in part inspired by the experience of Vietnam and by the resort to violent resistance of guerrilla movements more generally. The ferocity of the assault on Iraq during the Gulf war also resulted from a determination to put into practice lessons learned during the Vietnam disaster. One of the main lessons being: spare no enemy casualties to ensure a quick victory before anti-war protest can gain momentum.

Experience makes clear that even when a vestige of freedom from oppression is won through violence, it is bought at the cost of much blood-letting elsewhere and in a strengthening of the forces of greed, hatred and ignorance. It is sometimes hoped that a violent, Vietnam-style rising up of popular resistance might lead to some kind of global revolution against corporate capitalism. Erich Fromm summed up the prospects for this idea well, noting that it was born:

> of despair, mixed with a good deal of romanticism, phraseology and adventurism. A general attack against the United States would end in the establishment of fascism within this nation and probably in all other industrialized countries, as well as in the most ruthless dictatorships in the rest of the world.[12]

The reflexive counter-argument is close at hand: 'Surely compassion isn't enough; violence is sometimes needed, for example to contain a monster like Hitler? After all, Hitler had to be stopped. Compassion is powerless to stop that kind of brutality.' And yet, arguably, it was just the *lack* of compassion—bitterness fostered by the blaming and humiliation of Germany after the Great War, the imposition of crippling war reparations contributing to the collapse of the German economy—that created the malignant conditions for Hitler's rise. Also, the problem with the Western response to Nazism was not so much that it involved appeasement, but that it involved collaboration. As we have seen, the West has a long and bloody history of working with and through fascist dictators against democracy and other impediments to profits. Hitler was a South American general writ large, a giant Noriega who was originally welcomed and supported by the West as a staunch anti-communist and moderate. The American chargé d'affaires in Berlin wrote to Washington in 1933 that the hope for Germany lay in "the more moderate section of the [Nazi] party, headed by Hitler... which appeal[s] to all civilized and reasonable people." [13] However, Hitler got out of hand, refused to play by the rules of the game, and had to be stopped.

Historian Howard Zinn supports Princeton historian Arno Meyer's contention that the war against Nazism helped to promote its worst horrors. Writing on the Holocaust in his essay 'Just and Unjust War', Zinn argues that Hitler's pre-war aim was the forced emigration of Jews, not extermination, with the policy degenerating into mass murder as the frenzy of war overtook the already deranged Nazi mind-set:

> Not only did waging the war against Hitler fail to save the Jews, it

may be that the war itself brought on the Final Solution of genocide. This is not to remove the responsibility from Hitler and the
Nazis, but there is much evidence that Germany's anti-Semitic
actions, cruel as they were, would not have turned to mass murder
were it not for the psychic distortions of war, acting on already distorted minds.[14]

Essentially the same point has been made by Noam Chomsky and
Edward Herman regarding another of the century's great geno-
cides: the mass slaughter in the 'killing fields' of Cambodia.
Chomsky and Herman quote David P. Chandler, former Foreign
Service Officer in Phnom Penh, who asks: "What drove the
Cambodians to kill?":

> To a large extent, I think, American actions are to blame. From
> 1969 to 1973, after all, we dropped more than 500,000 tons of
> bombs on the Cambodian countryside. Nearly half of this tonnage
> fell in 1973... In those few months, we may have driven thousands
> of people out of their minds. We certainly accelerated the course of
> the revolution.[15]

Elsewhere, Chomsky quotes correspondent Richard Dudman, who
was held captive by the Khmer Rouge:

> The [US] bombing destroyed a good deal of the fabric of pre-war
> Cambodian society and provided the CPK (Khmer Rouge) with
> the psychological ingredients of a violent, vengeful and unrelent-
> ing social revolution... The party encouraged class warfare between
> the 'base people,' who had been bombed, and the 'new people' who
> had taken refuge from the bombing, and thus had taken sides, in
> CPK thinking, with the United States.[16]

If the argument is that inhumanity was needed to stop Hitler's
inhumanity, then we clearly failed: the world is beset as never before
by the forces of inhumanity: hatred, violence, selfishness and greed.
Again, Zinn has this to say:

> A war that apparently begins with a 'good' cause—stopping aggres-
> sion, helping victims, or punishing brutality—ends with its own
> aggression, creates more victims than before, and brings out more
> brutality than before, on both sides. The Holocaust, a plan made and
> executed in the ferocious atmosphere of war, and the saturation
> bombings, also created in the frenzy of war, are evidence of this.[17]

Moreover, as discussed, the legitimization of violence by authority figures has a profound demonstration effect throughout society as a whole. In which case, we might reflect on the extraordinary repercussions of those six years of global slaughter from 1939-45. Few would argue against the need for violent resistance to Nazism and, particularly with victory, virtually the entire world felt convinced that violence is therefore 'a necessary evil'.

The Second World War continues to be presented as the great proof of the occasional 'hard-headed', 'realistic' need for violence, and has been used by any number of individuals and organizations to justify any number of subsequent monstrous individual, familial, social and international acts: the demolition of Vietnam, the wrecking of Iraq, the slaughter of 'communists' in South America, for example.

That 'righteous' war against Nazism, that perceived triumph for 'good killing', was a tremendous setback for the notion that killing is always a disaster, and for the credibility of the kind of unconditional compassion on which our hope for the future depends. As the memory of that 'victory' fades, so too, it seems, does our faith in necessary violence: the conviction that we need to crush 'evil', so characteristic of the forties and fifties, has steadily lost ground to the possibility of negotiated settlement.

This compassionate way might initially strike us as incredibly difficult, but it is at least possible, and therefore preferable to the impossible attempt to achieve a compassionate society through violence and hatred. Feelings of hatred and anger do not even bring peace in relationships between friends, spouses, families; they prevent even dedicated people from forming cohesive movements for social change. How then can they bring anything but chaos and disaster to a whole world?

The above may well seem unrealistic, as it may seem to suggest that all resistance is to be abandoned, and that we should simply stand by and accept our exploitation and even destruction. The standard related question, of course, is 'Well, what should we have done in the face of Hitler? Should we have simply stood by as he ravaged the world?'

But the question itself is without real meaning. If the global cultural and political environment in 1939 had been such that a compassionate allied response to the threat of Hitler would have been possible, then presumably the historical conditions leading to

Hitler's rise would also need to be reconfigured, perhaps sufficiently to make such a rise implausible and even impossible. Hitler, and the response to him, grew out of a European culture rooted in centuries of greed, hatred and revenge. What we *can* say, however, is that by recognizing that violence is always a disaster, that compassion is the only effective antidote to greed, hatred and ignorance, we can work to ensure that the conditions conducive to violence now and in the future are reduced in the world.

Tantalizing clues to genuine resistance, to the antidote to the horrors of concentrated power, lie in the goals of concentrated power itself. Theodore Roosevelt's perception of a political need for war is significant in this regard: whatever is discouraged by power should be embraced wholeheartedly by those who seek to dissolve that power. If power seeks to overcome our compassionate feelings through war, the creation of enemies, the doctrine of original sin, and so on, then we can be sure that freedom and humanity are not served by acceptance of, and participation in, those deceptions.

Instead, weak and passive though we might initially imagine it to be, the generation and practice of unconditional compassion for all living beings is, I believe, the answer to the problem of exploitative power.

To understand how this might be possible we need to turn to societies relatively free from the necessary cultural illusions supporting Western exploitation.

Seeing the Dog

Asanga, we are told, decided to remove himself to the seclusion of the mountains to meditate as a hermit and devote himself to achieving the blessing of a vision of the Buddha Maitreya (that is, an experience of truth, wisdom and compassion). For twelve years, Asanga meditated in extreme hardship and appeared to achieve nothing. In dismay he eventually decided that enough was enough and abandoned his retreat. That very afternoon, however, as he descended from his mountain, Asanga came across a terribly injured dog lying by the side of the road. Though alive, the dog's front legs were missing, the lower half of its body a seething mass of maggots. Despite its pitiful condition, the dog snapped aggressively at passers-by, trying to bite them by dragging itself along the ground with its two remaining legs.

At the sight of such dreadful suffering, Asanga was overwhelmed by compassion. In an attempt to provide some relief he cut a piece of flesh from his own body and fed it to the dog. Then, seeing that the dog was literally being eaten alive by the maggots, he bent down to remove them from its rotten flesh. But fearful that the delicate bodies of the larvae might be damaged were he to prise them off with his fingers, Asanga determined that the only way to remove them safely was with the tip of his tongue. Kneeling down, he took in the terrible, writhing mass, closed his eyes, put out his tongue and... found his tongue touching the ground where the dog had been, but was no more.

Opening his eyes, the hermit looked up and beheld an awesome sight: before him stood the Buddha Maitreya, shining in an aura of light.

"At last," said Asanga, "why did you never appear to me before?"

Maitreya spoke softly: "It is not true that I have never appeared to you before. I was with you all the time, but your negative karma and obscurations prevented you from seeing me. Your twelve years of practice dissolved them slightly, so that you were at last able to see the dog. Then, thanks to your genuine and heartfelt compassion, all those obscurations were completely swept away, and you can see me before you with your very own eyes." [18]

Maitreya then demonstrated to Asanga how few people were able to perceive the vision of the crippled dog—not only could they not feel compassion for the suffering animal, they could not even see it. Asanga put Maitreya on his shoulder. "What have I got on my shoulder?" Asanga asked. "Nothing," most people replied. Only one old woman answered "You've got the rotting corpse of an old dog on your shoulder, that's all."

Now at last, it seems, Asanga finally understood the transforming power of compassion.

It is surely not difficult to translate these symbols into modern terms. The monstrous and pitiful dog writhing in agony represents the horror and suffering of our world. It is, for example, the monstrous truth of Third World torture and suffering, of environmental collapse, of the misery and despair of our own hedonistic lifestyles, and the origins of these tragedies in our own greed and ignorance. Our inability to perceive or care about these tragedies is conditional not merely upon our self-deceptive aversion from anxiety, but on our lack of compassion, on our unwillingness to see the truth behind our greed.

Compassion, then, as the tale of Asanga makes clear, is not merely about giving money from a position of ignorance, but about overcoming our selfishness sufficiently to want to see the truth—it is not a lack of charity but a lack of understanding born of a lack of desire to understand that is at the root of Third World torture and environmental collapse. It is compassion, and the understanding of the causes of suffering it brings, that is the greatest gift we can offer those suffering innocents.

The obstacles to compassion are, of course, greed, hatred and ignorance.

In an earlier chapter we witnessed, not mythical, but actual living examples of these obstacles at work in the flesh and blood persons of people like Robert Key and Elliot Abrams (see Chapter One) in their responses to the reality of human rights disasters. How, in all honesty, we may well find ourselves asking, can human beings dismiss suffering on this scale so casually, so cynically, and reject the desperate attempts of other human beings to seek help against the overwhelming might of political and economic forces with a vested interest in our not caring?

The answer is that Key and Abrams cannot "see the dog" because, quite simply, priorities other than the relief of suffering are at the top of their lists. Not consciously perhaps—for greed, pride and hatred have an almost unlimited capacity to blind us to the reality of our actions—but certainly unconsciously. Key and Abrams are hardly alone in this and the objective is certainly not to heap blame and invective on them, or on anyone else, merely to leave the final significance and effect of their position in no doubt.

Here, indeed, I believe, is the real test of compassion, and where we in the West move into what is often, for us, an almost completely alien world. We reach, actually, in my view, the limits of dissent and the limits of the power of dissent in the West to generate change. A measure of our ignorance may be indicated by our (presumably bemused) response to the following excerpt from a Buddhist text dating back some fifteen hundred years:

> As if a treasure had appeared in my house
> without my making any effort to obtain it,
> I must rejoice in my enemies,
> who help me to perform enlightened actions.[19]

The argument being that it is our 'enemies'—our very exploiters, oppressors and torturers—who provide us with the chance to strengthen our compassion, and so increase our clarity of understanding and so our capacity to transform the world in all its greed, hatred and ignorance.

It is hardly that Tibetan Buddhists, say, are ignorant of the levels of suffering currently being opposed by Western dissidents. Consider, for example, Palden Gyatso, who was imprisoned for thirty-three years by the Chinese, tortured into unconsciousness with electric batons and regularly beaten:

> He pulled the electric baton from the socket and began to poke at me with this new toy. My whole body flinched at each electric shock. Then, shouting obscenities, he thrust the baton into my mouth, took it out, then rammed it in again. [He] went back to the wall and selected a longer baton. I felt as though my body were being torn apart.[20]

Of the torturer who did this, Gyatso has this to say:

> I don't bear him a grudge. I simply want to illustrate the system that allows such things to happen. He was an ordinary person working in a system that encourages and rewards people who are prepared to torture. For his survival he follows orders. If the system punished people like that they wouldn't continue... I have no right to hate the Chinese. But I have a right to tell my story.[21]

It is a remarkable, and compassionate, insight. We know for sure, of course, that Gyatso is correct: if the system punished rather than rewarded the torturer, there would be little or no torture in the world. It is the system that is the primary cause, not individuals—like Gyatso's torturer—who are merely symptoms. We would do well to be extremely careful before declaring 'hateful' any individual required to live in a society that systematically seeks to deny him or her freedom, truth, understanding, compassion and happiness. What we rail against as 'evil' may well be simply an attempt at survival or escape from a terrible situation. It really is no good treating human destructiveness, servility and mendacity as a kind of stereotyped evil; these are natural phenomena that need to be understood.

The system cannot be fought with hate and violence, but the illusions that maintain it can be dissolved, so that the system and its torturers can be deprived of power and fall away. It is understanding the system, not hating Gyatso's torturer, that is the compassionate response. If we can realize the inappropriateness of hating even torturers, then who is there left that we should hate?

In similar vein, the Dalai Lama has said:

> I think that now I have almost no hatred towards anybody, including towards those Chinese who are creating misery and suffering for Tibetans. Even towards them, I really do not feel any kind of hatred.[22]

It will be argued here that the transforming power of dissent—the desire for change—which begins in compassion for the victims of oppression, collapses at the point where our compassion breaks in a wave of anger and hatred over those we take to be responsible for the horrors that have befallen humanity.

If nothing else, hatred of individuals implies responsibility, which implies power, which might actually fool us into imagining that our leaders are the controllers, rather than the functionaries, of a state-corporate system which selects or rejects 'leaders' according to their ability to follow its requirements, and which has long transcended the power of mere individuals. It might even persuade us to imagine that such people—and not we ourselves—have the power to reform the system, to lead us to Koestler's "promised land"—one of the most potent controlling delusions of all.

A Galaxy of Charms

Can we face ugliness on the modern scale with compassion? Is it in our interests to do so? What might be the benefit for us as individuals and as a society? Again, mythical tales the world over seem to leave us in little doubt. That proves nothing in itself of course, until we find ourselves sensing that there are indeed great and unsuspected truths hidden behind these colourful and often dramatic metaphors.

Consider, for example, a tale from the other side of the globe from Asanga: that of the five sons of the Irish King Eochaid, in which the former set off in a desperate search for water (their Buddha, their capacity for compassion, their understanding). After much travelling, the sons finally come upon an old well guarded by an altogether awesome old woman.

Blacker than coal every joint and segment of her was from crown to ground; comparable to a wild horse's tail the grey wiry mass of hair that pierced her scalp's upper surface; with her sickle of a greenish looking tusk that was in her head, and curled till it touched her ear, she could lop the verdant branch of an oak in full bearing...[23]

Once again, it is the horror of the world that stands before us. Once again, it is this same revolting creature who can give the brothers what they need, what we all need—wisdom, understanding, the power to relieve the terrible suffering and chaos of our lives and world—here symbolized by water. There is one small condition:

Only that I have of thee one kiss on my cheek.

As with Asanga, it is a kiss, kindness, compassion in the face of horror, that can overcome that horror. And the response:

"Not so!" said the first brother with a grimace.
"Then water shall not be conceded by *me*," declares the hag.

Appalled, the first brother declares he would sooner die. And so it shall be, the old woman affirms. And so it goes with all the first four brothers, none of whom will consider embracing the monster in front of them, not even to gain the desperately needed water from the well—though it represents nothing less than the water of life.
    Finally, the fifth son, Niall, steps forward and says:

"Let me have water, woman!"
"I will give it!" she replies. "And bestow on me a little kiss."

And, with the life-affirming kindness and compassion of a Buddhist saint, Niall answers:

"Forby giving thee a kiss, I will even hug thee!" and so embraces her.

In an instant, the image of ugliness is transformed into a great beauty, one comparable

... to the last-fallen snow lying in trenches every portion of her was, from crown to sole; plump and queenly forearms, fingers long and taper, straight legs of a lovely hue she had, two sandals of the white bronze betwixt her smooth and soft white feet and the earth...

"Here, woman," the young hero sighs, "is a galaxy of charms."
    It is the same transformation that was taught by the Buddhist

Teacher of Restraint when he assured his audience that compassionate restraint:

> is a coat of mail for the virtuous, for it blunts the arrows shot by wicked tongues and transforms those weapons into flowers of praise, garlands of glory.[24]

Weapons into flowers, writhing dogs into Buddhas, hags into galaxies of charms, greed into kindness, self-deception into self-awareness, fractured, impotent dissident movements into powerful cohesive forces for compassionate change.

The mythical trial of Niall and his brothers is far more than an amusing fantasy. It is a symbolic representation of a reality with which you and I are confronted every day of our lives: We are always standing before that dreadful creature and her precious well of water, and we are always accepting or turning our backs on her one small condition.

"May all Beings be Happy!": Unconditional Compassion

What fate might befall a world where the individual capacity for compassion has been all but banished from society, and replaced by greed, selfishness and hatred all wrapped up in a blinkered unwillingness to appreciate the reality and suffering of others?

The Path of Heroes, a Buddhist text written some 1,500 years ago, makes some dire predictions:

> Unbearably fierce winds arise...
> Fierce robbers and enemies of the land abound,
> and those with wealth and ease cannot enjoy it.
> Truly beings suffer: all aspects of their lives become frightful.
> The rains fall out of season, and hailstorms endanger travellers.
> Cows do not give milk, the seasons are disrupted,
> and grain does not grow upon the earth.
> Medicines become ineffective: the more essential
> they are, the weaker they become.
> Controversies proliferate; arguments lacking logic
> or truth take over, and evil prevails.[25]

As the globalization of capitalist greed proceeds apace, as huge smogs hang over entire nations in South East Asia, as giant plumes of low-level ozone swirl around the globe and we experience extreme phenomena associated with an unusually fierce El Niño weather system linked to rising global temperatures, these predictions make arresting reading.

And the solution to these problems caused by the madness of unrestrained selfishness?

Alternately practice unconditional giving and taking on all suffering.[26]

Should our response to a system of institutionalized exploitation be to adopt an attitude of unconditional giving?! Our instinctive, typically Western, combative response is to batten down the hatches, to try to make it harder for that system to take so much through sabotage, terrorism and so on; to concentrate on giving less ourselves and to start taking from it.

It also seems bizarre to advise us to give everything we have to others and to endure all their suffering—we want the good things in life!

But Buddhists do not merely demand that we take ourselves as we are and stoically choose to suffer for the sake of others. As Westerners, you and I are likely to be full of selfish desires, desperate to find happiness through satisfying our ambitions. It would be mere wishful thinking to expect us to sacrifice our hedonism for the sake of others.

Instead, Buddhism urges us to experiment with generating opponent forces, powerful antidotes to our greed and hatred (I cannot over-emphasize the importance of this point, particularly in the light of the fact that so many Western Buddhist commentators have failed to appreciate the critical role of opponent forces in helping us to generate compassion and restraint).

For example, if we experiment with some of the Buddhist techniques for generating a loving mind in the face of frustration and anger (see below), we may find ourselves actually able to prevent anger arising, so avoiding much stress and chaos, to the benefit of all parties. We may find that patience and kindness are indeed a more powerful and preferable response to the misery of angry revenge, which is in fact not at all empowering.

In this way we can learn to un-learn the self-seeking egotism that we cling to, on which we imagine our happiness depends, and in which, in fact, our unhappiness, concentrated power, and the torture of the world, are rooted. It is then that we can start to choose, rather than force ourselves, to seek happiness in generating kind thoughts and actions for others rather than fleeting pleasures for ourselves.

Notice that, according to the view cited above—"alternately practice unconditional giving and taking on all suffering"—a healthy life, society and planet is based not on the overthrow of an élite class, but on the overthrow of greed and hatred in the individual. It is certainly not based on fighting injustice with violence. It is not even based on meeting injustice and oppression with restraint and tolerance; it is based on meeting them with tender-hearted thoughts and kindness.

Note, also, that a healthy society is based not on equality but on compassion. The famous Western prescription, that we should seek the greatest happiness of the greatest number, is rejected for the promotion of the greatest kindness in the greatest number.

Depending on your view of human nature, the Western prescription might be seen to justify a large number of people being extremely happy with a few people being extremely miserable—the greatest sum of feasible happiness thereby being attained in an imperfect world. According to Buddhism this is like trying to build a house on rotten foundations: a happy society can never be built on, and in the presence of, the misery of others.

It is compassion—the concern for others over any personal material concerns, over even a concern for basic equality of wealth—that brings us well-being individually, as a society and as a planet.

A concern for equality might seem 'just', but it is compassion that brings happiness, sanity and health. To be concerned primarily with equality in material wealth is, after all, merely a watered-down version of the greed and conditional compassion that is wrecking the world today. This of course does not mean that extreme inequality—such that some are overfed while others are dying of starvation—is at all acceptable; it means that the primary work is not that of fighting for equality, but of promoting compassion for everyone, both rich and poor.

In truth there is no such thing as a political revolution. Ultimately, the struggle is always between self-cherishing and compassion; between the idea that happiness can best be sought through selfishness, and through kindness. There is no revolution in taking from one to give to the other, in expropriating from the élite to give to the working class; there is no revolution in catering for selfish needs more equitably. The real revolution lies in understanding that the extent of our happiness and well-being, as individuals and as a society, is determined by the extent of our compassion for others.

Compassion: The Basis of Happiness

To Western eyes, the recommendation that we give unconditionally to others and take on all their suffering might appear to be made out of some masochistic desire for self-mortification. In fact it is made in the understanding that compassion is the sole basis and cause of all happiness.

In Buddhism, concern for others, rationality and happiness, are deemed to be incompatible with greed, hatred, ignorance and unhappiness. To the extent that we are selfish, we will be afflicted by the suffering inherent in desire, anger and hatred.

For Buddhists, desire and anger are poisons to be recognized and treated, not indulged or vented. The first problem with desire, or greed, for example, is that to the extent that we are devoted to satisfying them, we will lose our ability to see clearly what is in our best interests; we will lose our rationality along with our compassion, and so wander into dangerous territory, guided only by our delusions.

> Sensual enjoyments bring with them endless suffering, sir. Listen now, and I will tell you precisely why the Munis [wise men] shun desire. People will undergo captivity and death, grief, fatigue, danger, and innumerable calamities, just to gain their desires. In order to gain what they desire, kings will eagerly oppress virtue...
>
> When friendships are suddenly broken; when wrong roads and unclean paths are travelled for the sake of expediency; when good reputations are lost and suffering arises—is it not always the result of desires? [27]

We may be used to imagining that selfish desire is a good thing, a source—perhaps the only source—of happiness and enjoyment. Our society continuously urges us, and with near religious fervour, to desire more, to seek happiness in the continuous satisfaction of desire.

One consequence of this propaganda campaign is that we are dramatically limited in our capacity to appreciate how we actually feel in any given situation. We have been told so often, so convincingly, that consumption, status and acquisition make us happy, that we remain certain regardless of our actual experience.

It is apparently very easy, when we are not in the grip of desire, to forget the extraordinary suffering that craving of any kind entails. To want anything that we cannot currently have, however small, is the cause of considerable unhappiness. On a small scale, sitting in a traffic jam wanting to be somewhere else is the cause of much frustration, even 'road rage'. The same is true when we are queuing for the cash point, at the bar, at the supermarket check out, sitting bored at our work desk, longing to escape. To desire some kind of possession, achievement, change in appearance, relationship, is to suffer exactly the same sensation of being torn between how things are and how we want them to be.

Desire is suffering. Compassion—the determination to promote the happiness of others—is the antidote to obsession with our desires, with our own happiness. It is compassion that has the capacity to extinguish the suffering of desire.

Unfortunately, desire is accompanied by many delusions, including the delusion that satisfying desire is a wholly good thing, without negative consequences. Yet satisfying any given desire is no solution because it only increases our appetite for repetition, or for something more pleasurable, and so cuts out a kind of habitual track around which our minds trundle, carving ever deeper. The deeper our addiction to desire, the more we lose our freedom and rational awareness, the more we are trapped in a circle of craving and self-deception.

The same effect is at work in all systems of concentrated power, in which the desire for selfish sensual enjoyments is institutionalized in an elaborate supply system—that is the central purpose of exploitative power. Once we are caught by the lure of greed, once we are inside the system designed, ultimately, to satisfy those enjoyments, we lose our capacity to perceive (or to want to perceive) the cruelty and self-destructiveness of what we are doing. This is the process of intellectual and moral corruption described by Chomsky with regards to mainstream media journalists:

> In order to progress you have to say certain things; what the copy editor wants, what the top editor is giving back to you. You can try saying it and not believing it, but that's not going to work, people just aren't that dishonest, you can't live with that, it's a very rare person who can do that. So you start saying it and pretty soon you're believing it because you're saying it, and pretty soon you're inside the system.[28]

The crucial difference, however—marking the point where Western dissidents alienate, disempower and become self-defeating rather than motivating—is that, unlike them, Buddhist analysts are not angered by this gradual erosion of integrity and rationality. On the contrary, as we noted above, they actually welcome enemies as a chance to strengthen their capacity for compassion; which is to strengthen the cause of their happiness and also the cause of the happiness of all living beings.

The logic is simple enough: if compassion, and the associated capacity to perceive the lies of power, are the true antidotes to the self-reinforcing suffering of greed and hatred in ourselves and others; if it is compassion that motivates dissidents to do enormous good in raising awareness of the suffering and destruction caused by the modern status quo, then the generation of compassion must be the highest good. And if compassion is such a potent antidote, then surely it becomes most potent when able to overcome our hatred even for those who are greediest and most violent. Were our compassion to cease at that point, then would not our motivation and power to alleviate suffering have been hobbled? From my own experience, I would suggest that feelings of anger tend to be followed by a feeling of despondency and a temporary abandonment of dissident efforts in a kind of 'To hell with everyone' response. Thus we should not hit back:

> When the time comes that you can retaliate, do not do so. Instead, do whatever you can to help. Even if the harm done to you was the most evil imaginable, *meditate only on love and compassion*, and do not act in any way to harm those who harmed you.[29] [my emphasis]

The italicized phrase marks the crucial point: without actively generating compassionate thoughts, the task is impossible.

The capacity to feel compassion for the individuals who run modern systems of institutionalized greed—corporations—opens our eyes to the reality of who these executives are and why they are doing what they are doing. What is so interesting is that without this compassion, such people remain unreal stereotypes, almost as if our imagination shapes them (and the wider reality) to satisfy the needs of our hatred. In a recent interview with David Barsamian, Chomsky commented on the anger he feels towards the élite ostensibly running the propaganda and corporate systems:

> I'm usually fuming on the inside... the only thing I ever get irritated about is élite intellectuals, the stuff they do I do find irritating. I shouldn't. I should expect it. But I do find it irritating.[30]

By contrast, Chomsky has no problem understanding the views of the majority of non-élite, non-intellectuals—"Joe six-pack"— whom he sees as victims of the propaganda system:

> When people live through all this stuff, plus corporate propaganda, plus television, plus the press and the whole mass, the deluge of ideological distortion that goes on, they ask questions that from another point of view sound inane, but from their point of view are completely reasonable.[31]

But, as Chomsky has stressed many times, it is the élite who are subjected to a far more intense "deluge of ideological distortion" for the simple reason that they read more, are educated longer, are subject to a more determined assault and have a vitally important role in running the system; also they are protected from the truth by a seemingly civilized, well-ordered, privileged world:

> There's maybe twenty percent of the population which is relatively educated, more or less articulate, plays some kind of role in decision-making. They're supposed to sort of participate in social life— either as managers, or cultural managers like teachers and writers and so on. They're supposed to vote, they're supposed to play some role in the way economic and political and cultural life goes on. So that's one group that has to be deeply indoctrinated. Then there's maybe eighty percent of the population whose main function is to follow orders and not think, and not to pay attention to anything...[32]

Surely it makes little sense to find the views of eighty per cent of the population understandable while "fuming" at the views of the twenty per cent of victims subject actually to a far more intense and effective propaganda barrage. Are we to imagine that the eighty per cent are helpless victims of the propaganda system filtering what they know and think, while the twenty per cent *choose* to be victims of far more intense propaganda?

Dissipating Dissent: The Price of Anger

Chomsky seems to recognize the contradiction between his forgiveness of the majority and his anger at the minority ("I shouldn't [get angry]. I should expect it"), but he also seems to feel that anger is nevertheless justifiable, appropriate, and even motivating, perhaps like a kind of fuel. But Chomsky's contribution lies in his determination to apply his extraordinary capacity for rational, independent thought in a compassionate way in defence of the victims of power. His anger, on the other hand, is deeply counter-productive. To refer to Buddhist thinkers, who have understood all of this for thousands of years:

> When fear and hatred motivate us in our attempts to destroy evil, the negative nature of such motivation, rather than destroying the forces of evil, lends them strength.[33]

Chomsky's uncomfortable arguments are infuriating enough to his opponents, but the often bitterly angry edge he gives them—for example, by denouncing the US administration for its "cowardly thuggishness"[34]—undoubtedly makes them even more so. More importantly, Chomsky's writing, and that of many other dissidents, delivers the reader brilliant ideas and profound understanding with anger deeply infused in the mix. What effect does this have on the reader?

I would imagine that most people taking in this heady cocktail come away feeling both inspired by the clarity of the analysis but also extremely angry at the cruelty and hypocrisy of our society. The question we need to consider is: where does this dissident anger begin and where does it end? Who *is* responsible for the horrors and supporting delusions of our world?

In his novel *The Grapes of Wrath*, John Steinbeck indicates the problem in his tale of a farmer whose land has been confiscated. The farmer aims a gun at the tractor driver who is about to demolish his house. But the tractor driver pleads that he is only taking orders from a banker in Oklahoma City, who in turn takes orders from a banker in New York. Confused, the farmer shouts out: "Then who can I shoot?"[35]

We can begin by being angry with the obvious targets, the chief executives of the major corporations; but, as Chomsky himself has acknowledged, these are actually merely the puppets of investors—one wrong (for example, virtuous) move and they may lose their positions. So we can hate the investors; but they in turn have been blinded by the greed that society has trained them to indulge and which they were often born into. We can hate the politicians. We can hate the lawyers who twist fact and reason and 'justice' to fit corporate profit-making. And then we can hate the media moguls and their senior editors for deceiving the population; and their senior journalists who 'should know better'; and junior journalists who turn a blind eye to the horrors and facts of the system of which they are a part. But where will this end? With the teachers, who pass on a business-friendly view of the world and of success and happiness to the young? With children's TV presenters who, collecting for charity and the Third World, give the impression that we live in a caring, eco-friendly society?

But why should we be angry with *any* of these people? Consider, after all, if an individual declares that we have a free and honest media system. Should we be angry with them for holding this view? On the contrary, given everything they have ever been told by parents, teachers, politicians and journalists, given the relative difficulty of transcending this propaganda to see the subtle truth, it is not at all unreasonable that he or she should believe that we have a free and honest media. Given that they do trust the media in this way, is it fair to revile them for swallowing the consensus media view on any number of other issues?

If we take the big step of deciding that it is reasonable to hate some people for their beliefs and actions, it is only a small step to then feel angry with the views of Chomsky's "eighty per cent", with their love of royalty, sports, holidays, mod. cons., nationalism, soap operas, and so on. They, also, could be accused of being 'sheepish', 'wilfully blind', of 'not giving a damn'.

It is a matter of common experience that when our minds are filled with anger, even at a single person, we tend to view everyone through rage-coloured spectacles: our husband or wife, children, friends, and other innocent bystanders, all seem to be mocking us, trying to provoke us. Moreover, the foundation stone of our hateful philosophy—that the 'bad' should be stopped by force, destroyed, rather than forgiven and loved and so transformed, has profound implications for every aspect of our lives. For, then, our friends and family who do not agree with us must be rejected, perhaps even seen as part of the problem: if we have no compassion for the powerful, then why should we have compassion for those who do not take up arms against them and who even side with them? If they are not with us then they must be against us, in effect.

And where does all this leave the aspiring dissident, perhaps originally driven to organize and act out of compassion for the wretched of the earth, but who is now drowning in anger?

The self-defeating and self-destructive end-point of runaway dissident hate has been well described by animal rights campaigner Carla Lane:

You feel a sense of injustice, a sense of failure, perhaps the arrival of insanity. You can't stop knowing about the horrors and soon after your arrival home you are hanging over the garden fence in undignified combat with your neighbour because they have left their cat out in the rain…. you develop the need to blow up the entire universe and to begin again, just yourself and a few insects in a desert.[36]

To be angry and full of hatred for so much of the world, so much of the time, is to suffer extreme levels of unhappiness, antagonism, isolation and confusion. These are not the bases for vibrant, co-operative, radical social movements. Rather, it seems reasonable to suppose that many young dissidents finding themselves plunged into this suffering will prefer to abandon all interest in dissident ideas, happy to dismiss it all as 'youthful idealism', a 'student thing', and will be eager to avoid any contact with former intellectual heroes who, they know, would consider them to have become 'moral cowards'. If anger is like picking up a hot coal to throw it at someone, then it makes sense that angry dissidents should drop dissent, drop the latest dissident book, and instead try to survive in the world without them as best they can. It also makes sense that the promotion of anger is hugely destructive of dissent. The real enemy, in fact, then, is anger itself.

Beyond the Pneumatic Theory of Anger

Our culture loves to pretend that revenge is an admirable, courageous and life-affirming response. The basic plot of many movies is set up as a justification for a vengeful bloodbath of this kind. Our soap opera characters respond to insults and injustice by exploding with anger and hitting back; they do not respond with patience and kindness.

Buddhists say that, when anger arises in our minds, we initially experience it as the arrival of a friend, a protector that has come to our aid. Moments later, we realize the truth: that after the first triumphant flourish, anger brings great pain, misery and also great mental confusion. Indeed, after the initial sense of enhanced power, and so control, we rapidly begin to realize that we are heading wildly out of control.

Psychotherapists, operating out of the pneumatic theory of Freudian psychology, like to encourage us to 'release' our pent-up, primal anger—we have energies that build up and need to be released to avoid destructive overload.

We are advised that bottling up our anger is stressful, and may even kill us; no doubt this is true in some cases. But what about the stress and danger to our mental health of releasing our anger, of letting our minds run riot? What about the stress caused to relationships torn to shreds by spiralling reductions of restraint, patience and self-control? True, too much anger in the system is unhealthy, but releasing it often makes angry outbursts more likely in the future.

After all, having responded angrily we will likely trigger an angry response which may in turn make us more angry and, given that we are now in full 'venting' mode, may result in a vicious circle persisting for many hours. In a close relationship there are of course long-lasting effects of this 'release' in terms of stored up feelings of bitterness and resentment in our partner, perhaps involving their desire to revenge our outburst in some way.

Nevertheless it is considered a truism between couples and in families with children that unacceptable behaviour must be deterred by punishment. Most famously it is assumed that smacking children is an unfortunate necessity for instilling discipline and self-control. According to Murray Straus of the Family Research Laboratory at the University of New Hampshire, however, this is exactly wrong: smacking, he reports, is "counter-productive; it makes things worse".[37] A view based on data analysed in 1988 and 1990 from 807 mothers of children aged six to nine, comparing levels of antisocial behaviour among smacked and unsmacked children. The research showed that the more punishment at the beginning of the period, the higher the antisocial behaviour at the end, regardless of traits such as socio-economic status or emotional support. Straus goes on:

> Many people believe if spanking is done by warm and loving parents, it has no harmful side-effects. That turns out not to be true.[38]

Too often the convenient belief that punishment deters bad behaviour has combined with the Freudian fear of restraining anger to the detriment of all concerned.

The point is that we are not simply human pressure cookers; yes, we become angry; yes, anger is unhealthy; but it is not simply an inevitable and indestructible atom of human psychology—the heat can be turned off by compassion for and understanding of the object of our anger.

Ancient Buddhist views support modern research by recognizing these facts, and suggesting a solution. Buddhism does not propose that we merely stand passively by while someone hurls abuse at us, that we merely absorb the abuse stoically without response. Self-restraint involves more than not doing something. For those of us accustomed to getting angry and retaliating, simply 'holding on to ourselves' will last up until about the third or fourth stream of abuse, after which we will no doubt decide enough is enough!

In support, we need to employ a counter force, an antidote, to the other person's anger and our own rising anger. This involves deliberately and very actively generating calm and compassionate thoughts towards a person with whom we are angry, in the understanding that anger necessarily brings with it great suffering for everyone.

Reflections on Kindness

In a marvellous little book entitled *Love and Sympathy in Theravada Buddhism*, Harvey B. Aronson outlines a technique for controlling anger:

> In this technique a practitioner tries to call to mind the pure [kind, generous, compassionate] physical, verbal, or mental activities that have been performed by the current recipient of his hostility. Through this, mindfulness and absence of hatred arise, and one's mind becomes clarified with regard to that person. Due to this mindfulness, absence of hatred, and clarity, the practitioner has a wholesome mind. Since an individual cannot have a wholesome mind and an unwholesome mind at the very same time, establishing a wholesome mind displaces the unwholesomeness.
>
> In practice, one makes the reflection on others' purity familiar by day-to-day repetition, even when one does not feel hostility, for it is of utmost importance that the practitioner experience the full emotive impact of these reflections in the quiet circumstances of daily practice. These reflections must not become empty verbalisations with no personal effect—mere distractions, as it were. When one actually becomes hostile, one then tries to call to mind a pure activity that the other person has performed.[39]

As Aronson intimates, we should not be disappointed if our first attempts to practice this technique in the face of anger ends in comic failure and low farce. As with any new skill, it is important to have patience with ourselves:

In the initial stages of practice, when one's anger is strong and the emotive force of reflection is weak, it often seems that one is failing. It may appear as if reflection has no power, that it has become a futile thought. Nevertheless, if one can maintain the mind on even the mere verbalisation of one's reflections in the heat of a hostile situation, one is training in strengthening mindfulness; it is not that one is having no effect at all in countering hostility. The few moments of mindfulness interspersed in the continuum of anger serve to dispel the anger, and the present moments of mindfulness serve as the causes for deepened mindfulness in the future. Gentle persistence and a tolerance for apparent failure must be maintained. Eventually, one is able to displace anger totally, whereupon one experiences the emotional satisfaction associated with a wholesome mind...

Thus, reflection on another's positive qualities is a method for consciously abandoning anger which, when practised correctly, does not result in physical or mental suffering. It stands as a challenge to those who assert that constraint of unwholesome attitudes necessarily leads to mental or physical damage.[40]

Alternatively we can stave off our own anger by focusing our mind on the self-destructiveness of an angry individual's behaviour by wishing as follows: *meditation*

> May this respectable individual abandon improper physical activities and cultivate proper ones. May he abandon improper verbal activities and cultivate proper ones. May he abandon improper mental activities and cultivate proper ones?[41]

These wishes are made out of concern for the suffering of the angry person—may he or she abandon the agony of anger for his or her own sake. Ideally, the victim of an angry tirade should be able to focus on the suffering inherent to an angry mind, a fact made easier by internally repeating, for example, the following phrases:

> May you be free from danger
> May you have mental happiness
> May you have physical happiness   *meditation*
> May you have ease of well-being

Focusing our minds on the deep unhappiness suffered by our angry individual—rather than on the 'injustice' of their actions and our own suffering and rising fury—can have a remarkable effect both on our own minds and that of our abuser. Our own anger can be dispelled and replaced by compassionate thoughts. The result is that the other person's anger can be met with kindness, calm and self-restraint, in the face of which their own anger cannot long be maintained. As the Buddha said:

> No matter how fiercely a fire [of hatred] burns, when it meets a great river filled with calming waters, it must die out. The fire which blazes within will lose its power when met by self-restraint.[42]

Giving and Taking: Tonglen

Another powerful meditation technique is the sublime tonglen technique of Tibetan Buddhism. Tonglen literally means 'giving and taking', and is intended to strengthen and broaden our capacity for love and compassion. In this technique, we begin by imagining the sufferings of a loved one. For example, we might imagine all the suffering experienced by our mother (or father, sister, brother, husband, wife) in her life: her illnesses, sadness at the death of her parents, spouse, friends; her suffering as she grows old, becomes ill and dies. Having generated compassion at the thought of all this suffering, we then imagine breathing this suffering into our heart in the form of grimy black smoke. As we do this we imagine that all of our greed, hatred, ignorance and self-cherishing are annihilated as our mother's misery is absorbed into our hearts. We then generate the conviction that we are purified of self-cherishing, and also imagine that our mother has been completely purified and is therefore in a state of blissful happiness. We focus on her feelings of happiness as long as we are able.

Subsequently, we imagine sending all our happiness and good qualities to our mother through a stream of light that enters her heart. Again we imagine that this causes feelings of overwhelming joy and happiness in her heart. We then imagine our mother's happiness as we give her everything she could wish for. We imagine, for example, that she is reunited with her parents and other loved ones, that she is young and healthy again, that she has everything she could possibly want and need. Having imagined this, we again focus for as long as possible on her intense feelings of peace, happiness and joy.

Readers will notice that the transition from imagining the great suffering of a loved one, to then imagining the great blissful happiness of the same person in this way, makes for an extraordinarily potent mental technique for generating both compassion and love.

It is of course significant that this focusing on the suffering and happiness of others involves a complete mental departure from obsession with our own desires, problems and suffering. The tonglen technique, if practised successfully, involves the temporary annihilation of our attempt to seek selfish happiness by maximizing pleasure and minimizing pain.

And yet, as the technique allows us to generate powerful feelings of compassion and love, practitioners report that they are filled with great feelings of happiness and tranquillity. The experiential results of this technique alone, therefore, stand as a very real challenge to the Western notion that happiness can be achieved via the pursuit of selfish desires. Instead, they suggest that happiness, tranquillity, contentment and mental health are achievable to the extent that we are compassionate and loving.

If someone insults us, we may well feel a surge of anger. This anger is the result of our self-cherishing, the source, according to Buddhists, of all our suffering. Yet if we reject anger, recognizing that patience and compassion are the source of incomparably greater happiness than any external factor, we may be able to generate compassion for our abuser, and so strengthen our compassion and patience, to our immeasurable benefit.

A remarkable practice of tonglen meditation involves imagining the inevitable sufferings in the lives of our 'enemies' in the same way as for our loved ones. To then mentally take their suffering into ourselves and imagine giving all our happiness and good qualities, say, to the person who has insulted us, filling him or her with great bliss and peace, can have a dramatic effect on the level of anger and hostility we feel towards them.

The significant point is that the source of insult can thus be seen as an actual cause of *good*, not harm—actually as a way of weakening our self-cherishing by testing and strengthening our tonglen meditation, our capacity for compassion. Thus our compassionate response is justified. Here, compassion is far from an indulgence, it is a rational defence of the source of all our happiness: our capacity for compassion, patience and kindness. (For a full explanation of the tonglen meditation, which the present outline is not intended to be, readers may like to refer to *Compassion: The Key To Great Awakening*, by Geshe Tsultim Gyeltsen, Wisdom Books, 1997. Also see *Universal Compassion*, by Geshe Kelsang Gyatso, Tharpa, 1997)

Your Cake: Having it and Eating it!

If our society had not been so adept at suppressing our under-standing of the nature and power of compassion, it would surely be obvious to us that compassion (unaccompanied by righteous anger) is hugely beneficial to both the recipient and practitioner. Aronson makes what should be an obvious point:

> Those who receive loving activities obviously benefit, but those who perform them also experience immediate benefit. Since lov-ing physical, verbal, and mental activities are initiated by a whole-some loving mind, the practitioner performing these activities would immediately experience the benefits associated with this state of mind.[43]

Arguably we Westerners are not very adept at perceiving how we actually feel at any given time. In my view, this is a result of the fact that we have been trained to recognize as real only socially acceptable forms of pleasure and happiness: the consumption of food, commodities, holidays, sex and so on. A concomitant of this is that plenty of what we imagine makes us happy actually has the opposite effect: endless gratuitous consumption at Christmas and on holidays generally, passive consumption of 'entertainment', and so on.

Given the exploitative nature of our social environment, it is hardly a surprise that for many Westerners generosity is experi-enced as an exhausting, agonizing loss ('compassion fatigue'), almost as a threat to be contained—we are terrified of giving some-thing up in case we later regret it.

Yet, if we are able to overcome our conditioning, we can become aware that acts of generosity inspired by kindness have a delightfully positive effect on our state of mind: they actually make us happy! In her excellent and accessible book *Lovingkindness: The Revolutionary Art of Happiness*, which is indeed revolutionary in the best sense of the word, Sharon Salzberg writes:

> Giving brings happiness at every stage of its expression. We expe-rience joy in forming the intention to be generous; we experience

altruism? - how do we purify our acts of giving?

This suggests we do it for 'feel-good' ie reward.

joy in the actual act of giving something; and we experience joy in remembering the fact that we have given.[44]

Yet these facts are apparently beyond the awareness of many, if not most, Westerners. The irony is that giving away money, for example, motivated by a feeling of genuine kindness (rather than duty), often makes us far happier than using that money to reinforce our sense of isolated selfishness. But our culture depends on our clinging to the fiction that getting what we want, rather than giving to other people, is the only way to mental health and happiness. As a result, we resist the kindness and generosity that would otherwise liberate us from much fear, craving, anger and general dissatisfaction. To understand that our happiness truly resides in our capacity for kindness, after all, liberates us from the fear of losing any particular material source of mere pleasure—a fact of potentially enormous significance for what has been termed the 'age of anxiety'.

Moreover, to be compassionate and kind is to be temporarily freed from greed and hatred, for compassionate and selfish states of mind cannot simultaneously coexist. To be free of the suffering associated with negative states of mind is to be happy and, quite apart from anything else, is to generate the kind of mental attitude conducive to working together with other people to change society.

This, indeed, appears to be a case of having our cake and eating it! For, alongside the clear social benefits and the positive experiences reported by practitioners of Buddhist mind training techniques, there is the intriguing evidence of Western medical science.

In *Healing Emotions*, Daniel Goleman argues that there is clear evidence that 'negative' emotions—greedy desire, anger and hatred—are destructive of mental and physical well-being. Goleman summarizes the work of Dr. John Barefoot at the University of North Carolina, who tested people who had symptoms of potentially serious heart disease:

> When they came in for a procedure to measure blockage in the arteries, they were given a psychological test to see how angry they were in general. They were asked, for instance, how often they yelled at their children. The lowest amount of blockage was found in the group that had the least anger, and the people that had the most anger had the highest blockage.[45]

Goleman also cites the work of Dr. Redford Williams at Duke University, who looked at a group of 2,000 factory workers who happened to have taken a test some twenty-five years earlier that included a measure of their level of hostility:

> Of those who had a very low score for anger, up to 20 percent had died. About 30 percent of those with a high level of anger had died, from causes such as heart disease, cancer, other diseases, and from causes not even related to health, such as accidents. This suggests that if you're a chronically angry person, you're one and a half times more likely to die, over a period of twenty-five years, than a person who's not angry.[46]

Elsewhere, summarizing the research in the field, Dr. Herbert Benson, Associate Professor of Medicine at Harvard Medical School argues that compassion is a great source of emotional, but also physical, well-being. Benson reviews the work of Allan Luks:

> In a survey of thousands of volunteers across the nation, Luks discovered that people who help other people consistently report better health than peers in their age group. Many also say that their health markedly improved when they began volunteer work... Ninety-five percent of those he surveyed indicated that helping others on a regular, personal basis gives them a physical, good sensation. Nine out of ten identified specific characteristics of the physical sensation or rush, including a sudden warmth, increased energy, and a sense of euphoria. They also reported long-term effects of greater calm and relaxation. Not only does the act of doing good bring about this helper's high, eight out of ten of the volunteers surveyed said that health benefits returned when they later remembered the helping act.[47]

The "helper's high" and the other beneficial effects are surely related to those experienced by meditators generating compassion for the beings around them. As Benson says, the lessons are clear:

> One of the healthiest things you can do for yourself is to volunteer to help your community, backing away from too much self-worry and fretting. Focusing our attention away from our own problems by helping others, we can experience physical benefits, instead of passively absorbing a deluge of bad news, panic and fear—the physical translation of which is very damaging.[48]

This appears to begin to confirm health benefits claimed by Buddhists for tonglen meditation and other techniques. According to Buddhists, these techniques are a kind of supreme medicine because they have the power to heal mental, physical, social and even environmental sickness (the latter being the result, ultimately, of an excess of selfish greed and lack of compassion).

Greed: the Price of 'Privilege'

It seems a matter of common sense, then, that we should generate a compassionate attitude. Even the tormentors of our world are human beings seeking happiness, and they also have their reasons for acting as they do. When we overcome our anger for them, we can open our minds to their real situation and real suffering.

This, in itself, would be a huge triumph for libertarian ideals, for up to this point we may well have assumed that the rich and powerful were selfish but happy, so that we have been unconsciously reinforcing the delusions we thought we were fighting. We need to understand that, at present, the greedy see no sane alternatives to choose:

> Those unaccustomed to detachment cannot but follow blindly after worldly desires; they see no difference between giving up the world and jumping off a cliff.[49]

People caught in the drive for selfish satisfaction cannot help but follow blindly after their goals. It achieves nothing to rail against the 'moral cowardice' of élites seduced, threatened and selected to think in a specific way. And the reward for their obedience?

> Worldly pleasures tend to destroy everyone, the highest, the middling, and the lowest... Therefore... in order to benefit themselves, the rishis [wise] keep their distance from desires as if from angry serpents.[50]

Note the key point, as discussed, that Buddhists do not at all perceive as privileges the rewards that drive this élite filtering process. These "tend to destroy everyone, the highest, the middling and the lowest", which is why the wise keep away from them. For Buddhism, it is one of the deluding effects of the pursuit of "worldly desires" to imagine that wealth and privilege constitute happiness.

Understanding the wounding nature of selfish living presents the possibility of transcending what otherwise appears to be an

intractable class war: if it is true that we can look deeper and see
that both rich and poor are united by suffering in a society based
on greed and violence, then the possibilities for change appear infi-
nite. If compassion really does form the only viable basis of our
own happiness and well-being, then, despite all appearances, there
would be no losers from revolutionary change, and no one to fight
or resist. Yes, there are ruthless, shameless exploiters, but there is
more to them than this:

> Alas for those shameless ones who, in the name of expediency,
> oppress humanity and extend amorality. I do not see that such
> actions have gained you either pleasure or joy.[51]

The key point here is not blame of the "shameless ones", but the
vital observation that such actions bring them neither pleasure nor
joy. Again, a notion in remarkable contrast to our own casual conviction that the greedy are happy, living lives of luxury: a view supported as much by dissident anger as media advertising and
propaganda.

Time and again, Buddhist texts emphasize the same point: it is
not just that selfish actions carried out in the name of expediency
oppress humanity and extend immorality, they also bring disaster to
those who carry them out. Of the Buddha, it is said:

> He understood that worldly pleasures can never give true satisfac-
> tion—that they are attended by the suffering of greed, quarrels,
> wars, and a host of other evils; that worldly pleasures are forever
> threatened by the fear of loss from acts of kings or thieves, from
> water, fire, one's enemies, and so forth. Therefore, avoiding worldly
> pleasures like poison and longing for Truth, he cut off his fair hair
> and beard, and exchanged the brilliant dress of a householder for
> the saffron robes of an ascetic.[52]

According to Buddhism, then, the horrors of our world are a kind
of terrible farce: the rich torture and oppress the poor for the sake
of selfish pleasures which bring them only misery, despair and bitterness. Utterly deluded by greed, the rich reject this suggestion
out of hand, just as they reject the idea that they are torturing the
poor for profit. The rich, then, are as ignorant of the suffering they
inflict on themselves as they are of the suffering they inflict on
other people:

Such is the way of the world: Like foolish moths drawn to a flickering light, people are lured by the prospect of riches. Little by little, the suffering they cannot bear erodes their integrity, until one day they fall, deluded by their desire. Take pity on this man, and restrain your anger.[53]

This "man" being none other than the average Third World tyrant, media mogul, corporate boss—these are the proper objects of our pity, our compassion. But for the torrent of deceptions from our propaganda system, it would be an obvious truth that selfishness, egotism, indifference to the fate of others, overweening ambition in pursuit of status and power, result in a devastated, embittered existence. We see it all around us: the fate of our wealthy celebrities provides anecdotal evidence every day of the cost of abandoning compassion for self-centredness.

Even when suffering unbearable agony, those lost in desire and hatred cannot identify the true source of their suffering, preferring instead to strike out at enemies presumed to be responsible. Though the real enemy is their own greed and ignorance, the powerful will leap at the chance to blame and vilify oppressed people who seek change.

Beyond the delusions of greed lies the truth: that a life of greed and hatred is a life of misery.

From Animal Rights to Human Rights—and Back Again

As we have discussed, for Buddhists all creatures are deserving of our kindness. Even if we do not always feel able to resist eating them, or exterminating them from our crops, the goal is that we should strive to be as kind as we are able to all beings. Buddhists, we should be clear, are not joking—they mean *all* beings. For example, sympathy for the gnat is urged:

Look at the tiny gnat. See him wringing his hands, wringing his feet.[54]

And ants should not be overlooked:

We must not ignore the population of ants, thinking that they are excluded: they are not.[55]

The Buddhist view is of particular interest at the present time as debate rages over the possible banning of fox hunting, indeed the hunting of all mammals.

The motivation of people in favour of such a ban is subject to considerable speculation. Writing in the *Guardian*, Henry Porter suggests that:

> At the back of our minds is the ruddy-faced squire and master of hounds trundling across the land in pursuit of the scared little fox, scattering all in his path. As an object of common loathing, he has a very old history... To eliminate hunting would be to eliminate the mounted arrogance of a certain class of people.[56]

Porter takes this analysis a step further, implying that, at heart, opponents are really upset because they hate the thought of people they dislike enjoying hunting:

> It is only when you know that people are taking some enjoyment from an activity that your interest picks up and you begin to make all sorts of judgements about the desirability of that enjoyment and the kinds of people who take part.

The bottom line being that

> people who enjoy such a sport are not as they should be and they must be brought into line.

Certainly it is natural enough that our interest should pick up when people gain enjoyment from an activity that involves an animal being torn limb from limb: the human capacity for deriving pleasure from the suffering of other people and animals is after all one of nature's more disturbing phenomena. Concern in the face of this activity cannot be cited as an example of some kind of killjoy tendency. It is, anyway, the suffering of the animal rather than the pleasure of the people that is surely the root of concern.

Porter decries this concern as "a rather hypocritical desire", on the grounds that, as a nation, we "ignore the palpable terror of the slaughterhouse."

In reality, as the BSE crisis has illustrated so well, we can't ignore what we don't know about. Also, occasional articles and documentaries can hardly compete with the advertising and communications propaganda of the farming industry. The deeper point is that anyone seeking to reform an exploitative and brutal society necessarily starts out a hypocrite. We are all 'part of the system', as taxpayers, road-users, company workers: to work for what should be is always to contradict our inevitable role in what is. This is not a fault, it is unavoidable. Moreover, assuming that it is good to be kind, then the argument that it is wrong to seek to be a little kinder if we cannot be perfectly kind, makes little sense.

But what are the rights and wrongs of this and related issues? Why is it wrong to gain pleasure from the suffering of animals? If we are to answer these questions rationally, we need to look in some depth at the issue of suffering, and the significance of our indifference, cruelty or compassion in the face of suffering.

Earlier, we reviewed some aspects of the suffering endured by animals in the modern factory farming system. The cruelty is enormous. But so what? We have to eat, insects have to be cleared from crops, anglers want to have their fun. Maybe we feel revulsion, but is there any merit in it? What benefit could result from acting on our revulsion?

According to a commonly held animal rights view, the very question is invalid—it is a matter not of benefits but of rights. In his recent book *The Price of Meat*, environmental journalist Danny Penman writes:

> Modern animal-rights philosophy is based on the belief that animals are sufficiently like humans for their interests to be taken into account.[57]

The argument is that if humans are considered inherently valuable, then animals possessing characteristics similar to those considered to be defining of human life should be judged of similar value. Specifically, humans have a memory of the past; they are capable of planning for the future; they have a capacity for rational thought; they feel pain and experience emotions. Animals which also have these capabilities should be accorded rights: "If there are no *morally significant* differences between an animal and a human", Penman argues (paraphrasing Professor Andrew Linzey), "then an animal has rights that should be respected." [58]

If not, then discriminating against non-humans is merely a kind of speciesism: a prejudice based, not on skin colour or sex, but on other morally insignificant features like the number of legs they walk on, or how they happen to feed. Penman and others argue that rights for higher animals should therefore be considered for reasons of "logical consistency",[59] if nothing else.

This idea of logical consistency as a basis for morality is a peculiar one, and a peculiarly Western one at that. In reality, it is not for reasons of logical consistency that we feel mortified at the sight of a Vietnamese soldier being shot through the head at point-blank range by a South Vietnamese general: 'I would feel sorry for myself, therefore it is only right that I should feel sorry for that similar individual over there'. We feel mortified because we feel spontaneous compassion for the terror and the suffering, for the extinction of hope and happiness. Most of us are filled with a strong desire that other people and animals should not suffer unnecessarily; sometimes we would risk our own lives to save them from suffering.

The reaction is emotional rather than logical, although of course compassion is strongly modified by what we believe. For example, if we feel a certain creature has no feelings, or that certain people 'deserve' their fate, then we may well not feel compassion, and may even be jubilant at the sight of suffering.

The point surely is that a creature may be of extremely limited intelligence, with no capacity to plan, no memory, no thoughts and ideas, with almost nothing in common with human beings at all, but if we are aware that it has the capacity to suffer, then that is all we need to feel compassion for that creature. It is not the issue of rights that is our primary concern—let alone logical consistency with regards to them—but the desire for an end to suffering.

Accepting compassion as the basis of animal and human rights answers the challenge sometimes levelled against both, based on reciprocity. In other words, rights must be mutually granted to be valid: if you don't respect my rights I don't need to respect yours. Thus John Mortimer writes:

> One sure thing about foxes is that they have absolutely no concern for animal rights. No one who has found their chickens slaughtered, for entertainment not food, or seen lambs with their stomachs torn out, doubts that foxes have to be controlled. Whether they are trapped, poisoned, shot or killed by a dog would seem, to a visitor from Mars, to be a question of no great moral or political significance.[60]

It is the same argument beloved of tabloid newspapers reporting the actions of human criminals: if they fail to show compassion, then we need not feel compassion for them. Yet, as we have discussed, it is in just these testing situations that our capacity to remain compassionate gains supreme moral and political significance.

First, it should be clear that our compassion for another person or animal should not be conditional on their level of kindness. If I understand the reasons underlying vicious human behaviour—violent abuse as a child, poverty, mental illness—I might well feel great compassion for that person regardless of their cruelty. Likewise, I do not wish a creature to suffer more because it has been less kind, and I certainly do not wish an animal to suffer more, or less, according to the relative cruelty (by my interpretation) of its instinctual programming. I do not, after all, feel less compassion for a carnivorous lion dying an agonizing death than for an herbivorous lamb. Mortimer seems to hold animals responsible for their instincts.

Instinct aside, in the real world, the cruelty of an individual says nothing about the appropriateness of a compassionate response. If we decide that compassion is at the heart of personal and social well-being, then arguably it is much *more* important to respond compassionately to a cruel individual or creature, because it is just here that our compassion is tested. From this perspective, it is the very fact of a person or animal's cruelty that means we should try particularly hard to respond compassionately. By so doing, we stop the cycle of hatred and also strengthen our own capacity for compassion.

So what of the gnat "wringing his hands", in the Buddhist quotation above. Why, as an individual perhaps concerned above all with human rights, or perhaps above all with my own rights, should I care about it? From the Penman perspective cited above, I may presume that it is logically consistent for me to accord the gnat no rights whatsoever: it is sufficiently dissimilar from me for it to be disqualified from entitlement to human rights. As an animal rights activist I may therefore ignore its fate. So why not allow a gnat drowning in the meniscus of a glass of water to simply drown?

The problem is that the gnat's waterlogged wings are lying flat in the water, trapped by the surface tension; its legs are moving frantically, trying to escape from the water. I know the gnat is suffering, that (at whatever level) it desires life and an end to suffering, and I would like it not to suffer. But even if I fished the gnat out, surely such compassion for such a tiny creature is of no consequence in the grand scheme of things. So why bother?

The intriguing answer, as we have seen, is that:

All the joy the world contains
Has come through wishing happiness for others

All the misery the world contains
Has come through wanting pleasure for oneself.[61]

So where does this leave the issue of animal rights generally? Why be kind to a gnat, or a pig, or a fox, or any other creature? Because they qualify for human rights by dint of their similarity?

From a Buddhist perspective, the real motivation is that being kind to anyone and anything is as beneficial for us as individuals as it is for the gnat, and as it is for everyone around us. From an immediate personal perspective, generating a compassionate mind means we are temporarily freed from the suffering of selfish thinking, the frustration of greed and hatred. Furthermore, we will have set down a kind of mental track that will make it easier for kindness to pass that way again in the future. Also, we will have set an example of kindness and restraint that will have ripple effects throughout society.

In a sense, then, it is indeed logically consistent to treat other creatures as we would treat human beings: not because human beings are more deserving of kindness, but because treating human beings with kindness makes us and everyone around us happy, as does treating foxes, pigs and insects in the same way. Animal rights are not a sentimental diversion from human rights, or should not be—concern for both is justified and united by the understanding that happiness is rooted in compassion for all living beings.

Chapter Seven

GENEROSITY IS DISSENT

Humble Daisy
Form a chain to hold all battleships in check
Humble Daisy
Knit a ladder down to nature's sunken wreck.
—from the song 'Humble Daisy' by Andy Partridge

"What Then Must We Do?"

As we begin to become aware of the true scale and causes of suffering, we quickly find ourselves confronted by the central question of what we as individuals can do in the face of the vast problems facing us: What can we do to make a difference?

There is, I think, more to this question than meets the eye. If Westerners were as intent on kindly behaviour as this question suggests, the question itself would surely be redundant—good causes in need of urgent assistance are hardly in short supply or difficult to find. In full, the real question perhaps should read: 'Is there some way I can reconcile my desire for personal happiness with my desire to do something about the suffering and destructiveness that afflicts our world?' That is 'I want to do something but not at the expense of my own happiness. How, then, can I find the motivation?'

The problem of motivation is surely resolved by the Buddhist conception of compassion. When we realize that a compassionate life dedicated to relieving the suffering of others is also far more conducive to our own happiness than a life of self-destructive greed, then we have discovered the motivation, the means and the goal.

The standard Western objection to seeking to 'do something' is, of course, the assertion that the problems facing us are just too big, too entrenched for us to be able to make any real difference. Why support Amnesty International by writing letters to despots in Tibet, when the world is anyway overflowing with torture and misery? Why campaign to protect the environment, when greed is so entrenched and so ably assisted by corporate power? Why try to reform the factory-farming system when every year hundreds of millions of animals are killed or die of natural causes all over the world? Why do any of these things, when all of us are doomed to grow ill and die—that is, to suffer? What is the point of doing something kind when the world is awash with pain?

Another similar objection, as we have discussed, is the idea that to seek to be a little kinder without being a perfect saint is hypocritical: to stop swatting flies while continuing to eat meat, for example. But whether or not we can become fully enlightened beings, or whether the world can be turned into some kind of utopia, is beside the point. The Buddhist assertion is that by reducing our selfishness and increasing our compassion and kindness we will make life better for ourselves and those around us. We do not refuse to keep ourselves clean because the world is full of unwashed bodies or because we will someday die. We wash because it is conducive to our current and future health and happiness. So, too, generosity and kindness can wash away some of the self-destructive selfishness and cruelty from our minds to the benefit of all. The difference is that, unlike physical washing, as we practice compassion we can become better at it, stronger, more all-inclusive, with increasing benefits for everyone.

The answer to the question of what we should actually do is found in the nature of the problems facing us, which fall into two categories. Firstly, the ultimate source of the destruction of the Third World and environment is in the individual human tendency to greed, hatred and ignorance. Secondly, these destructive forces have become institutionalized in political, economic and media forces which depend upon the promotion of these same forces for their survival. Both aspects of the problem need to be tackled simultaneously. As Stephen Batchelor writes of Buddhism:

> The contemporary social engagement of dharma practice is rooted in awareness of how self-centred confusion and craving can no longer be adequately understood only as psychological drives that manifest themselves in subjective states of anguish. We find these drives embodied in the very economic, military, and political structures that influence the lives of the majority of people on earth.[1]

I agree that if we are serious about the relief of suffering, we need to combat greed, hatred and ignorance as manifested in ourselves as individuals but also as manifested in these institutions. The two tasks are inseparable: understanding the goals and nature of the institutions of power is a key factor in combating greed, hatred and ignorance in ourselves. For example, to rely on the corporate media for a credible source of views about the world is to lay ourselves open to massive indoctrination: we will be critically and compassionately disabled by political deceptions such as the notion that we are free, that the West supports human rights around the world, that real action is already being taken to protect the environment. We will also be ensnared by deep personal deceptions such as the idea that unrestrained satisfaction of personal desires is conducive to our happiness, to social harmony, environmental security and the economic well-being of our country. Trained to stand in awe of our 'superiors' and experts generally, we may well have great difficulty taking ourselves seriously, and the idea that we might have some role to play will strike us as an embarrassing and presumptuous fantasy.

An ability to appreciate the true nature and drives of corporate capitalist institutions frees us from the business-friendly version of reality, allowing us to take a genuinely critical look at the nature of what is and is not conducive to happiness and social reform. We can come to appreciate, for example, that the idea that a more compassionate society is 'impractical' and 'unrealistic' from an economic point of view, is a deception designed to perpetuate inequality.

The Myth of 'Tough Love': Sacrifice, Ancient and Modern
In his book *The Buddha*, Trevor Ling notes that the brahmanical sacrificial system into which the Buddha was born was based on the idea that the world "was kept in existence, and the important aims of human life were achieved, by the operation of the sacrifice".[2]

Because the brahmans alone understood how the sacrifice was to be effectively performed, they deemed it their duty to perform this task and consequently considered themselves to be the most essential class in society.

Both of these claims were rejected by the Buddha. He is said to have criticized the tradition of sacrifice "on the grounds of economic wastefulness, cruelty to animals, forced labour, with harsh treatment of the labourers, and oppressive taxation of the people in order to pay for it all."[3]

Buddhists have rightly argued that this attitude to sacrifice is indicative of the Buddha's rationalism, his rejection of all unfounded superstition. We could also interpret his rejection in another way, however, by considering the practice of sacrifice in the modern context.

After all, is not our entire social, economic and political system built on the idea of the need for sacrifice? We are all of us aware that our nation is filled with poor, disadvantaged people, and families struggling to survive. We know also that the world's 358 billionaires possess as much wealth as 45 per cent of the world's population. We know that a billion people are living in abject poverty, suffering the effects of starvation, disease and other miseries. So why do we not do something to help those who need help?

Because, as in the Buddha's time, we are told (and convinced) that the world is kept in existence, that the important aims of human life are achieved, by an economic and political system dependent on this necessary sacrifice. To tinker with this system too much, to spend too much on the poor, to spend too much on housing, education and health, would bring the whole structure crashing down. It is possible, we are told, to be too kind: compassion for all would simply lead to disaster.

Thus Britain's role as a supplier of £5 billion worth of arms a year, constituting almost a quarter of total world sales (22.1 per cent to be precise, second only to the United States) is defended on the basis of the need to preserve 'jobs' (actually profits), regardless of the possibilities of conversion to peaceful production and the complete moral redundancy of an argument that pits lives against jobs. After disingenuously declaring that Labour would put "human rights at the heart of our foreign policy",[4] Foreign Secretary Robin Cook announced that "the government is committed to the maintenance of a strong defence industry, which is a strategic part of our industrial base...",[5] which, of course, puts arms manufacturers' profits at the heart of our foreign policy.

Corporate attempts to block limits on greenhouse gas emissions are ultimately based on the same notion of the need to sacrifice others for the sake of 'jobs' and 'economic growth' (for which read, once again, profits). Similarly, in Britain, cuts are being made in single parent benefits, with further cuts planned for disabled people. These cuts are said to be necessary to stop the welfare budget spiralling out of control and stifling the economy.

The basic principle at work throughout is the idea that some people just have to be sacrificed, that not everyone can be treated compassionately if basic stability and prosperity are to be maintained.

It is exactly this idea that the Buddha rejected. His insistence was always that happiness could not be built on the suffering of others:

> Don't try to build your happiness on the unhappiness of others. You will be enmeshed in a net of hatred.[6]

As we have seen, the Buddhist view is that individual happiness can only be based on the promotion of happiness for all.

In one tale of the Buddha's former lives, the Buddha-to-be is said to have ruled over a land afflicted by great drought and disaster. In the tale, ministers and religious advisers insist that a large sacrifice, that is 'tough love', is required to save the people (that is, 'our industrial base'). The Buddha is unimpressed; he might almost have been referring to our own political and economic leaders when he says:

> Truly, those who are proclaimed the best refuge among men are often those who do the most harm, all in the name of religion [in our time, 'national prosperity'!]. Alas for any who follow such a path, for they end in desperate straits, surrounded by the evils they think to avoid! What connection can there possibly be between virtuous behaviour and the killing of animals? [7]

Instead, the Buddha had a different kind of sacrifice in mind:

> The protection of my subjects has always been my highest aim. Now... my people have themselves become worthy to receive the gifts of sacrifice... Let anyone who seeks to fuel his happiness by wealth come and accept all he wishes from my hand.[8]

As a result of his great kindness and generosity, "all his subjects grounded their lives in virtue, and the powers of evil faded away." [9] For how could a nation not prosper where the people were inspired by an example of generosity on this scale?:

> The people of that land indeed enjoyed the wonders of a Golden Age, for their practice of virtue, self-control, good conduct, and modesty continued unabated. The strength of the king's sacrifice, performed in accordance with the spirit of the law, put an end to the sufferings of the poor. The country teemed with a thriving and happy populace...[10]

Significantly for our own time, the story notes that this revolution in generosity and virtue also had the effect of resolving all environmental problems: "The seasons succeeded one another in due course, gladdening everyone with their regularity. The earth produced all kinds of food in abundance." [11]

This is a kind of deep libertarian view, arguing that the growth of compassionate values in society has effects that go far beyond what we might immediately expect or imagine, even to the point of healing the environment. These profound effects, though hard to divine and impossible to quantify, are very real, and the same is true for individual acts of compassion. Superficially, giving money to other—maybe unknown—people might seem a kind of waste. But the effects of such actions on our lives can go far beyond merely having less money to spend. To be consistently more generous will radically affect the kind of thoughts and emotions we experience, the kind of impression we make on other people, the kind of reception we receive, the kind of relationships we develop. According to Buddhism, the same is equally true for whole societies and their relationship with their environments.

This deep libertarian view rejects the idea that suffering is an unfortunate necessity that must be tolerated. No one needs to be sacrificed for some spurious notion of 'stability', or 'strategic' necessity. The stability that exists in our own time is stability for a wealthy few, and chaotic instability for the rest of us. Stability nowadays means maintaining state and corporate pipelines of exploitation, stifling critical thought and compassion with ceaseless propaganda, and the systematic repression of impoverished, men, women and children in the Third World. This is the stability of a prison regime.

Real personal, social and global environmental stability can only be rooted in a commitment to kindness and compassion for all. If only one of those 358 billionaires learned this lesson, it would do more than will ever be achieved by a thousand benefit cuts, a million 'welfare to work' schemes. The world is not maintained by economic management alone: it is maintained by kindness and compassion. To strengthen that understanding and commitment is to improve and strengthen all human relations, including economic relations, immeasurably.

Generosity and Dissent

We have discussed how power has a vested interest in promoting a cynical view of human nature, suggesting that happiness and selfishness are compatible, indeed that human beings are incapable of rising above selfish concerns. It therefore strikes a great blow for freedom and true democracy when we question such assumptions, when we investigate, say, the issue of generosity from a Buddhist perspective:

> Generosity is a great treasure. No thief can steal it, no fire destroy it, no water can ruin it, no king can command it. Generosity cleanses the mind of selfishness and greed, relieving our weariness as we travel through life. It is our best and closest friend, constantly giving pleasure and comfort.[12]

The logic of generosity is that it helps maintain a mental environment conducive to the happiness of ourselves and the people around us. By being generous, we are keeping our minds free from the initially sweet, but finally long and painful habit of self-centredness.

There is a strange, disabling Western notion that giving would only be truly worthwhile if total altruism were possible. We tend to see displays of generosity as simply another kind of selfishness: there is always some greedy ulterior motive (ego, status, self-righteousness, pay-back). We imagine this because we believe the giver receives no personal benefit from the act of giving itself, and so we perceive no genuine motivation for giving. Therefore there must be some selfish agenda underlying any pretence of kindness. So while we are feigning concern, in fact we are simply dressing up our selfishly motivated mutton as altruistic lamb—every time we are kind, we are, as it were, just politicians picking up babies. In which case isn't it more honest simply to dispense with such pretence and be openly selfish and self-centred? As usual, Buddhism is well aware of these objections and counters them with ease:

> Generosity is associated with a wholesome mind, and though one might not have a wholesome mind during every moment of an act of almsgiving, one would for some moments. Since a wholesome mind is associated with the feeling of either happiness or equanimity and is completely devoid of mental suffering, an individual who naturally maintains or makes efforts to maintain the wholesome mind associated with acts of generosity benefits immediately.[13]

It is not necessary that our acts of generosity be entirely altruistic; indeed the understanding that we also gain from giving is a major motivation to begin experimenting with increased generosity.

Even though an act of giving might seem to us to be contaminated by selfish motivation, we will still be promoting elements of compassion and equanimity that are of great benefit to us. Through these acts, we can gradually develop and strengthen our capacity for generosity.

The relationship between generosity and dissent is simple: dissent is one of the most important and powerful kinds of generosity. Such dissident generosity is a source of great well-being for both dissidents and those around them. To weaken the force of the illusions that permeate society, even to a small extent, is to relieve suffering somewhat. In this situation, everything we do counts. To even gain a basic understanding of the destructive nature of anger and greed, or an understanding of the benefits of generosity, is an act of generosity. Why? Because an understanding of the truth of anger, for example, will reduce the anger in our lives, to the benefit of those around us.

Guess Who's Coming to Dinner?

In the light of the fact that so many have been persuaded to see generosity and kindness as a loss and a sacrifice, acts of kindness can have a dramatic effect on cynical people who have been deprived of inspiring examples. This is communicated with wonderful effect in the mythical Jataka tales. In one of them, the future Buddha promises to return to the lair of a flesh-eating ogre and sacrifice his life out of compassion for others, including the ogre himself. The ogre is the embodiment of the cynicism we see all around us, symbolic of the utter contempt so many people have for even the idea that human beings can be genuinely compassionate and courageous:

> Do you expect me to believe such nonsense? It goes beyond belief! Who, once released from the jaws of Death, would willingly return there? [14]

As a kind of sport, the ogre agrees to let the Buddha go: "Well, then, go ahead. We will see your great truthfulness in action, we will see how you keep your promises. We will see your great righteousness." [15]

And yet the Buddha does return, and not merely in order to keep his promise but in the hope of actually helping the monster who "deserves only pity, who is immersed in the mire of wicked habits… and has no one left to protect him". [16]

Astonished by this display of compassion and courage, the ogre, surrounded by the half-consumed and decaying corpses of previous victims, is sufficiently impressed so that "not even his cruel nature, however deeply rooted in his defiled mind, could prevent him from thinking: 'Ah! Ah! Wonder of wonders! Truly a miracle!... To me, a man as cruel as Death, he returns of his own free will, without fear or anxiety. What constancy!" [17]

To be sure, the ogre is not immediately converted by the Buddha's compassionate actions and words. Coyly, he announces: "I am in no hurry to eat you. What's more, this funeral pyre is still smoking, and flesh isn't worth eating unless it's roasted on a smokeless fire. Tell me some more..." [18]

On hearing more of the Buddha's gentle words, something remarkable happens: the ogre is moved to tears. And there is more:

> The hairs of his body stood on end; the darkness of his wicked nature vanished. Looking with reverence on the Bodhisattva, he exclaimed: 'Beware! May evil be averted! O foremost of princes, may those who wish evil on beings such as you wilfully swallow the poison of Halahala. [19]

It is an awesome story, with awesome implications for our own time. Indeed, it is far more than just a story. It is an attempt to revolutionize our entire attitude to the world and, through us, to revolutionize that world. It tells us that insolence, cruelty, cynicism and brutality of the most outrageous kinds really can be subdued by compassion and reason, that these really do have the power to dispel the "Terror of the World".

Here, personal belief and personal action can clearly be seen to be political—if we take the system of concentrated power as a whole, even a small act of kindness *here* loosens the grip on society of cynicism, selfishness, hatred and greed slightly *there*, which in turn loosens the grip of corporate capitalism on our minds, the Third World and the environment. While dissidents are sometimes critical of Buddhists for being apolitical, it is in fact not possible to be entirely apolitical: the 2,000 or more Buddhist centres in the United States, for example, are 'doing something' to combat the greed, hatred and ignorance on which the madness of corporate capitalism absolutely depends.

If illusions are responsible for suffering, then what greater kindness can there be, what greater act of generosity, than combating those illusions by whatever peaceful means? To even sit down and spend our time discussing these ideas together is a kind of generosity, a kind of giving.

Consider the advice of a Tibetan Buddhist sage:

> If somebody uses very harsh words against you at some time, and you don't return them and instead, if you are able to smile at it, then suddenly that makes it less heavy for that person. That will reduce the whole intensity of the anger. For our part, it is a wonderful thing, to be able to accept that kind of defeat gracefully, because even though it is a defeat in that moment, in a true sense it is a victory on our part. In the Eight Verses on Thought Training by Langri Tangpa it says, 'To be able to accept a defeat on our part and offer the victory to the other is one of our practices.' [20]

To be insulted and not retaliate, as Gyeltsin makes clear, is a kind of defeat, but it is a defeat that is simultaneously a great victory for us and for the forces of freedom and happiness. By absorbing hatred, restraining ourselves and meditating on compassion and kindness (see the previous chapter and also Sharon Salzberg's book *Lovingkindness: The Revolutionary Art of Happiness*) we have taken that hatred out of the system.

Or consider Joseph Campbell's words:

> Social pressure is the enemy! I've seen it happen. How in heaven's name are you going to find your own track if you are always doing what society tells you to do? I also spent a year teaching in a boys' prep school and that was a crowd that was trying to make up their minds, you know? I've seen them since and those who followed their zeal, their bliss, they have led decent, wonderful lives; those who did what Dad said they should do because it's safe found out it's not safe. It's disaster. [21]

For many people, particularly young people on the point of leaving school or college, these words are an act of enormous generosity. What Joseph Campbell meant by "following your bliss" is that we should follow what gives us deep and lasting satisfaction, as opposed to short-term sweetness and long-term misery. In my view, to follow your bliss is simply to follow the hunches that we all sense: that compassion, kindness, generosity, and tender-heartedness are indeed the true sources of bliss.

To encourage people to think for themselves is one and the same thing as recommending that people follow their bliss: it is mindless obedience, believing what we are told, that persuades us to ignore the suffering of the self-centred soul. It also persuades us to overlook the tremendous happiness we gain from truly helping someone, truly relieving someone's suffering, as somehow unimportant and unreal. To encourage young people to think for themselves is an act of great kindness and generosity which, again, is not compatible with the systems of power that stand over us.

In contrast to these examples, it seems to me that the promotion of cynicism, selfishness, greed, hatred and confusion, that are staples of most media commentary and advertising, are acts of great unkindness.

Conclusion: On the Magic Mountain

We began this book with an indication of the true causes at work behind the holocaust currently overtaking the people of Algeria. With this tragedy again very much in mind, let us conclude by turning to consider an individual by the name of Hans Castorp, standing utterly alone, high in the Swiss Alps where, we might almost imagine, "among twenty snowy mountains, the only moving thing was the eye of the blackbird." [22]

And perhaps not even that. The stillness and silence of this, the Magic Mountain of Thomas Mann's imagination, was such, Mann tells us, that Castorp "would halt for a moment, to quench the sound of his own movement, when the silence about him would be absolute, complete, a wadded soundlessness, as it were, elsewhere all unknown."

It was almost as if Castorp had indeed wandered onto a magic mountain—one paradoxically emptied of all the illusion and nonsense of the world. A void, perhaps, into which something real could enter. If so, the silence, we are told, seemed to portend something less than pleasant:

> No, this world of limitless silences had nothing hospitable; it received the visitor at his own risk, or rather it scarcely even received him, it tolerated his penetration into its fastnesses, in a manner that boded no good... [23]

But Castorp was courageous, and eager for a challenge. He, a mythical hero in the classical mould, "was bound to no path, none lay behind him to take him back whence he had come. At first there had been posts, staves set up as guides through the snow—but he had soon cut free from their tutelage, which... seemed inconsistent with the attitude he had taken up toward the wild." [24]

Indeed, for some reason unknown even to him, it seems, Castorp had "deliberately set out to lose his way".[25] An objective fully realized with the arrival of a giant, and potentially fatal, snow storm which bursts with such ferocity that all visibility and even his breath are torn away from him.

Half-frozen and delirious from the cold, Castorp stumbles in a futile circle around the mountain eventually chancing upon a small, locked hay hut where he takes shelter against a wall. There, foolishly, he takes several fortifying swigs from his hip flask. His tenuous hold on reality is soon broken completely, and he finds himself engulfed in a hallucination of startling intensity and clarity.

Standing in a swirl of snowflakes by his little hut, he gazes out at a breath-taking paradise of deep blue southern seas, at a beautiful bay enclosed by mountains, with white houses gleaming among palm trees and cypress groves. The preternatural beauty of it all, Mann tells us, is "too much, too blest for sinful mortals".[26]

Castorp finds human creatures of equally astonishing beauty populating this dream world. "How joyous and winning they are, how fresh and healthy, happy and clever they look!" But it is not merely their outward appearance that beguiles him: "They seem to be wise and gentle through and through." [27]

It is as if Castorp has stumbled on utopia, the perfect harmony of humanity and nature. But then he catches the eye of someone different, an individual, like Castorp, "apart from his companions". This boy looks directly at Castorp and then past him, and "in his gaze there came a solemnity... which gave the scarcely reassured Castorp a thorough fright". Following the direction of the boy's gaze, Castorp spies a huge and forbidding temple.

With a heavy heart, following an inner compulsion, Castorp rises and enters the temple. Inside, the sight awaiting him is almost enough to make his knees give way. For, here, far from the appearance of sunlit perfection outside, lies the truth on which this dream world is somehow built:

> Two grey old women, witchlike... were busy there, between flaming braziers, most horribly. They were dismembering a child. In dreadful silence they tore it apart with their bare hands—Hans Castorp saw the bright hair blood-smeared—and cracked the tender bones

between their jaws, their dreadful lips dripped blood. An icy coldness held him. He would have covered his eyes and fled, but could not.[28]

He would have covered his eyes, as so many of us would, and do. But is it not exactly this that the heroic Castorp, "bound by no paths", has deliberately set out to lose his way for: the truth?

Could there be a more accurate set of symbols to describe the reality of our own world? Our society, too, gives every appearance of being "wise and gentle through and through". We, too, are supposed to be healthy and happy in our corporate wage slavery. And as we have seen, the truth of Third World suffering is very much the stuff of Castorp's nightmare: our society is built on suffering in exactly this way.

Castorp—that is, Mann—interprets the meaning of his dream in this way:

Love stands opposed to death. It is love, not reason, that is stronger than death.[29]

But surely love is the greatest inspiration and protector of reason. It is love and compassion that help us overcome the greed and hatred that blinker our desire to see the true effects of our actions. It is love and compassion that lend us the motivation to plunge through metaphorical snowdrifts, freezing half to death in a world at war with the 'unnecessary overhead' of compassion, in order to try to identify and remove the true causes of the suffering of those around us. Equally, as we have also seen, angry dissent, reason without compassion for all, is a cure that kills.

If reason rooted in love and compassion stands opposed to death, then reason based on mere self-interest may well actually collude with the forces of death. To be successful in this culture, it is not necessary to round on official enemies as in days of old, it is necessary merely to stay within the bounds of respectability. There is leeway, of sorts: sadistic violence and pornography of the most freakish kinds are respectable, indeed celebrated as art. Yet the questioning of the accepted, business-friendly status quo is considered 'extreme' and 'offensive'.

The point is that it is up to us, and no one else: we can direct our efforts, meagre though we might (falsely) imagine them to be, to attempting to reduce the suffering of others, or we can seek our fortune and leisure by merely attempting to entertain and be entertained. As Ken Saro-Wiwa pointed out, this is not nearly enough:

> In this country [Britain] writers write to entertain, they raise questions of individual existence—you know the angst of the individual—but for a Nigerian writer in my position you can't go into that...You cannot have art for art's sake. This art must do something to transform the lives of a community, of a nation.[30]

We can fritter away our lives in self-centred careerism if we like, fixing our blinkered gaze on the blue sea, bay and little white houses of paradise-pretend, but we will never find much interest, happiness or fulfilment here. We will find what we call 'meaninglessness', which, if we did but know it, is the name we give to the oppressive atmosphere that gathers in a life dedicated to the pursuit of selfish happiness. No surprise, then, that the more 'successful' we become in this pursuit, the closer we come to the terrible pointlessness of it all. By contrast, 'meaning' is the name we give to the feeling that fills our lives and relationships when we know we are engaged in at least trying to do something to relieve the suffering of others.

We tend to imagine freedom solely in terms of our ability to satisfy our personal needs. But this is a very limited kind of freedom. Materially free, we may still be dragged through bushes backwards by selfish desires, imprisoned in the solitary confinement of hatred, shut away in the half-light of self-deceptions—deceptions which are a necessity for all who cannot face the fact that the price of the few consuming everything they could possibly want, is the denial of the most basic needs of the many who produce it.

Compassion allows us to recognize that, paradoxically, freedom and happiness can only be won when we work for the freedom and happiness of others. Every time any one of us understands this, truly the world is shaken by a compassionate revolution.

> Conquer anger through gentleness, unkindness through kindness, greed through generosity, and falsehood by truth. Be truthful; do not yield to anger. Give freely, even if you have little. The gods will bless you.[31]

References

Preface
1. Howard Zinn, *The Zinn Reader*, p.506.
2. Shantideva, *The Way of the Bodhisattva*, pp.36-37.
3. Zhechen Gyaltsab and Padma Gyurmed Namgyal, *Path of Heroes, Birth of Enlightenment*, p.460.

Introduction
1. The *Guardian*, 1.10.97.
2. Quoted in the *Guardian*, 5.12.97.
3. John Sweeney, the *Observer*, 16.11.97.
4. Ibid.
5. Ibid.
6. Quoted in the *Guardian*, 16.10.97.
7. Quoted in the *Observer*, 18.1.98.
8. The Pentagon, quoted the *Guardian*, November 26, 1997.
9. Robert Dahl, quoted Alex Carey, *Taking the Risk out of Democracy*, p.36.
10. Tolstoy, Leo, *Government is Violence: Essays on Anarchism and Pacifism*, p.95.
11. Quoted in Stephen Batchelor, *The Awakening of the West: The Encounter of Buddhism and Western Culture*, p.348.
12. Aryasura, *The Marvellous Companion*, p.65.
13. Ibid., p.67.
14. Quoted in Harvey B. Aronson, *Love and Sympathy in Theravada Buddhism*, p.89.
15. Shantideva, *A Guide to the Bodhisattva's Way of Life*, p.120.
16. Quoted in Lama Surya Das, *Awakening the Buddha Within*, p.341.
17. Mark Curtis, *The Ambiguities of Power*, p.3.
18. Aronson, op. cit., p.49.
19. Geshe Tsultim Gyeltsen, *Compassion: The Key To Great Awakening*, p.60.
20. Norman Mailer at a talk in Shaftesbury Avenue, the *Guardian*, September 23, 1997.
21. Ibid.

Chapter 1
1. BBC TV, Nine O'Clock News, December 1, 1995.
2. Quoted in Howard Zinn, *Failure To Quit*, p.132.
3. Quoted in Noam Chomsky, *Powers and Prospects*, p.170.
4. Henry Kissinger, the *Guardian*, December 29, 1992.
5. *Financial Times*, January 7, 1991.
6. Quoted in Mark Curtis, *The Ambiguities of Power*, p.1.
7. Ibid., p.1.
8. Ibid., p.2.
9. Quoted in Chomsky, *Power and Prospects*, pp.210-11.
10. Rousseau, *Emile*, p.118.
11. Charles Glass, *New Statesman*, November 15, 1996.
12. Glass, ibid.
13. Quoted in Chomsky, *Turning the Tide*, p.48.
14. Quoted in Paul Farmer, *The Uses of Haiti*, pp.19-20.
15. Quoted in Noam Chomsky, *World Orders, Old And New*, p.122.
16. Ibid., p.122.
17. Quoted in Noam Chomsky, *On Power and Ideology: The Managua Lectures*, p.14.
18. Quoted in Edward Goldsmith, 'Development as Colonialism', *The Ecologist*, March/April 1997.
19. Winston Churchill, January 1914. Quoted in Clive Ponting, *Churchill*, p.132.
20. Martha Gellhorn, the *Observer*, November 10, 1996.
21. Evans, *Dependent Development*, p.4.

22. Petras and Pozzi, *Against The Current*, March/April 1992.
23. *Z Magazine*, September 1995.
24. Quoted in *New Internationalist*, June 1996, p.31.
25. Ibid.
26. *The Guardian*, July 15, 1996.
27. Quoted in *Death On Delivery*, Campaign Against the Arms Trade, 1989, p.37.
28. Quoted in Edward Herman, *The Real Terror Network*, p.3.
29. Piero Gleijeses, *Politics and Culture in Guatemala*, p.392.
30. Mark Zepezauer, *The CIA's Greatest Hits*, p.12.
31. The *Nation*, October 28, 1978.
32. Quoted in Paul Farmer, op.cit., p.241.
33. Immerman, *The CIA In Guatemala*, pp.158-159.
34. Quoted ibid., p.176.
35. Quoted in Chomsky, *What Uncle Sam Really Wants*, p.50.
36. Amnesty International Briefing on Guatemala, London, 1976.
37. Quoted in Mark Curtis, op.cit., p.153.
38. Quoted ibid., p.154.
39. Quoted in Farmer, op. cit., p.243.
40. Kinzer and Schlesinger, *Bitter Fruit*. Quoted in Edward S. Herman, *The Real Terror Network*, p.35.
41. Quoted in *Z Magazine*, May 1995.
42. Quoted, ibid.
43. *The Nation*, October 28, 1978.
44. Quoted in Noam Chomsky, *Keeping The Rabble in Line*, p.295.
45. Quoted ibid., p.295.
46. Quoted in Curtis, op.cit., p.130.
47. Quoted in the *New York Times*, March 7, 1981.
48. Quoted in Blum, op. cit., p.363.
49. Quoted ibid., p.353.
50. Quoted ibid., pp.364-5.
51. Quoted in Edward Herman and Frank Brodhead, *Demonstration Elections*, p.167.
52. Ibid., p.137.
53. Ibid., p.125.
54. Letter to President Carter, February 17, 1980, cited Pearce, *Under The Eagle*.
55. Quoted in Blum, op. cit., pp.358-9.
56. Quoted in Curtis, op.cit., p.94.
57. *New York Times*, July 10, 1953. Quoted in Blum, op. cit., p.67.
58. Quoted in Curtis, op.cit., p.91.
59. Quoted ibid., p.92.
60. Quoted ibid., p.93.
61. Quoted ibid., p.93.
62. Quoted in Barry Rubin, *Paved With Good Intentions: The American Experience and Iran*, p.67.
63. Dorman and Omad, 'Reporting Iran the Shah's Way', *Columbia Journalism Review*, January-February, 1979.
64. *Time*, June 5, 1978.
65. Quoted in James Bill, *Foreign Affairs*, Winter 1978-79.
66. *New York Times* editorial, August 6, 1954. Quoted in Blum, op. cit., p.71.
67. Quoted in John Pilger, *Heroes*, p.179.
68. Ibid., pp.179-180.
69. Quoted ibid., p.31.
70. Schoultz, *Comparative Politics*, January 1981.
71. Herman, *The Real Terror Network*, p.126-7.
72. W.E. Gutman, *Z Magazine*, September 1995.
73. Quoted ibid.
74. Quoted ibid.
75. Quoted ibid.
76. The *Guardian* March 30, 1996.
77. Curtis, op. cit., p.235.
78. Quoted ibid., p.29.
79. Quoted ibid., pp.31-32.
80. Quoted ibid., p.35.
81. Quoted ibid., p.35.
82. Ibid., p.36.
83. Quoted ibid., p.38.
84. Quoted ibid., pp.58-59.
85. Quoted ibid., p.57.

86. Quoted ibid., p.58.
87. Quoted ibid., p.78.
88. Quoted ibid., p.77.
89. Quoted ibid., p.79.
90. Lyrics by Andy Partridge of XTC, from the album 'English Settlement', Virgin, 1982.
91. The *Guardian* 23.9.96.

Chapter 2

1. Quoted by Wayne Grytting, *Z Magazine*, June 1997.
2. Quoted in *Boston Herald Traveller*, January 15, 1972.
3. David Chaney, Process of Mass Communication, 1972. Quoted in James Curran and Jean Seaton, *Power Without Responsibility: The Press And Broadcasting in Britain*, p.7.
4. Quoted in the *Guardian*, October 11, 1995.
5. Curran and Seaton op. cit., p.13.
6. Ibid., p.13.
7. Curran and Seaton, op. cit. p.25.
8. Quoted in Curran and Seaton, p.87.
9. Andrew Neil, *Full Disclosure*. Quoted in the *Guardian*, October 24, 1996.
10. Alan Rusbridger, the *Guardian*, October 24, 1996.
11. Curran and Seaton, op.cit., p.94.
12. Quoted in Sharon Beder, *Global Spin: The Corporate Assault Against Environmentalism*, p.15.
13. Quoted ibid., p.181.
14. Quoted in Herman, *The Real Terror Network*, p.146.
15. Lee and Solomon, *Unreliable Sources*, p.61.
16. James Twitchell, 'But First A Word from Our Sponsor', *The Wilson Quarterly* 20, 1996, pp. 69-77.
17. Lee and Solomon, op. cit., pp.60-61.
18. Quoted in Beder, op. cit., pp.182.
19. *The Economist*, December 5, 1987.
20. Quoted in Chomsky and Herman, *The Washington Connection*, p.380.
21. Ibid.

22. *Z Magazine*, February 1995.
23. Quoted in the *Observer*, June 9, 1996.
24. Quoted ibid.
25. Quoted ibid.
26. Quoted ibid.
27. Nyhan, *Boston Globe*, January 4, 1990.
28. Quoted in Alexander Cockburn and Ken Silverstein, the *Observer*, May 26, 1996.
29. Walter Karp, quoted Lee and Solomon, op. cit., p.106.
30. Quoted in Curran and Seaton, op. cit., p.105.
31. Anthony Sampson, *The Essential Anatomy of Britain*, p.166.
32. Quoted in Mark Achbar, *Manufacturing Consent*, p.149.
33. Quoted in Milan Rai, *Chomsky's Politics*, p.27.
34. Ibid., p.27.
35. Tom Wolfe, quoted in Achbar, op.cit., p.61.
36. Edward Bernays, *The Engineering of Consent*, quoted ibid. p.41.
37. Walter Lippmann, *Public Opinion*, p.195.
38. Quoted in Beder, pp.168-9.
39. Vance Packard, *The Waste Makers*, p.27.
40. Milan Rai, op.cit., p.23.
41. Quoted ibid., p.23.
42. Quoted, ibid., p.23.
43. Edward Herman, *The Real Terror Network*, p.11.
44. Ibid., pp.11-12.
45. Beder, op. cit., p.203.
46. Mark Curtis, *The Ambiguities of Power*, pp.116-117.
47. Cockburn and Silverstein, op.cit.
48. R.D. Laing, *The Politics of Experience*, p.64.
49. Quoted in the *Guardian*, November 23, 1996.
50. Ibid.
51. Ibid.
52. The *Guardian*, November 23, 1996.
53. Richard Sambrook, Head of BBC

News gathering, quoted in the *Guardian*, November 23, 1996.

54. Alan Rusbridger, Editor of the *Guardian*, quoted in the *Guardian*, November 23, 1996.

55. The *Guardian*, August 5, 1997.

56. Howard Zinn, *Failure to Quit*, p.30.

57. Quoted in John Pilger, *New Statesman*, August 2, 1996.

58. Pilger, op. cit.

59. Quoted in Curran and Seaton, op.cit., p.167.

60. The *Observer*, December 1, 1996.

61. Goleman, op. cit., p.107.

62. Psychologist Donald Spence. Quoted ibid., p.107.

63. R.D. Laing, quoted ibid., p.175.

64. Ibid., p.175.

65. Yevgeny Yevtushenko, quoted ibid., p.230.

66. Ibid., p.123.

67. Irving Janis, quoted ibid., p.186.

68. Janis, quoted ibid., p.186.

69. Goleman, ibid., p.188.

70. Tolstoy, *Writings on Civil Disobedience and Non-Violence*, p.103.

71. Goleman, op. cit., p.158.

72. Ibid., p.232.

73. Ibid. p.114.

74. Ibid. p.232.

75. Chomsky, *Deterring Democracy*, p.79.

76. Goleman, op. cit., p.226.

Chapter 3

1. The *Guardian*, December 7, 1996.

2. Quoted in Howard Zinn, *A People's History of the United States*, pp.252-253.

3. Simon Finch. Personal correspondence with the author, April 25, 1998.

4. Quoted in the *Observer*, 19.5.96.

Chapter 4

1. Quoted in *Z Magazine*, October 1995.

2. Chomsky, *Powers and Prospects*, p.113.

3. Quoted ibid., p.113.

4. Quoted ibid., p.117.

5. John Pilger, *New Statesman*, October 25, 1996.

6. The *Guardian*, December 11, 1996.

7. Eric Shaw, *New Statesman*, April 26, 1996.

8. Brown, the *Guardian*, June 21, 1997.

9. Quoted in the *Guardian*, October 4, 1997.

10. Quoted by Milan Rai in *Freedom*, June 21, 1997.

11. Ibid.

12. Quoted in John Pilger, *Heroes*, p.528.

13. Ibid., p.528.

14. Quoted in John Pilger, *Heroes*, p.489.

15. Ibid., p.489.

16. Quoted in the *Guardian*, December 7, 1996.

17. Lyrics from Funk Pop-A-Roll, from the album *Mummer*, 1983.

18. Quoted in Alex Carey, *Taking the Risk out of Democracy*, p.149.

19. The *Guardian*, October 1, 1997.

20. Ibid.

21. Ibid.

22. The *Guardian*, October 4, 1997.

23. Quoted in the *Observer*, July 28, 1996.

24. Ibid.

25. The *Observer*, July 27, 1996.

26. Quoted in John Pilger, *Distant Voices*, p.302.

27. Quoted in John Pilger, ibid., p.307.

28. Ibid., p.303.

29. Quoted in John Pilger, *New Statesman*, April 5, 1996.

30. Quoted in Chomsky, *Powers and Prospects*, p.216.

31. Quoted in *New Statesman*, April 5, 1996.

32. Quoted ibid.

33. Roy Greenslade, the *Observer*, August 4, 1996.

34. *Webster Collegiate Dictionary*, 1945. Quoted in Herman, *The Real Terror Network*, p.21, original emphasis.

35. *The Concise Oxford English Dictionary*, Ninth Edition, p.1440.
36. Herman, op. cit, p.201.
37. The *Observer*, July 28, 1996.
38. Ibid.
39. Quoted in Mark Curtis, *The Ambiguities of Power*, pp.219–220.
40. Quoted ibid., p.221.
41. Quoted ibid., p.221.
42. The *Guardian*, March 13, 1996.
43. Quoted in Maria Lopez Vigil, *Envio*, June 1995.
44. Quoted in Chomsky, *Power And Prospects*, p.81.
45. *New Statesman*, August 9, 1996.
46. *Amnesty* magazine, British Section, September/October 1994, p.5.
47. Quoted in the *Observer*, July 28, 1996.
48. Amnesty International, 'Indonesia: Workers' rights still challenged,' June 1995.
49. William Blum, *Killing Hope: US Military and CIA Interventions Since World War II*, p.197.
50. Letters From Lexington, *Reflections on Propaganda*, p.51.
51. Edward Herman, *Beyond Hypocrisy: Decoding The News in an Age of Propaganda*, p.68.
52. Quoted in Chomsky, *Powers and Prospects*, p.178.

Chapter 5
1. Jeff Hogan, *Otherwise*, Winter 1996.
2. Zhechen Gyaltsab and Padma Gyurmed Namgyal, *Path of Heroes, Birth of Enlightenment*, p.540.
3. Anarchist Emma Goldman at her trial, 1917. Quoted in Howard Zinn, *A People's History of the United States*, p.363.
4. Quoted ibid., p.337.
5. Victor Lebow, retailing analyst, quoted Beder, p.1.
6. Quoted in Beder, op. cit., p.4.
7. Norberg-Hodge, *Ancient Futures*, p.84.
8. Aryasura, *The Marvellous Companion*,

p.115.
9. Sir Francis Bacon. Quoted in *The Oxford Book of Aphorisms*, p.22.
10. Mike Jempson, *A Glimpse of Hell*, p.73.
11. Quoted in Rose, Lewontin & Kamm, *Not In Our Genes—Biology, Ideology and Human Nature*, p.86.
12. Quoted in Kirkpatrick Sale, *The Conquest of Paradise*, pp.99–100.
13. Ibid., p.127.
14. Ibid., p.127.
15. Quoted ibid., p.99.
16. Ibid., p.129.
17. Quoted ibid., p.131.
18. Ibid., p.135.
19. Ibid., p.151.
20. Linnaeus. Quoted in Rocker, op. cit., p.303.
21. Quoted in Rose, Lewontin and Kamm, op. cit., p.30, my emphasis.
22. Cited in Noam Chomsky, *Year 501*, p.158.
23. Quoted in Chomsky, *Deterring Democracy*, p.38.
24. Quoted in R.C. Lewontin, *The Doctrine of DNA*, pp.25–26.
25. Quoted in Rocker, op. cit., p.219.
26. Quoted in Rocker, op. cit., p.220.
27. Curran and Seaton, op.cit., p.47.
28. Quoted, Edward Herman, *Beyond Hypocrisy: Decoding The News in an Age of Propaganda*, p.61.
29. Quoted by Mark Curtis in the *Observer*, July 28, 1996.
30. Ibid.
31. *Boston Globe*, March 10, 1991. Quoted in Chomsky, *World Orders, Old And New*, p.12.
32. *Greenwood Leaves*, 1850. Quoted in Howard Zinn, *A People's History of the United States*, p.112.
33. Quoted in Rose, Lewontin and Kamm, *Not In Our Genes*, p.143.
34. Ibid.
35. Ibid., p.143.
36. Sharon Salzberg, *Lovingkindness— The Revolutionary Art of Happiness*, p.174.

37. Quoted in Jeffrey Masson and Susan McCarthy, *When Elephants Weep: The Emotional Life of Animals*, p.33.
38. Ibid., p.20.
39. Ibid., p.20.
40. Ibid., p.21.
41. Ibid., p.40–41.
42. Quoted in Danny Penman, *The Price of Meat*, p.82.
43. Quoted ibid., p.83.
44. Quoted ibid., p.86.
45. Quoted in Penman, ibid., p.82.
46. Quoted by George Monbiot, the *Guardian*, 9.7.97.
47. Ibid.
48. Machiavelli. Quoted in Rocker, p.188.
49. Kant. Quoted in Rocker, p.184.
50. Rocker, p.55.
51. Chomsky, writing in 1979. Quoted in C.P. Otero, ed.,*Radical Priorities*, pp.19–20.
52. Quoted in the *Observer*, October 26, 1997.
53. Ibid.
54. Ibid.
55. Ibid.
56. Peter Singer, Mandarin, 1994, *How Are We To Live? Ethics in an Age of Self-Interest*, p.144.
57. Ibid., p.139.
58. Quoted in Felicity De Zulueta, *A Glimpse of Hell: Reports on Torture Worldwide*, p.97.
59. Ibid., p.98.
60. Ibid., p.98.
61. Quoted in the *Observer*, October 26, 1997.
62. The *New York Times*, March 1991.
63. Edward S. Herman, *Beyond Hypocrisy: Decoding The News in an Age of Propaganda*, p.79.
64. Quoted in Trevor Ling, *The Buddha*, pp. 142–143.
65. Aryasura, *The Marvellous Companion*, p.257.
66. De Zulueta, op. cit., p.96.
67. Ibid., p.96.
68. Quoted ibid., p.90.

Chapter 6
1. Bakunin. Quoted in Marshall, *Demanding the Impossible*, p.270.
2. Quoted in Zinn, *A People's History of the United States,* p.290.
3. Quoted in Marshall, op. cit., p.292.
4. Bakunin. Quoted ibid., p.299.
5. Engels. Quoted ibid., p.637.
6. Arthur Koestler, *Darkness At Noon.*
7. Marshall, op. cit., p.633.
8. Quoted in John Pilger, *Hidden Agendas*, p.573.
9. Ibid., p.576.
10. Quoted ibid., p.573.
11. Quoted in William Blum, *Killing Hope: US Military and CIA Interventions since World War II*, p.197.
12. Erich Fromm, *On Being Human*, p.53.
13. Quoted in Noam Chomsky, *Deterring Democracy*, p.41.
14 Howard Zinn, *The Zinn Reader*, p.247.
15. Quoted in Chomsky and Herman, *After the Cataclysm*, p.154.
16. Quoted in *The Chomsky Reader*, ed. James Peck, p.290.
17. Howard Zinn, op. cit, p.259.
18. Quoted in Sogyal Rinpoche, *The Tibetan Book of Living and Dying*, p.192.
19. Gyaltsab, Zhechen and Padma Gyurmed Namgyal, *Path of Heroes*, p.415.
20. Palden Gyatso, *Fire Under The Snow—Testimony of a Tibetan Prisoner*, p.195.
21. Quoted in the *Guardian*, September 29, 1997.
22. Dalai Lama, *The Power of Compassion*, p.44.
23. Quoted in Joseph Campbell, *The Hero With A Thousand Faces*, p.116.
24. Aryasura, *The Marvellous Companion*, p.276.
25. Gyalstsab, op. cit., p.360.
26. Ibid., p.328.

27. Aryasura, *The Marvellous Companion*, pp. 170-1.
28. Chomsky, *Chronicles of Dissent*, p.69.
29. Gyalstsab, op. cit., p.492.
30. *Class Warfare*, Pluto Press, p.27.
31. Ibid., p.27.
32. Mark Achbar, *Manufacturing Consent: Noam Chomsky and The Media*, p.52.
33. Gyalstsab, op. cit., p.416.
34. Chomsky, *Powers and Prospects*, p.209.
35. Quoted in Howard Zinn, *The Zinn Reader*, p.373.
36. Carla Lane, the *Guardian*, January 31, 1998.
37. The *Guardian*, August 15, 1997.
38. Ibid.
39. Harvey B. Aronson, *Love and Sympathy in Theravada Buddhism*, 1996, p.19.
40. Ibid., pp.19-20.
41. Ibid., p.21.
42. Aryasurya, *The Marvellous Companion*, p.275.
43. Aronson, op. cit., p.38.
44. Sharon Salzberg, *Lovingkindness: The Revolutionary Art of Happiness*, p.155.
45. Daniel Goleman, *Healing Emotions*, p.35.
46. Ibid., p.36.
47. Herbert Benson, *Timeless Healing*, p.181-2.
48. Ibid., p.278.
49. Aryasura, op. cit., p.165.
50. Ibid., p.171.
51. Aryasurya, op. cit., pp.225-226.
52. Ibid., pp.185-6.
53. Ibid., p.256.
54. Quoted in Lama Surya Das, *Awakening the Buddha Within*, p.235.
55. Gyeltsen, op. cit., p.102.
56. Danny Penman, *The Price of Meat*, p.166.
57. The *Guardian*, July 10, 1997.
58. Ibid., pp.166-7.
59. Ibid., p.166.
60. The *Observer*, November 23, 1997.
61. Shantideva, *The Way of the Bodhisattva*.

Chapter 7
1. Stephen Batchelor, *Buddhism Without Beliefs*, p.112.
2. Trevor Ling, *The Buddha*, p.67.
3. Ibid., p.68.
4. Quoted in the *Guardian*, October 16, 1997.
5. Quoted ibid.
6. The Buddha. Quoted in Eknath Easwaran, *The Dhammapada*, p.167.
7. Aryasura, *The Marvellous Companion*, p.99.
8. Ibid., p.102.
9. Ibid., p.103.
10. Ibid., p.103.
11. Ibid., p.103.
12. Ibid. p.25.
13. Aronson, op. cit., pp.9-10.
14. Aryasurya, op. cit., p.315.
15. Ibid., pp. 316-17.
16. Ibid., pp. 319-20.
17. Ibid., p.320.
18. Ibid., p.321.
19. Ibid., p.323.
20. Geshe Tsultim Gyeltsen, *Compassion—The Key To Great Awakening*, p.120.
21. Joseph Campbell, *The Hero's Journey*, p.65.
22. Wallace Stevens. Quoted in *The Little Zen Companion*, p.137.
23. Thomas Mann, *The Magic Mountain*, p.476.
24. Ibid., pp.480-1.
25. Ibid., p.481.
26. Ibid., p.490.
27. Ibid., p.492.
28. Ibid., p.494.
29. Ibid., p.496.
30. Ken Saro-Wiwa, the *Independent*, November 14, 1995.
31. The Buddha. Quoted in Eknath Easwaran, *The Dhammapadda*, p.148.

Bibliography

Achbar, Mark. *Manufacturing Consent: Noam Chomsky and The Media*, Black Rose Books, 1994.

Americas Watch. *A Year of Reckoning*, 1990.

Amnesty International. 'Guatemala', Briefing, London, 1976.

Amnesty International, 'Indonesia: Workers' rights still challenged,' June 1995.

Aryasura. *The Marvellous Companion*, Dharma, 1983.

Aronson, Harvey B. *Love and Sympathy in Theravada Buddhism*, Motilal Barnasidass, 1996.

Barsamian, David. *Class Warfare*, Pluto Press, 1996.

Batchelor, Stephen. *Buddhism Without Beliefs*, Bloomsbury, 1997.

Batchelor, Stephen. *The Awakening of the West: The Encounter of Buddhism and Western Culture*, Aquarian, 1994.

Beder, Sharon. *Global Spin: The Corporate Assault Against Environmentalism*, Green Books, 1997.

Benson, Herbert. *Timeless Healing*, Pocket Books, 1998.

Blum, William. *Killing Hope: US Military and CIA Interventions Since World War II*, Common Courage Press, 1995.

Campaign Against the Arms Trade. *Death On Delivery*, 1989.

Campbell, Joseph. *The Hero With A Thousand Faces*, Paladin, 1968.

Campbell, Joseph. *The Hero's Journey*.

Carey, Alex. *Taking The Risk Out Of Democracy*, University of New South Wales Press, 1995.

Chaney, David. *Process of Mass Communication*, Macmillan, 1972.

Chomsky, Noam. *Chronicles of Dissent*, AK Press, 1992.

Chomsky, Noam. *Deterring Democracy*, Hill & Wang, 1992.

Chomsky, Noam. *Keeping The Rabble in Line*, AK Press, 1994.

Chomsky, Noam. *On Power and Ideology: The Managua Lectures*, South End Press, 1987.

Chomsky, Noam. *Powers and Prospects*, Pluto Press, 1996.

Chomsky, Noam. *The Chomsky Reader*, ed. James Peck, Serpent's Tail, 1987.

Chomsky, Noam. *Letters From Lexington: Reflections on Propaganda*, AK Press, 1993.

Chomsky, Noam. *Turning the Tide*, Pluto, 1985.

Chomsky, Noam. *What Uncle Sam Really Wants*, Odonian Press, 1993.

Chomsky, Noam. *World Orders, Old And New*, Pluto Press, 1994.

Chomsky, Noam. *Year 501*, Verso, 1993.

Chomsky, Noam and Edward Herman. *After the Cataclysm*, South End Press, 1979.

Chomsky, Noam and Edward Herman. *The Washington Connection*, South End Press, 1979.

Clark, Ramsey. *The Fire This Time*, Thunder's Mouth Press, 1994.

Concise Oxford English Dictionary, Ninth Edition, Oxford University Press, 1995.

Curran, James and Jean Seaton, *Power Without Responsibility: The Press And Broadcasting in Britain*, Routledge, 1991.

Curtis, Mark. *The Ambiguities of Power*, Zed Books, 1995.

Dalai Lama, The. *The Power of Compassion*, Thorsons, 1995.

Das, Lama Surya. *Awakening the Buddha Within*, Bantam, 1997.

De Zulueta, Felicity. *A Glimpse of Hell: Reports on Torture Worldwide*, Amnesty International, Cassell, 1996.

Dorman and Omad, 'Reporting Iran the Shah's Way', *Columbia Journalism Review*, January–February, 1979.

Easwaran, Eknath. *The Dhammapada*, Arkana, 1986.

Evans, D. *Dependent Development*, Princeton, 1979.

Farmer, Paul. *The Uses of Haiti*, Common Courage Press, 1994.

Fromm, Erich. *On Being Human*, Continuum, 1997.

Gleijeses, Piero. *Politics and Culture in Guatemala*, Michigan, 1988.

Goleman, Daniel. *Healing Emotions*, Shambhala 1997.

Gross, John (ed.). *Oxford Book of Aphorisms*, Oxford, 1981.

Gyaltsab, Zhechen and Padma Gyurmed Namgyal. *Path of Heroes, Birth of Enlightenment*, Dharma Publishing, 1995.

Gyatso, Palden. *Fire Under The Snow—Testimony of a Tibetan Prisoner*, Harvill, 1997.

Gyeltsen, Geshe Tsultim. *Compassion: The Key To Great Awakening*, Wisdom Books, 1997.

Herman, Edward. *Beyond Hypocrisy: Decoding The News in an Age of Propaganda*, South End Press, 1992.

Herman, Edward. *The Real Terror Network*, South End Press, 1982.

Herman, Edward and Frank Brodhead. *Demonstration Elections*, South End Press, 1984.

Immerman. *The CIA In Guatemala*, University of Texas Press, 1982.

Kinzer, Stephen and Stephen Schlesinger, *Bitter Fruit*, Doubleday, 1981.

Koestler, Arthur. *Darkness At Noon*.

Laing, R.D. *The Politics of Experience*, Penguin 1990.

Lee and Solomon. *Unreliable Sources*, Carol Publishing Group, 1990.

Lewontin, R.C. *The Doctrine of DNA*, Penguin 1993.

Ling, Trevor. *The Buddha*, Wildwood House, 1973.

The Little Zen Companion, Workman, 1994.

Lippmann, Walter. *Public Opinion*, Free Press, 1965.

Mann, Thomas. *The Magic Mountain*, Penguin, 1988.

Marshall, Peter. *Demanding the Impossible: A History of Anarchism*, HarperCollins, 1992.

Masson, Jeffrey and Susan McCarthy. *When Elephants Weep: The Emotional Life of Animals*, Vintage, 1996.

Melrose, Diana. 'The threat of a good example?' Oxfam Report, Oxfam, Oxford, 1985.

Norberg-Hodge, Helena. *Ancient Futures*, Sierra Club, 1992.

Otero, C.P. (ed.). *Radical Priorities*, Black Rose Books, 1981.

Packard, Vance. *The Waste Makers*, Penguin, 1960.

Parker, Phyllis. *Brazil and the Quiet Intervention*, University of Texas Press, 1979.

Pearce, Jenny. *Under The Eagle*, Westview, 1982.

Penman, Danny. *The Price of Meat*, Gollancz, 1996.

Petras and Pozzi, *Against The Current*, March/April 1992.

Pilger, John. *Distant Voices*, Vintage, 1994.

Pilger, John. *Heroes*, Pan, 1989.

Pilger, John. *Hidden Agendas*, Vintage, 1998.

Ponting, Clive. *Churchill*, Sinclair-Stevenson, 1994.

Rai, Milan. *Chomsky's Politics*, Verso, 1995.

Rinpoche, Sogyal. *The Tibetan Book of Living and Dying*, Rider, 1992.

Rose, Lewontin & Kamm, *Not In Our Genes: Biology, Ideology and Human Nature*, Penguin, 1990.

Rousseau, *Emile*, Everyman's Library, 1974.

Rubin, Barry. *Paved With Good Intentions: The American Experience and Iran*, Oxford University Press, 1980, p.67.

Sale, Kirkpatrick. *The Conquest of Paradise*, Papermac, 1992.

Salzberg, Sharon. *Lovingkindness: The Revolutionary Art of Happiness*, Shambhala, 1995.

Sampson, Anthony. *The Essential Anatomy of Britain*, Cornet, 1993.

Schoultz, *Comparative Politics*, January 1981.

Shantideva. *A Guide to the Bodhisattva's Way of Life*, Dharamsala, translated by Stephen Batchelor, Library of Tibetan Works and Archives, 1979.

Shantideva. *The Way of the Bodhisattva*, Shambhala, 1997.

Singer, Peter. *How Are We To Live? Ethics in an Age of Self-Interest*, Mandarin, 1994.

Tolstoy, Leo. *Government is Violence: Essays on Anarchism and Pacifism*, Phoenix Press, 1990.

Tolstoy, Leo. *Writings on Civil Disobedience and Non-Violence*, New Society Publishers, 1987.

Twitchell, James. 'But First A Word from Our Sponsor', *The Wilson Quarterly* 20, 1996.

Zepezauer, Mark. *The CIA's Greatest Hits*, Odonian Press, 1994.

Zinn, Howard. *A People's History of the United States*, Harper Perennial, 1990.

Zinn, Howard. *Failure To Quit*, Common Courage Press, 1993.

Zinn, Howard. *The Zinn Reader*, Seven Stories Press, 1997.

Index

East Timor 89-90
  British arms and 112-28 *passim*
  Death of a Nation 95
  genocide in 89-90, 113, 161
  oil 115
  Zelter/Key *Guardian* correspondence
  112-28 *passim*
  see also Indonesia; Suharto, Thojib
Economist 66
Eden, Anthony 40
Edsell, Thomas 104
education, anti-environmentalism and
68
Eisemann, C.H. 143
Elliott, Michael 99-100, 101
Ellul, Jacques 110
El Niño 171
El Salvador 36, 42-5, 50, 108-9
  elections 43-5
  media and 43-4
  US intervention in 42-3, 45, 50, 109
  see also South America
Engels, Friedrich 158-9
Eochaid 169-71
Evans, Peter 32-3
Eyal, Jonathan 105

factory farming 145-7, 193
  dairy industry 146-7
  pigs 146
  poultry industry 145-6
  see also animals
Falklands War, media and 77
Fallows, James 98-9, 101
Farmer, Paul 37
farming *see* factory farming
FBI (Federal Bureau of Investigation) 92
Ferguson, Thomas 104
Filene, Edward 72
Financial Times 74, 106
Fones-Wolf, Elizabeth 68
Ford, Gerald 161
Foreign Office (UK) 39-40, 53
Foster, Christopher 113
fox hunting 191-2, 194-5
Fromm, Erich 162

Galtieri, Leopoldo 50
Galton, Francis 140
Gelles, 155
Gellhorn, Martha 32
gender stereotypes 142
General Strike 77
generosity 201-2
  dissent and 202-4
  see also compassion; kindness
genocide

in Cambodia 163
  in East Timor 89-90, 113, 161
  the Holocaust 162-3
Gilchrist, Andrew 142
Gingrich, Newt 93
Glass, Charles 28-9
globalization 16-17, 103, 160, 171
global warming 13, 106, 107, 111-12,
171-2
Godoy, Julio 39
Goenka, Satya Narayan 20
Goldman, Emma 132, 134
Goleman, Daniel 20, 79-86, 187-8
Grasser, John 13
greed, hatred and ignorance 167, 168,
169, 174-6, 189-91, 198-9, 205
  see also compassion
Greenfield, Jeff 71
greenhouse gas emissions 13, 200
Greenpeace 67
Greenslade, Roy 116
Guardian 25, 63, 74, 75, 98-9, 106, 121,
122, 123
  Zelter/Key correspondence 112-28
  passim
Guatemala 33, 36, 37-41, 50
  land reforms 37
  military coup in 38-40
  trade unions 39
  United Fruit Company (UFCO) 37-
8, 39, 40
  US intervention in 37-41
  see also South America
Gulf War 142, 161
  media coverage 91-2, 98
Gunson, Phil 34
Gusmao, Jose 115
Gutman, W.E. 50, 51
Gyatso, Palden 168
Gyeltsin, Geshe 206

Haig, Alexander 43
Haiti 36
Hamilton, Archie 114
Hawke, Bob 27
Heath, Edward 77
Helmore, Edward 68
Helms, Richard 42, 92
Heritage Foundation 68
Herman, Edward 40, 44-5, 49, 56, 65,
69, 71, 72-3, 82, 104, 116-17, 127, 153,
163
  see also propaganda model of the
media
Herschbach, Dudley 111
Higson, Mark 115
Hiroshima 108

Paul Emerson.